RAIN FOREST EXCHANGES

SMITHSONIAN SERIES IN ETHNOGRAPHIC INQUIRY
William L. Merrill and Ivan Karp, Series Editors

Ethnography as fieldwork, analysis, and literary form is the distinguishing feature of modern anthropology. Guided by the assumption that anthropological theory and ethnography are inextricably linked, this series is devoted to exploring the ethnographic enterprise.

ADVISORY BOARD
Richard Bauman (Indiana University), Gerald Berreman (University of California, Berkeley), James Boon (Princeton University), Stephen Gudeman (University of Minnesota), Shirley Lindenbaum (City University of New York), George Marcus (Rice University), David Parkin (Oxford University), Renato Rosaldo (Stanford University), and Norman Whitten (University of Illinois)

WILLIAM H. FISHER

INDUSTRY AND
COMMUNITY
ON AN
AMAZONIAN
FRONTIER

RAIN FOREST EXCHANGES

SMITHSONIAN INSTITUTION PRESS
Washington and London

COPY EDITOR: Marsha A. Kunin
PRODUCTION EDITOR: Robert A. Poarch
DESIGNER: Janice Wheeler

Library of Congress Cataloging-in-Publication Data
Fisher, William H. (William Harry)
    Rain forest exchanges : industry and community on an Amazonian frontier /
    William H. Fisher.
      p.   cm. — (Smithsonian series in ethnographic inquiry)
    Includes bibliographical references and index.
    ISBN 1-56098-958-0 (alk. paper) — ISBN 1-56098-983-1 (pbk.: alk. paper)
    1. Xikrin Indians—Commerce.   2. Xikrin Indians—Cultural assimilation.
    3. Cayapo Indians—History.   I. Title.   II. Series.
  F2520.1.X5 F57   2000
  981.004′984—dc21   00-028516

British Library Cataloguing-in-Publication Data available

Manufactured in the United States of America
06 05 04 03 02 01 00   5 4 3 2 1

FOR MY MOTHER,
ELIZABETH LEUCHAK FISHER

CONTENTS

PREFACE AND ACKNOWLEDGMENTS

I found the final inspiration for this study in November 1994 as bathtime found me crouching naked in the shallow river's edge, while a thoroughly besotted man waved a pistol in my face. Under these conditions the ordinary fare of anthropology receded quite far down my list of priorities. Most pressing was to explain the presence of this frontier figure in the Amazonian community where I was doing fieldwork. Besides being an immediate threat, I wondered why he (and other backland logging and mining profiteers) were tolerated at all in indigenous communities when their business activities seemed to undercut the basis traditional reservation life.

I had previously done fieldwork in the same village of Bakajá Xikrin people between 1984 and 1986 and knew that the easy answer, Indian naïveté or venality, was ultimately unconvincing. I realized how little I knew of the sociology of the Brazilian reservation system that would account not only for Indian lives but also for this drunken son of a rich landowner I was desperately hoping would not shoot me or, less seriously, crush my eyeglasses underfoot. It was all here: alcohol, violence (or the threat of violence), the seeming acceptance of logging and mining within the community, and the ease with which the Xikrin seemed to fall for the enticements of junk food in return for their valuable natural resources of gold and mahogany. Madness was in the air. I realized that any account of reservation life would have to face up to the absurdity and desperation of contemporary reservation life as well as its moments of elation and beauty, placing it within the context of the frantic boom-bust mentality that grips much of the Amazonian frontier.

I resolved to try and see the community with fresh eyes and search for a perspective that would allow me to confront, rather than sanitize, what I knew to be a not uncommon experience on Brazil's reservations. I am certainly not alone in this effort, and recent works on Brazilian Indians, many notably by Brazilian authors (e.g., Ramos 1995, Caiuby Novaes 1997, and Graham 1995), have set their descriptions firmly within the contradictory realities and crises of reservation life.

It seems to me that such works depart from a previous anthropology. By embedding descriptions in larger sociological realities beyond the village and its surrounding landscape, all descriptions of ongoing tradition and change become implicitly tied to a dialogue concerning the future of indigenous communities within nation-states. This future entails both the recreation of distinctiveness, and dependency, with all its associated problems and complications. I wrote the present work in the spirit of such a dialogue.

After consulting with different Xikrin about the feasibility of my proposed project, I began to intensively examine the role of trade goods within the life of the Bakajá-Trincheira reservation. Most of my research of 4.5 months during 1994 and 1995 centered on this issue, although the time I had spent in the village almost a decade previously for my doctoral research greatly facilitated this subsequent project. I focused on the historical origins and social complexities of relations between the Xikrin, the Brazilian Indian agency, and the mining and logging firms who so often found their way onto reservation territory. At the time, the population of the two communities in the reservation included 51 persons at Trincheira and 275 at Bakajá and I owe a debt of gratitude to all of them. In particular, the Bakajá community, where I was based, put up with and even encouraged an intrusive research methodology that involved poking through the manufactured goods of every household. I subsequently thank individuals, but I must also express a debt of gratitude to the forthrightness with which so many Xikrin—male and female, young and old—freely aired their own questions, doubts and disagreements about the present and future of their community.

The funding for the present study was provided by a Smithsonian postdoctoral fellowship, a grant from the Timbira Foundation, and a faculty summer research grant from the College of William and Mary. While at the Smithsonian Institution I was greatly helped by the guidance and sponsorship of William H. Crocker. Gail Solomon, Barbara Watanabe, and Betty Meggers, along with Carl Hansen, Henry Solomon, and Chip Clark, helped make the Smithsonian a great place to work. In Brazil the support and wisdom of Dr. Lux Vidal, who has dedicated herself to the Cateté Xikrin for over thirty years, was invaluable. Many anthropologists, employees of the Brazilian National Indian Foundation (FUNAI), and others went out of their way to make research possible and provide me with information and hospitality: Benedito Pessoa Marques, Walter Avelino da Silva,

Caetano Ventura, Ocirema de Oliveira, Otília Escócia, Neila Soares, Lúcia Van Velthem, Marcio Mieira, Clarice Cohn, Raimundo Amaral, and Neide Xavier. The Instituto Socioambiental and its predecessor, CEDI, provided access to their archive of materials on indigenous people. Marcio Ferreira da Silva freely gave insightful counsel and hospitality, beyond what anyone has a right to expect.

I also wish to acknowledge the people who read and commented on drafts of material that went into the book: Bill Merrill of the Smithsonian; Jim Axtell; Katie Bragdon; Beth Conklin; Jim Greenberg; Martha Houle; Ken Kensinger; Marco Lazarin; Debra Picchi; Rich Price; and two classes of students in my Native Cultures of Latin America course at William and Mary. Eduardo Viveiros de Castro and Jack Hammond also offered valuable academic guidance. Along the way students of the Kayapó—Lux Vidal, Terry Turner, Isabel Murphy, Vanessa Lea, Gustaaf Verswijver, and Darrell Posey—have given me the personal benefit of their knowledge.

At my home institution of William and Mary, support of the anthropology department is gratefully acknowledged, as is the help of Professor Jack Martin, Fredrika Teute, Jean Belvin, Karen McCluny, and Marilyn Lewis. Many librarians, especially those of the interlibrary loan variety, are superior human beings and should be recognized as such. Art and Annick Ensley, Jack Hart, and Keith Harver intervened at a crucial point in the writing process, as did John Frechione and John Sydenstricker-Neto. At Cornell University, the Latin American studies program provided some writing facilities, and Mary Jo Dudley, Tom Holloway, and Barbara Lynch made sure the project moved forward. Ann Peters labored over the illustrations, offered critical commentary on the project, and extended generosity too great and varied to enumerate.

With few exceptions, the entire elder generation of Xikrin have been important interlocutors in my life over the past decade. Without the help of the following people, the present book would not have been possible: Bep Tok, Bep Éti, Bep Kêti, Komrê, Bep Krô, Bemôro, Mêx-ti, Bep Djôti, Bep Djô, Bekôjri, Bemoypa, Karangré, Bemnibeti, Bep Pydji, Kayre, Kanaipô, Coronel, Màd ma, Bep Krã, Katinô'ôk, Bep Pumati, Pedro, Kupato, Nhojprê, Tucum, Mauré, Tchuya, Ngreikôti (untiring reciter of genealogies), Nhàgdjô, Ire'ô, Ngreikaro (wife of my formal friend who bailed me out with obscene jokes whenever things got tense), Irete, Huire, Irepron, Irepunu, Nhàkrin, Nhàkati, and Dona Oswalda. For reasons of confidentiality, I have mostly changed their names in the account that follows. As I write this I realize a whole younger generation has come of age since I began working with the Xikrin. I interacted much less with them, although many of them readily extended hospitality and assistance. They are the future and are sure to surprise. I thank them as well.

My father and mother have also given home and child care help for sometimes lengthy periods during the course of writing. My mother, in particular, is to be thanked for a couple of heart-stopping car trips when, despite being loaded down with field gear, we always just made the plane. It seems trite to thank my wife, Monique, and my daughters, Diana and Melanie. They are part of this book and have shaped it and been shaped by it. Better to ask for their forebearance. I ask the same from the many whom I have surely forgotten to mention here.

A NOTE ON ORTHOGRAPHY

Except for names, non-English words are italicized at first usage in the text. The inconsistent use of *k* and *c* in the spelling of the Bakajá and Pacajá rivers should not only help the reader distinguish between two bodies of water that are easily confused but also respects local usage in which *Bakajá* appears more frequently than *Bacajá* and *Pacajá* more frequently than *Pakajá*.

The system of orthography most recognized among Kayapó speakers with formal instruction in their own language has been developed by the Summer Institute of Linguistics based on phonological studies carried out over a number of years (Stout and Thomson 1974). I used their phonemic analysis to guide my transcriptions in the field. With slight modifications this system has been used in a number of anthropological works on the Kayapó (e.g., Lea 1986; Verswijver 1992; and Turner 1992). There are both lexical and phonological differences that may distinguish Xikrin from other Kayapó communities. The following list is offered as a rough guide to pronunciation of words encountered in the text.

CONSONANTS

p, t, b, d, k, g, m, n, w, r approximate the sounds of English; *p, t, k* lack aspiration
dj like *j* in *jar*
x like *sh* in *shingle*
nh like *ny* in *canyon*
ng like *ng* in *song* (nasal velar)
j like *y* in *yahoo*
An apostrophe (') indicates a glottal stop

VOWELS

i like the *ee* in *bee*
e like the *e* in *wet*
a like the *a* in French *table*
u like *oo* in *boot*
o like *o* in *off*
y like *oo* in *boot* said while smiling (high back unrounded vowel)
à like *o* in *off* said while smiling (low back unrounded vowel)
The preceding vowels may all be nasalized (symbolized with a tilde, e.g., ã)
The following vowels may only be oral:
ê like *a* in *hate*
ô like *oa* in *boat*
ỳ like *oa* in *boat* said while smiling (medium back unrounded vowel)

RAIN FOREST EXCHANGES

1 INTRODUCTION

As a doctoral student embarking on fieldwork with the indigenous Xikrin Kayapó community in the Brazilian Amazon, I had assumed I would give some presents as tokens of friendship and goodwill to my hosts. As weeks and months wore on I spent what seemed to be frustrating stretches of time listening to discussions of machetes, plastic beads, and electric motors. The seemingly indefatigable desire of my hosts for certain kinds of goods was something I put aside in order to proceed with my doctoral research, which involved traditional disciplinary concerns with kinship, social organization, and factionalism. Returning to the field in 1994 after an eight-year hiatus, I found that the desire for trade goods of various types had only increased. Unlike during the mid-1980s, however, the region of southern Pará, where I worked, was in the middle of a mahogany boom. Much of the timber came from indigenous reserves, either with or, in most cases, without the consent of indigenous peoples. When Indians acceded to this activity, however, they inevitably offered their need for trade goods as a rationale.

If anthropologists are to understand this facet of indigenous life, concern with trade goods has to be elevated from a field methods footnote on useful field supplies to a full-blown research concern. There are some classic precedents for this type of study involving the adoption of steel axes (Sharp 1952; Salisbury 1962), and in the Amazon, Peters (1973), Hugh-Jones (1992), Ferguson (1995), and Ramos (1996) have considered indigenous peoples' adoption of firearms, steel tools, and other trade goods. The present study looks at trade goods and frontier relations as part of a long-term process of change within the boom-bust cycles that mark the collecting of natural commodities in the Amazon. I wish to get beyond the image of indigenous peoples as either environmental heroes or villains to consider in detail their changing relationship with their environment and the choices and challenges they face in their relations with the larger world. What follows is my attempt to make sense of the complex social context in which trade goods play such a large role. In the remainder of this introduction I present a brief overview of the problem of trade goods before considering the larger stakes relating to forest conservation efforts and some relevant background material on the indigenous peoples involved. I also present a brief overview of the specific approach used in this work as a prologue to exploring the impact of frontier industries on the Xikrin community.

Xikrin depend on an infusion of trade goods while living an apparently traditional lifestyle. Trade goods are necessary for carrying on traditional subsistence activities, such as hunting and gardening, while they stimulate inevitable challenges to those very same traditions.

Anthropologists with symbolic and interpretive orientations have described how native Amazonians incorporate concepts of trade goods and technology into their own symbolic constructs (Albert 1988; Giannini 1996; Da Matta 1970; Lea 1986; Turner 1988). But understanding the mythical origins or taxonomies offered by native peoples does not explain the preponderance of attention paid to such goods in daily life. For example, this literature did not help me understand those days in the field when I experienced a seemingly single-minded collective attention to trade goods as a massive obsession.

Indisputably, people desire goods that are useful, and steel axes are vastly more efficient than stone axes in opening forest garden plots, as Carneiro's experiment among the Yanomami proved (1979). However, the intrinsic attractiveness or innate superiority of Western manufactured products can explain neither the relatively restricted list of desired goods nor the quantities of goods considered satisfactory by the Xikrin. Moreover, Xikrin make no distinction between what we understand as necessities and luxuries, and the latter can hardly be judged in relation to measures of efficiency.

The implication is that the allure of trade goods themselves explains the Indians' desire for them. This sort of explanation, resting on the assumed inherent quality of the goods themselves, transforms indigenous people into rational consumers who are merely expressing a preference among alternative uses of their time or resources. Such an approach obscures the question of how goods are acquired and incorporated into the lives and societies of indigenous peoples operating with different regimes of value and social structures. In addition, the perspective of "Indian as consumer" does little to inform our understanding of change in indigenous societies, beyond implying that once natives are released from the narrow confines of choices available in their own society, they will take their place among the rest of us in the global marketplace. Conversely, such a perspective may lead some romantics to suggest that a preference for western trade goods represents a corruption of the system of aboriginal beliefs and values. Both perspectives, deriving as they do from the focus on the quality of the product itself, downplay the active transforming power exercised by native belief systems and organization and their role in determining the logic and circumstance of the adoption (and refusal) of different types of trade goods.

An additional factor complicates any notion that the desire for Western trade be interpreted in terms of individual consumer preference; where I did fieldwork, the acquisition of goods was so often a collective endeavor that I was suspicious that many goods were incorporated precisely because they could be consumed "socially" and hence were best seen as an emblem of group achievement. Since exclusion from consuming collectivities amounted to exclusion from society, it seemed clear that little or no individual choice could be involved. In other words, a particular repertoire of Western trade goods reflected conditions of Xikrin life rather than individual desires for certain items.

Goods that found their way into the Xikrin village were distributed and consumed in accordance with Xikrin traditions and social units. An outsider could not observe the Xikrin's mode of hunting, foraging, and horticulture and deduce from this a list of items, such as steel axes and fishing line, that would be considered necessities for all. Leaving aside for the moment that the Xikrin refused to make a distinction between luxuries and necessities, it was clear that one could never predict how goods would be used, owned, or apportioned merely by examining the abstract requirements of the horticultural or hunting process itself. Xikrin social organization distributes social labor and its products and determines the conventions for the circulation and utilization of trade goods. One cannot possibly begin with the character of the goods themselves to deduce the specific social units (e.g., households, age grades) that establish the parameters for trade-goods use in the processes of production, distribution, and consumption. Here one has to rely on careful ethnography that pays attention to ideas and behavior as well as to the collective consequences of behavior that may lie beyond the consciousness of the actors involved.

As presented thus far, the study of trade goods and indigenous peoples promises to shed light on the interrelated changes in indigenous belief systems, social forms, and relations with the larger dominant society. However, conservationists and environmental policy makers and the rest of us should pay attention to such cases for other reasons as well. Both the population of indigenous peoples in Latin America, some 40 million (and their number is rising) (Wearne 1996, 3), and the resources over which they are entitled to exercise control suggest that we need to envision diverse ethnic groups or peoples, each with distinct needs and even ecologies, coexisting within nation-states. For example, researchers estimate that in 1987 "69 percent of the mahogany exported from Brazil" came from Kayapó reservations in the eastern Amazon (CEDI 1991, 312). Some of this was stolen, but the impulse for some of this economic movement, from the Amazon to global markets, resulted from the Kayapó desire for trade goods, or, more properly, from the part that such goods play in the relations between and among Indians and non-Indians as a result of the history of contact.

The respected ecologist Philip Fearnside calls mahogany a "catalytic species," claiming that logging of this valuable hardwood sets in motion a series of events, from road building to land occupation, that "eventually leads to destruction of the entire ecosystem" (1997, 305). He singles out the Kayapó as one of a number of tribes who have been corrupted by loggers and who continue to defy attempts to implement a moratorium on mahogany exports. According to Fearnside, Indians are not merely hapless victims but are active abettors of loggers and hence agents in the environmental destruction unleashed by logging activity. Rather than sweep this issue under the rug, as Fearnside accuses many environmental and indigenous rights advocacy groups of doing, I believe we need to confront it squarely and develop tools to understand cross-cultural transactions on the boom-bust frontier. A blanket condemnation of indigenous corruption will prove less effective in conservation efforts than an understanding of the sociological complexities. Ecological effects are part of a complex web of causality (Vandermeer and Perfecto 1995), the understanding of which lies not only in listening to indigenous voices but in analyzing the configurations of social relations and institutions both forged by and forced on indigenous peoples.

Before describing the method used to examine the multifaceted processes involved in the relation between trade goods, Indians, and logging, let us take a closer look at the main protagonists of this work.

THE KAYAPÓ

Living Kayapó in today's Amazon are descendants of the "Northern Kayapó," so-called to distinguish them from the now vanished "Southern Kayapó" who inhabited extensive areas from the central Brazilian savannas as far south as the state of São Paulo. The Bakajá Xikrin-Kayapó share a common origin and cultural tradition with other Kayapó peoples, currently divided between fifteen communities scattered widely over the southern part of the Brazilian state of Pará and the northeastern portion of Mato Grosso. All communities trace their origin to a single ancestral village that lay on the rolling savanna between the Araguaia and Tocantins Rivers, in what is now the state of Tocantins (Verswijver 1992). Whatever differences in language and organization exist between the diverse Kayapó and Xikrin populations have arisen during a century and a half of separation, tempered by the friendly and unfriendly contacts in the interim. The Xikrin split from the main body of Kayapó fairly early (perhaps as early as 1810 or as late as 1850) and have received less global scientific and media attention than the remainder of the Kayapó. The war clubs, feather headdresses, large lip disks, and colorful body paint sported by Kayapó warriors have furnished arresting imagery for countless newsreels, papers, and magazines worldwide.

The Kayapó themselves are part of a wider linguistic and cultural tradition that includes a number of other indigenous peoples classified by linguists as part of the Macro-Gê language stock. The designation *Gê* originated with the German explorers Martius and Spix, who, in the course of their natural history travels between 1817 and 1820, met many Indian peoples in the Brazilian hinterlands. Apart from language, Gê peoples share many cultural similarities. They are horticulturists and hunters whose lifestyle often combines both sedentary villages and seasonal mobility in the form of organized treks. Among notable Gê features are circular village forms, elaborate social organization predicated on a dualist cosmology, the use of age and gender divisions to group people for both ritual and quotidian purposes, and the use of rituals to create differently endowed ceremonial persons within an overall framework of material equality (cf. Mayberry-Lewis 1965, 1979; Carneiro da Cunha 1993). The relationship between the myths of different Gê peoples has been carefully probed in Lévi-Strauss's monumental four-volume *Mythologiques* (1969–81).

The Kayapó are one of the larger lowland indigenous groups in South America, numbering around five thousand, and have successfully obtained demarcated reservations totaling tens of thousands of square hectares. Many Kayapó communities have been fieldwork sites for anthropologists, and the resulting ethnographic studies have shed light on many aspects of Kayapó culture and social life. In addition to the attention to symbolism, ritual, and social organization, specialists have studied Kayapó classification and manipulation of their environment (Posey 1979, 1985).

The Xikrin, along with all other Kayapó, refer to themselves as the "people of the watery place" or "Mebêngôkre." As is common in the cases of many tribal peoples, both "Kayapó" and "Xikrin" are labels originally applied by outsiders that have stuck (Fried 1975). In tribal councils and conversations within Kayapó communities, "Mebêngôkre" continues to be the term of choice. Different labels are used by indigenous peoples to make many subtle sociological distinctions in a variety of contexts. To simplify matters, during the remainder of the book, I will use the terms "Xikrin" or "Kayapó" when referring to specific Mebêngôkre communities with a prefix indicating the name of the community of which they are a part (e.g., Gorotire Kayapó, Cateté Xikrin).

The arrangement of Kayapó communities reflects their ideas about the proper creation of social persons. According to native ideas, such persons develop physical and cultural powers through their own actions and, as important, those of relatives and age mates. Only intact functioning communities may recreate the knowledge, social ornaments, and bodily potencies of the different ages and genders necessary for the continuation of Kayapó society. Residences form a circle around a central open plaza (or occasionally along a street) that is a site for dancing, singing, ceremony, and speechmaking. Under normal circumstances, the center is reserved for collective male activities from which females are excluded or act as adjuncts. Females gather outside of domestic houses or outside the village proper. However, in certain ritual contexts, this disposition of gendered space is inverted and males and females take up the place of their gender opposites.

The distinction between male and female space allows a contrast between maleness and femaleness, and the qualities and activities associated with each are part of a scheme that is at one and the same time a moral taxonomy, a natural history, and an organizational hierarchy. Most students of Gê societies agree that binary oppositions appear in many guises and are a key to understanding both the village layout and the natural and supernatural worlds within which it is set. Among the Kayapó, as among other Gê, the use of principles of opposition or contrasts is pervasive, and binary contrasts figure prominently in both social structure and systems of classification. Within Kayapó communities the domestic sphere of the house is contrasted with the collective public space; unmarried people, especially males, are contrasted with married folk; chiefs are contrasted with commoners; people without ceremonial inheritances are arrayed against those with such birthrights. Whereas all cultures use exclusion and contrast to create categories, in Kayapó society such contrasts are conceptualized in terms of antithetical qualities that both oppose and complement one another. Both are equally necessary for the recomposition of the encompassing order or totality of which they are a part. Kayapó understand the reality of society, nature, and the cosmos to be forged from a unity of opposites.

As an example of this basic outlook, I have written elsewhere (Fisher n.d.) about the contrast between married and unmarried men. Both are dependent upon each other in a personal kinship sense and in a larger collective sense. All men, indeed, all Xikrin, benefit from complementary activities organized according to age. However, both the diet and the activities of unmarried men are

Figure 1. Aerial view of the Bakajá Xikrin village in 1985 with landing strip in the foreground. (Photo by author)

thought to be the opposite of those of married men. In order to prepare themselves for the transformative experience of fatherhood, bachelors do not emulate fathers; they sleep, work, and dance in ways that distinguish them from what they will become. This opposition has major organizational consequences, since married and unmarried men often act as separate collectivities. However, studies from many different communities reveal the flexibility inherent in this system of age organization. Demographic factors, factionalism, competition for leadership, and the availability of different extra-village sources of trade goods may produce organizational variants, as the collected group of males is subdivided in different ways. Sometimes unmarried and married men are united and opposed to other groups of similar makeup, or finer age distinctions form the basis of collectivities, such as the contrast between men with few children and those with many children. Elders may form a separate group or assimilate with a group of fathers. On their own, the logical principles used to distinguish separate age categories are insufficient to describe the actual groups of agemates one will encounter in a given village.

Anthropologists have long been fascinated with dualist systems of thought and have sought to understand the specifics: how are opposing categories mediated? How are different pairs of oppositions conjoined, either in the human mind or in human social arrangements? How are notions of both equivalence and hierarchy ordered through simple binary contrasts? Anthropologists find these issues relevant for understanding the prevalence of dualist thought and organization in the societies, religious thought, and cosmologies of many peoples. Although seemingly abstract, they are central to a comparative understanding of human social arrangements.

I will not systematically explore these aspects of Kayapó society in this book, but I discuss social organization inasmuch as it plays a part in understanding the transformations that have occurred in the lives of the Xikrin. Part of the difficulty stems from anthropology's treatment of thought and social relations as a system in and of itself, where every relationship and component is held to be indispensable for the re-creation of a total system. We lack models and hypotheses about which aspects of tradition react to, participate in, and generate changes in response to both social contradictions and larger ecological and social circumstances. Yet we cannot ignore the logic behind social forms. Every permutation of Kayapó age organization discussed herein would then appear sui generis as an adaptation to immediate circumstances rather than a reflection of a culturally specific Kayapó social order that itself comprises a part of broader networks of relationships.

Rather than attempt to describe Kayapó thought as a system of logical abstractions, I try to show how indigenous ideas and organization have played a part in shaping processes of frontier contact and change in village work organization. Village social institutions reflect both widespread regional processes, such as the Brazil nut trade, and homegrown developments within villages. I believe an in-depth focus on a single community best describes the way community institutions have interacted with the specific spatial displacements and extra-community relations induced by the boom-bust frontier. Kinship, friendship, and a shared identity link Kayapó of different villages, although Kayapó acknowledge the unique experience of each village.

Some of the recent ties between Kayapó villages and the wider world have taken place in full view of a global public. The actions of Kayapó leaders together with environmentalists and defenders of Indian rights—in protest and lobbying initiatives in Brazil and around the world—have made the Kayapó one of the most widely portrayed indigenous people in the popular media.

The Kayapó have made hundreds of newspaper headlines over the past decades. Kayapó mobility, readiness to take up arms, and the successive waves of economic interlopers on Kayapó land—rubber tappers, cattle ranchers, squatters, gold prospectors, road builders, and loggers—resulted in many confrontations. In 1980

Kayapó warriors appeared on front pages around Brazil after they clubbed eleven ranch hands. The public largely accepted this action as a legitimate defense of the Xingu National Park, home to the Kayapó and some thirteen other indigenous communities, from the owner of the São Luis ranch and other large landowners who sought to expand into park lands (*Jornal do Brasil* 14 August 1980).

Thereafter Kayapó militancy brought them attention throughout the country. Warriors occupied the ferry along the roadway through the northern portion of the Xingu National Park, holding its crew hostage. Several hundred kilometers to the east, Kayapó occupied a gold mining site with 196 men, detaining some five thousand miners until they were guaranteed 5 percent of gold production (*Veja* 6 November 1985). Subsequently, Kayapó leaders made good use of their reputation and newfound wealth, taking their actions to the heart of Brazil's political establishment. They successfully demonstrated against the dumping of nuclear waste in the Serra do Cachimbo near Kayapó lands. During the long months of drafting Brazil's new democratic constitution, Kayapó men lobbied the halls of congress and gathered in the galleries and hearing rooms as their leaders and advocates testified during the drafting of the new constitution. They sought to ensure that the interests of indigenous peoples were addressed and especially that subsoil rights to the mineral wealth on reservation lands were not extended willy-nilly to large mining concerns.

As a result of their activity, the Kayapó were arguably the most visible indigenous group in Brazil during the 1980s and became international celebrities as well. In February 1988 Kayapó leaders Payakan and Kube'i, along with anthropologist Darrell Posey, spoke out against a Brazilian power sector loan under consideration by the World Bank at the bank's headquarters in Washington and in media covered events in the United States. The loan was to fund a series of hydroelectric dams along the Xingu River that threatened to disrupt at least eleven indigenous reserves (Santos and Andrade 1988). Upon their return to Brazil all three faced legal charges stemming from the authorities' anger at the threat to Brazil's economic interests. These charges were eventually dropped, although not before a spirited demonstration of four hundred Kayapó warriors in front of the courthouse in Belém also made international headlines (Posey 1989).

Dwarfing all this coverage, however, was the February 1989 protest against the dam project held in Altamira, Pará. The protest was orchestrated by Kayapó leader, Payakan, and publicized as the "First Meeting of Indigenous Peoples of the Xingú." At the event five hundred Kayapó and one hundred invited representatives from forty other tribes were almost equaled in number by news media, politicians, and NGO supporters (Turner 1993). The demonstration appeared to be crucial in the eventual rejection of the power sector loan. To the media and politicians Payakan presented the Kayapó's struggle against the dam as part of a larger effort to avert ecological catastrophe. This stance converged with that cultivated by other Kayapó leaders. For example, Chief Ropni (Raoni) had previously surprised many Brazilians who thought of him primarily as a warrior when he dedicated himself to learning healing ceremonies and attempted to cure the cancer of widely known Brazilian naturalist Augusto Ruschi in 1986. With the blessing of Indian supporters, the media coronated the Kayapó as "guardians of the rain forest." The Kayapó were able to attract support from environmentalists and NGOs. They were key players in generating enthusiasm surrounding participation of indigenous peoples in efforts to reforge relationships between governments, NGOs, and local populations seen at the gathering of the United Nations Conference on Environment and Development in Rio de Janeiro in 1992.

Throughout the 1980s prominent Kayapó leaders—Payakan, Ropni (Raoni), Pombo, Kube'i, Megaron—became accomplished speakers before nonindigenous audiences. They appeared in Brazil and also traveled to Europe and North America. As far back as 1977, a film featuring Ropni had been shown outside of competition at the Cannes Film Festival. Ropni later appeared on the TV program of talk show host Phil Donahue. Payakan graced the cover of the *Parade Sunday Magazine* (Whittemore 1992) inserted in newspapers nationwide. The headline "A Man Who Would Save the World" appeared beneath his ochre-painted countenance. Megaron, a relative of chief Ropni, rose to administrator of the Xingu National Park and later was appointed to head the cabinet of the Brazilian Indian Agency (FUNAI) in the mid-1980s.

Clearly, charismatic and forceful leaders are a key to Kayapó successes in securing demarcation of their reservations as well as health care, education, and basic food and trade goods. Such leaders bargain with the FUNAI and other government agencies, environmental NGOs, and frontier entrepreneurs. Within the Amazon, these latter include miners, loggers, and Brazil nut gatherers; internationally, the Body Shop cosmetics firm contracts for natural products supplied from Kayapó reserves. Leaders seek to make contacts with the outside world in order to forward the interests of their communities and bolster their standing within the village. The leaders are the visible symbols of Kayapó identity and culture consumed by the public and media, and the Kayapó's ability to deal with the outside world and attract allies and supporters hinges on them. Unfortunately, reliance on public opinion for prestige and resources means the loss of the same when public approval evaporates. Those who supported the Kayapó because of the part they played in protecting the rain forest turned against them when their role as forest protectors was called into question.

The backlash against the Kayapó's ecological image was inevitable once it became public knowledge that leaders were making money from logging and gold prospecting within their reservations. This pulled the rug out from under the image of the Kayapó as allies of ecologists. In some cases, the same leaders were playing both sides of the street, soliciting sustainable projects from environmentalists while simultaneously negotiating the exploitation of timber and minerals within their own reservations. The fall from grace was compounded when it was revealed that chiefs were squandering much of the wealth they had accumulated as brokers for their community on luxuries such as cars, real estate, and mistresses.

A scant year and a half after being touted as world savior, Payakan was back in the North American press, this time portrayed as a scoundrel. "Amazon Tribe Takes Villain Role: Chiefs Cash in on Rain Forest," reads the headline to Katherine Ellison's article in the *Times-Picayune* (23 September 1993), an example of dozens of similar-sounding articles published around this time. Some of the more conservative press could hardly disguise their triumphal tone at the downfall of ecological standard-bearers: "Kayapó Indians Lose Their 'Green' Image" trumpets a front-page *Wall Street Journal* article by Matt Moffett (29 December 1994). The ironies of this dramatic turn, in which the media and Western public seem incapable of rising above their stereotypes of Indians, have been thoughtfully discussed in recent popular works on the Amazon (Rabben 1998; O'Connor 1998).

The present account deals with a Xikrin community that has remained largely removed from the notoriety and extravillage ties of many other Kayapó communities. Nevertheless, Xikrin have had to contend with many of the same problems and regional trends. If logging and gold mining became a fixture among many Kayapó communities in the mid-1980s, a short half a decade later, these same industries were a prominent part of Xikrin lives. While there are similarities and differences in the experience of each village, events in one indigenous community tend to have ripple effects in other communities, since the Kayapó form a network throughout Central Brazil. Villages are poles of attraction for young men from other Kayapó communities seeking excitement, marriage partners, or access to trade goods. Loggers and miners move from one reservation to another, and their entrance may be helped by introductions furnished by Kayapó leaders from other villages. Some Kayapó villages have also formed regional associations to assert control over the economic development affecting their reservations (Turner 1995). Sometimes chiefs from different villages unite to consult one another, ongoing soccer rivalries heat up relations between villages, and shortwave contact over hundreds of kilometers are frequent occurrences. Despite these ties, each village retains political autonomy over its own future, and a common store of tradition has not generated identical developments in all villages. Indeed, one of the fascinating things about the present study is that it allows us to see factors influencing the history of specific indigenous communities and to begin to explore the limits of a purely cultural analysis for understanding the complexities of indigenous life on the reservation.

THEORY AND METHOD

This study rests on the premise, put forward with increasing sophistication and clarity in recent years, that far from being pristine isolates, indigenous communities are always part of a wider social field. In particular, it may be said that up until quite recently, the Xikrin occupied an area Ferguson and Whitehead (1992) would label a "tribal zone," an area continuously affected by the proximity of a state yet escaping direct state administration. While indigenous people within the particular tribal zone considered here contributed to its overall dynamic, a central feature is its character as an extractive frontier. The exchange of natural resources such as timber, minerals, fruits and nuts of undomesticated trees, animal and plant oils, and other products, such as rubber and wild cacao, along with medicines, dyes, spices, and even the "collection" of slave labor, has shaped the settlement, social organization, and lifestyle of both Europeans and native inhabitants.

The tribal zone within which Xikrin found themselves experienced boom-bust cycles linked to extractivist production whose commodities were taken directly from nature with only minimal processing. Rubber is a familiar example, and mahogany is simply the latest natural product in a long line of others that tie the Amazon to global markets. Extractivist activities can be contrasted with manufacturing in which raw materials are transformed through production processes that require the continual input of capital and labor. These activities may likewise be contrasted with the domestication of plants and livestock, since extractivists must follow the natural distribution and regeneration of commodities rather than shape them to their own requirements. The extractive economy of the Amazon expands and contracts in cyclical fashion because the expansion phase is inevitably self-limiting as the natural commodity becomes scarce, depleted, or rises in unit cost to the point where cultivated or synthetic alternatives are developed (Bunker 1985, 25). Bunker (1985) contends that the collapse of a particular commodity undermines subsequent expansion of productive forces predicated on further extraction since each extractive product embodies a different natural form and thus demands a different set of extraction skills and application of labor as well as a different disposition of administration, settlement, and infrastructure. Rather than developing out of previous activities, each successive wave of production represents a "new beginning" and not an expansion or redirecting of existing production capacity.

This work examines the relationship between the Xikrin community and the boom-bust frontier in terms of the changes wrought within the indigenous community itself. Beginning with the present state of affairs in the community, I worked both with historical sources and with Xikrin informants to understand the process that has produced deep-seated anxieties regarding horticulture and other subsistence activities. While not always visibly linked to frontier activities, the external events of Brazilian development have been experienced within the Xikrin village in terms of what I call "the frontier within": familiar indigenous institutions have taken on a different feel and begun to work in different ways. Over the course of time social relationships have acquired new meanings, diet and work have changed radically, and the Xikrin have begun to see themselves in a new way.

If changes within Xikrin communities correlate in some fashion to larger frontier processes, the end result has been a dependency on certain tools and utensils that Xikrin were not able to manufacture themselves. The Xikrin became "dependent" in the classic sense that on their own, they could no longer produce all the necessary preconditions for the reproduction of their social relations. In order to recreate relations within the village, Xikrin had to develop relations beyond the village through which they could acquire what they needed. However, in their case, the possibility of developing enduring articulations with the outside world was precluded by the very boom-bust trends that shaped social relations on the frontier.

During the process of colonial expansion, autonomous communities have been incorporated into larger systems and rendered "dependent" through such practices as barter or trade, wage labor, debt peonage, as well as taxation and tribute, sumptuary laws, and other legal and extralegal compulsions. In some cases, Europeans adapted ideological and organizational forms for generating wealth and empire building that had been cultivated by pre-Columbian indigenous states (e.g., Spalding 1984; Stern 1982). In the case of the Xikrin, these possibilities were rendered moot by a combination of the proclivities of the Xikrin themselves and the nature of the extractive commodities found in their region. While such relations as debt peonage or trade with extractive bosses tied indigenous peoples to extractive fronts in other areas of the Amazon, such as the Mundurucú of the Tapajós (Burkhalter and Murphy 1989), Kayapó peoples were only rarely involved in such relations and only for brief periods. Missionaries have been much more effective agents among the Kayapó in this regard, although in contrast to other Kayapó, the Bakajá Xikrin have only sporadically been visited by priests from the prelate in Altamira, and then for only a few days at a time.

Within the boom-bust frontier context, Xikrin developed ways of exercising their collective power that were primarily based on their ability to disrupt or threaten disruptions of extractivist production or, in more recent times, on development initiatives by the Brazilian government or corporations (Fisher 1994). This implies that the Xikrin had an awareness of regional events beyond their ordinary social sphere and developed collective social forms and mobility as a means to shape the terms of their existence within larger social, economic, and political networks. The organizational power of Xikrin social forms shaped the context of contact with extractivists and others in the region and created conditions to resist or escape the power of the extractive industries and the Brazilian state. Social organization was forced to work in two senses, to establish connections beyond the village and to create mechanisms to preserve autonomy.

In order to reconstruct the correlation between changes in the frontier situation and Xikrin organization, I first was obliged to construct a periodization of the boom-bust cycles of the Xikrin tribal zone based on nonindigenous sources. Initially this periodization was compiled in order to grasp the variety of tactics employed by Xikrin to achieve their aims over a number of boom-bust cycles (Fisher 1994). Subsequently, in the field once again, I used my knowledge of the different periods of extractive cycles to engage the Xikrin in discussions regarding the larger regional structures they had confronted over the course of their history. While I brought the questions to the table, the discussion was not entirely on my terms, since the Xikrin raised all kinds of considerations that would have been unforeseen by a cultural outsider. The history that follows, therefore, does not resemble a history told in a spontaneous native idiom, but is the fruit of an extended dialogue over a period of months during which the issue of Xikrin relations with the outside world and changing forms of society and work organization were discussed in a number of venues. In lieu of a complete chronological sequence of events and settlement locations, I present what the Xikrin offered as illustration of the crucial episodes that reveal their relations with the wider world. Once Xikrin interest in the topic had been ignited, I could scarcely avoid discussing their previous contacts with the world beyond the village or the features of village work life during different historical epochs.

The historical chapters that follow, particularly as we move closer to the present, describe how work has been modified and how new sorts of contradictions and tensions emerged as a result of these modifications. Beginning with the culturally specific Xikrin framework for social action with its implicit rules and limits, I sought to document the background against which strategies are formulated. In this effort I tried to build on the existing understanding of Gê social organization (e.g., Maybury-Lewis 1979) while resisting the idea that organizational forms were ends in themselves. All social arrangements indicate both a social order and ways in which this order is inadequate. Individuals and groups within a sociocultural order learn what is desirable and necessary and the means at their disposal, sanctioned or not, to strive for these. I document some of the factors that differentiate Xikrin from one another while positioning each within a common network of social relations and symbols that make their different visions intelligible. In this I followed Bourdieu's (1977, 21) suggestion that

Only by constructing the objective structures (price curves, chances of access to higher education, laws of the matrimonial market, etc.) is one able to pose the question of the mechanisms through which the relationship is established between the structures and the practices or the representations which accompany them, instead of treating these "thought objects" as "reasons" or "motives" and making them the determining cause of the practices.

The anthropologist attempts to understand how relationships involving cultural, technological, and ecological dimensions, among others, are both conserved and changed by people with different stakes in the existing order. For example, through a survey of trade goods in households I show that all Xikrin do not have equal access to trade goods. Furthermore, the size and location of kinship networks, including relations in other Kayapó communities, patterns of past sponsorship of name-confirmation ceremonies, as well as personal work and marriage histories, play a part in making Xikrin a common community and in determining options available to differently situated individuals. Being part of a kin network implies being either well or poorly positioned with kin for certain purposes. Such considerations helps us understand the pressures and opportunities faced by differently positioned individuals (or sets of individuals) and how they contribute to the process of change.

When different individuals derive different benefits from collective social organization and face the task of fulfilling work obligations with different resources at their disposal, the sheer act of making a living involves what we can call "political" considerations. The fact that organizational forms benefit some more than others imbues collective activities with their political content. The insight that subsistence activities are not only a culturally specified means to make a living but also arenas of intracommunity as well as extracommunity politics has been well made by Smith (1989). From this perspective we are able to more fully see the effect of the frontier on community life, since we focus not only on the sensational, such as the raids on mining camps or the openly defiant confrontations with the FUNAI and extractivists, but also on the day-to-day activities. Workaday life turns out to be exquisitely expressive of the tensions and frustrations as well as the triumphs of ordinary people who still confront within their village a social world and physical infrastructure they have largely crafted with their own muscle and mind.

Although we have described social life in terms of social relations, relations with the environment are equally key. In fact, a central piece of wisdom from the nascent field dubbed "political ecology" holds that any human engagement with nature or the environment simultaneously expresses a social relationship and a position within a network of social power. This insight suggests that subsistence is a good place to begin examining how, in challenging the power of the FUNAI, the extractive industries, and the reservation system, the Xikrin Kayapó have developed organizational forms to act collectively within the frontier context.

A previous study of growing native Amazonian reliance on trade goods and markets ingeniously compared the relative difficulty of making a living in several communities, as measured by the ratio of labor input to food output. The study found that increased sedentarization and pressure on local resources forced indigenous groups to intensify their production effort. Trade goods and metal tools, obtained through market activities, facilitated intensification. The intrinsic attractiveness of Western goods was less important than relationships with the environment, and the length of exposure to Western goods did not correlate with differences in community market involvement. Rather, market partici-pation appeared to be an "adaptation to environmental forces" (Gross et al. 1979, 1049).

The study suggests a feedback loop in which increased habitat degradation and/or population increases require greater intensification of labor effort, which in turn depend on larger inputs of Western manufactures. Follow-up research has not borne out this scenario of spiraling environmental degradation and dependency and suggests that indigenous ecologies are also shaped by historical factors and relations with larger Brazilian society. The Xavante community included in the study by Gross and his collaborators actually dedicates less time today to horticulture and more time to collecting wild resources than during the time of the original study (Santos et al. 1997). Social change, intensification, and reliance on trade goods cannot be explained solely as a response to the environ-ment. Rather, the interplay between local factors and the larger regional context is shaped by indigenous practices whose ramifications are both political and eco-logical (e.g., Picchi 1995).

We begin our examination of the Bakajá Xikrin, far removed from their pres-ent village, in a time and place in which they found themselves enmeshed in a regional diplomacy and conflict that would propel them to their present location. The historical background sets the stage for an understanding of their present dilemmas.

2 | THE RISE OF RUBBER AND RELIGION

Brazilian frontier expansion was never a sustained steady push westward of people, farms, or industry. Instead, sporadic nuclei of Europeans became irregularly sprinkled over the landscape, as colonists leapfrogged from one area to another, wherever patchily distributed resources could be found. They sought whatever products—animal, vegetable, or mineral—could be exploited for commercial value, anything from human slaves to cacao or gold. European nuclei were often fleeting, established and later disbanded during the pulse of outward movement and subsequent reflux of return migration.

While Brazil's full territorial limits were known quite early, its great interior was crisscrossed, flooded, and emptied over the course of centuries, as different products entered their commercial heyday, only to be exhausted or supplied more cheaply to the world market by other regions. Historian Russell-Woods (1989, 5) has described the Brazilian frontier, such as it was, as "hollow," in contrast with the progressive westward expansion in North America. He suggests that the Brazilian interior might best be treated as a metaphorical frontier consisting of overlapping cultures rather than as a solid expanding front. Curtin (1968, 92) coined the term "transfrontiersmen" for European inhabitants of the Brazilian frontier zone, since they lived beyond the reach of legal and administrative state control.

BRAZIL'S HOLLOW FRONTIER

Thus for centuries the Brazilian frontier was what Ferguson and Whitehead (1992) have termed a "tribal zone." While operating within a larger system of influences, indigenous peoples living in the tribal zone had (and continue to have) their own resources, traditions, and social organization to draw upon in formulating the decisions they make in such circumstances.

Much of the genesis of Kayapó society took place within Brazil's hollow frontier, where the reach of state institutions was weak, fleeting, or nonexistent. Moreover, European colonies did not merely seek native labor. Native knowledge of the terrain and its resources was sought by entrepreneurs in the caucho rubber trade. As we will see, the history of the Xikrin must be seen as more than a mere reaction to Europeans' actions, threats, and trade goods.

The Xikrin were apparently one of the first large factions to break off from the ancestral Kayapó. Whether this split occurred during the time the Kayapó inhabited the triangle formed by the Araguaia and Tocantins Rivers or after their migration to the western bank of the Araguaia is not known. Vidal (1977, 13) suggests that by 1859 when the Kayapó entered into contact with the New Mission of Santa Maria, the faction that gave rise to the Xikrin had already separated from the main group. By this date the Kayapó were settled on the western bank of the Araguaia. They established themselves here sometime between 1824 and 1859, when they had been reported as living on the eastern side of the river by Matos (1874), a military officer loyal to the newly independent Brazil. Xikrin histories seem silent on the reason for their initial separation from the Kayapó village. However, the remainder of the non-Xikrin Kayapó are still occasionally called "snake children" referring to the prolific offspring resulting from the mythic union between a Kayapó women and a snake.

INTERTRIBAL TRADE

Narratives regarding contact and trade point to a time after the separation from the main body of Kayapó. Such tales provide a means for the Xikrin to interpret their current relations with the wider world and are framed to provide insights on the motivation of the ancestors. Most important, they reveal the degree to which elder Xikrin regard their present community as a product of long-standing interactions with others.

Jaguar, who was the dominant chief during my fieldwork, relates that the village of his ancestors was very populous and situated in proximity to a Karajá Indian settlement. During this period, the Karajá and Xikrin got along quite well. An adventurous (ancestral) aunt of Jaguar's visited the Karajá village in order to observe their customs. Whether this was her only motivation or not, during her time in the Karajá village she maintained many amorous liaisons and, indeed, almost married into the village.[1] In telling the story Jaguar claims a direct kin tie to the story's protagonist. He substantiates this claim by reciting three different names she used. "Ngreinibeti," as she was commonly called, made several journeys to the Karajá village. At this time the Xikrin were involved in trading several natural items highly desired by the Karajá that were apparently rare around their own settlements close by the Araguaia River in what is now the Brazilian state of Tocantins. Xikrin were able to offer *bàjkà* (unknown sp.), a vine used along with beeswax to bind projectile tips to arrow shafts, macaw tail feathers, and macaw and parakeet hatchlings, which the Karajá could rear for feathers. In return the Xikrin received beads, machetes, and axes. According to Jaguar, this was not a one-time deal. Many trading excursions were made between Xikrin and Karajá settlements, but the items traded never varied. Neither did the direction of travel, for the Xikrin always went to the Karajá village while the reverse was never the case. The Karajá presumably had to stay closer to home if they wished to continue their river trade with Brazilians. At least one historical report (Coudreau 1897), however, states that Karajá were found in Xikrin villages.

Be that as it may, the pattern of trade seems clear: Xikrin furnished natural products, predominantly from forested regions, in return for manufactured goods. The Karajá almost certainly received these from passing river traffic, as Brazilian settlements in the region were few and far between until close to the turn of the century. On hearing the story today, Xikrin commented that the one-way traveling for trade purposes made sense since their ancestors, not having manufactured goods, had to go in pursuit of them.

Many published sources report that the lower Araguaia River had many Karajá villages strung along its banks and that these villages were essential stopovers for river travelers during the middle of the nineteenth century. Published travel memoirs for the 1840s (Castelnau 1949; Segurado 1848), 1860s (Magalhães 1975), and 1880s (Ehrenreich 1948) are very consistent in this regard. When a steamship line was inaugurated to facilitate trade between Goiás and Pará in 1871, attempts were made through both missionary and governmental actions to have the Karajá provide dependable supplies for the effort. "All along the Araguaia, the Karajá were encouraged to bring logs for the steamers' boilers and were to be paid in tools, tobacco, clothing and salt" (Hemming 1987, 394). It would not be surprising if some of the ax heads and machetes delivered to the Karajá found their way into the hands of the Xikrin along trade networks that extended between the factories of Europe and the forests and savannas that remained outside of Brazilian government administration.

This sort of trade, spanning numerous cultural boundaries, is of the same type that is carried out by other Kayapó with peoples other than the Karajá. At the turn of the century, Verswijver (1982) relates how the Mekrãgnoti Kayapó traded with the Juruna, offering arrows, parrots, and genipap fruit (used for body paint-ing) in return for glass beads. The parallel is very close, since the Juruna, like the Karajá, were river-dwelling peoples and hence had much better access to European wares. Both Mekrãgnoti and Xikrin women participated in travels between villages, and intergroup marriage was clearly a possibility in both cases.

But manufactured goods, however attractive, were not the sole reason to visit the Karajá village. Ceremonial needs prompted Karajá to seek feathers for decora-tion of the costumes used in their Aruanã ritual, and Karajá ceremonial life also proved of great interest to the Xikrin. This again has parallels with the Juruna trading partners mentioned above since the Kayapó have adopted Juruna songs in the *kwỳrỳ kangô* (manioc liquid) ritual dedicated to name confirmation and cur-rently celebrated in all Kayapó villages (Turner 1965). According to Jaguar, the Karajá have many versions of the Aruanã ceremony. Ngreinibeti closely observed the dance and other customs of the Karajá, which she faithfully recounted in much detail to the assembled Xikrin village. Although Ngreinibeti was profoundly familiar with various versions, the Xikrin ended up adopting only two of the cere-monies. These were labeled *bô* after the eponymous Xikrin term for the babassú palm, which was used to confect the costume. When the aunt gave up any idea of marrying into the Karajá village, she returned permanently to the village of Jaguar's ancestors and continued to oversee the correct performance of the festi-val she had imported. There is no doubt that the continued trade between the Karajá and the ancestors of the Xikrin must have kept the palm dance in vogue.

Intertribal trade did not continue indefinitely, according to Jaguar. The actions of one Xikrin man, A'ire, compromised the friendly relations enjoyed between the two peoples. A'ire's offense consisted of stealing from the Karajá village or being ungenerous with his own trade goods. Jaguar's version of the story has the Karajá calling thief after the fleeing A'ire as he raced from their village. Henceforth, trade was cut off, although Jaguar's account of this one episode of intertribal thievery segued into another far more serious sort of thievery be-tween Kayapó themselves.

FACTIONAL WARFARE

The incident that detonated what became a war of extermination had its roots in the absconding of the garden harvest from a plot apparently worked by two closely related groups of Kayapó. That members of two different villages should be cooperating on a single large garden plot is not too surprising given the typi-cal pattern of settlement evident during other periods of Kayapó history. As I

Figure 2. The Bô dance adapted from the Karajá as performed in 1994 under a non-functional floodlight. (Photo by author)

document more fully, at times large settlements give way to smaller, more temporary settlements whose residents visit each other for ceremonial feasting and the like (see Chapter 3). The separate settlements do not properly constitute autonomous communities, as they are bound together by ties of kinship, ritual responsibilities, and the expectation that under the proper conditions, inhabitants could easily reunite in a single settlement. Each settlement, however, does have distinct chiefs and age organization, although leaders from one community may subsequently become leaders of other similarly constituted communities and people may move freely between villages.

Splits in Kayapó communities are caused by tensions within the village, and relations between newly formed offspring settlements and their parent community are usually hostile. While the large ancestral village, whose population probably numbered in the thousands, did not disintegrate at once, over the course of perhaps thirty to forty years the site of the mother village was abandoned and the Djore or Xikrin, Irã'ãmrajre, and Gorotire factions were solidified. The Gorotire subsequently underwent several fissions in turn giving rise to the Mekrãgnoti, Kararaô, and other groupings. At least for the Djore or Xikrin, ongoing raids between former neighbors and kinsfolk became, perhaps, the overriding fact of life after the split, even overshadowing the push of Europeans into the savanna and forest regions on either side of the Araguaia.

That the inhabitants of two neighboring settlements considered themselves "Djore," in Jaguar's account, is evidence of their past unity as a faction within the larger Kayapó settlement. However, one settlement was referred to by the name of its men's club, "Mekukakĩnhti," or alternately by the plentiful cane for making arrows in the vicinity, "Kruakrô," or "Porekrô," while the other settlement was referred to by its prodigious gardens, "Purukarôt" (garden-constipated, full). Upon their return from an extended trek, this group was confronted by a garden stripped bare of its crops, which the hungry Djore had been expecting to feast on. The sight of the bare garden, with no sweet manioc, sweet potatoes, or squash, was so devastating that one man broke out in tears. Anger rapidly overcame his sadness, however, and he began to manufacture a war club to go after the culprits. While planing the wood down to a smooth finish with a broken mollusk shell he severely cut his finger. On seeing his mangled finger, his brother exclaimed that gripping the club in battle was now out of the question and offered to take up the club in his sibling's place. Thus began a full-scale mobilization, as the Djore prepared clubs and arrows for use against the depredators of their gardens.

When pursuing the offending party, one Djore recognized a song wafting back as the personal composition of a kinsman and concluded that the culprit was none other than the allied village! When the two sides met the battle was relentless, as only disputes between kin can be. The object was not only to make off with the desired goods as is the case with ordinary foes but to kill in order to erase the feelings of hatred that had built up in response to previous slights and offenses. In the course of battle the Purukarôt were decimated and their village of origin left empty *(me mõrõdjà kapry)*. While the adult men were killed, women and children were captured and taken to the Mekukakĩnhti settlement of the other Djore group. Left behind was the single escapee of the massacre, a man named "Nhojre," who belonged to the men's club "Ngànhỹtykti." He became so consumed with hatred for the killers of his comrades and relations that he devoted the rest of his short life to wreaking vengeance on warriors of the victorious settlement. He actually had the entire body of Mekukakĩnhti men in fear as

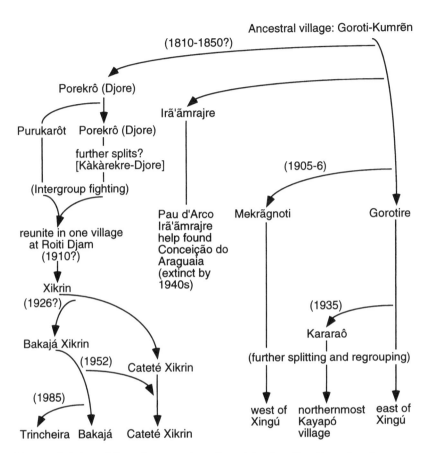

Figure 3. Relations of Kayapó community splits and timeline. (Ann Peters, based on Verswijver 1992, Vidal 1977, Turner 1992, and author's field notes)

he inflicted casualties one by one. Finally, he was tracked down and killed by a group of four men as he bathed in a small stream. Even to the end, his inner fury almost allowed him to prevail over such overwhelming odds.

The fathers of several elder members of the present-day village of Bakajá were children captured by the Mekukakĩnhti, according to Jaguar. In retrospect we can see that it was these children (and their mothers) who told the story to Jaguar, who recounts it from the point of view of the vanquished rather than the victors. Indeed, Jaguar identifies the present-day village with the defeated Purukarôt. Sympathies clearly lie with the heroic Nhojre who mounted his campaign of personal vengeance against an entire village. If the Purukarôt village was extinguished, how do they continue to figure in Xikrin identity?

PERSONAL HISTORY AND GROUP IDENTITY

Setting Jaguar's narrative against the present-day culture and social organization of the Xikrin points out the danger of simply using names of groups or factions to trace a history of splits between Kayapó groups. Anthropologist Eric Wolf (1982, 6) warned us against "turning names into things," because in this manner named entities become the only recognizable historical agents and the processes by which they are constituted may be rendered invisible. In the case of indigenous histories we cannot assume that simply because villages or men's clubs possess names that they are enduring corporate entities from which contemporary identity is derived. Men's club membership may be fluid, and village names, which often refer to the village's physical setting, are usually applied after the village has been abandoned. Moreover, there is no effort made to standardize village appellations, and different persons may persist in using different names. From the perspective of a child or a woman, the men's club allegiance of spouses may determine some activities and even village of residency. However, there is ample reason to avoid making the leap that the public identity of males overrides other sorts of identifications that due to the norm of uxorilocality tend to be reckoned through females. The standard ethnohistorical practice followed by Verswijver (1992), Turner (1992), and Vidal (1977), as well as the information conveyed in Figure 1 and some of the accounts in the present work, chart Kayapó history primarily in terms of men's organizations and village names. While village fissions and place names give us an idea of the locations of groupings in the recent historical past, such movements are not windows into processes of identity formation or sorts of historical agents considered vital to the Kayapó themselves.

Jaguar's story of the Djore internecine massacre is a case in point. The women and children of the defeated men never considered themselves assimilated to the public men's-club identity of their captors. Nor, it should be added, do village locations (or names, which often amount to the same thing) stand for groups of kin. Kayapó do not have unilineal descent groups of any kind, and even a very superficial examination of the kinship system shows that relations to both mothers' and fathers' families are quite important; kin ties cross-cut settlements as well.

Jaguar's summary that *"Jãnh kam Purukarôt"* (Those here have come from Purukarôt), or at other times *"ibê Djore"* (I am Djore) means neither that the existing Bakajá settlement is best described as "Purukarôt" or "Djore" or that past connections with people identified with these labels reveal something about the contemporary character of village inhabitants. In fact, at other places in Jaguar's narrative, he exclaimed that the Djore are no more *(Mebê Djore aʾyp kêt)*. There are certainly residents who would not claim identical Djore, Purukarôt, or

Porekrô antecedents as does Jaguar. But all inhabitants, with a couple of recent exceptions to be explored later, consider themselves "Xikrin." In this sense, of course, all these prior labels are irrelevant to group identity even while retaining an important place in individual narratives, and we should not assume names for villages or political factions signify perpetual corporate entities.

The origin of the term "Xikrin" remains a mystery. Vidal (1977, 14) believes that this term was used by the Irã'ãmrajre Kayapó to refer to the Djore faction and later became applied to the Purukarôt grouping as well. Variant spellings are encountered in historical and contemporary documents: Usikrin, Chricrîs, Tchikrin, among others. The stories recounted by Jaguar vary on different points from the evidence gathered by Vidal (1977, 13–42) regarding the history of the Xikrin. The accounts are in agreement that the group (Porekrô or Djore, depending on the source) that split from the Goroti-kumrẽn split again in its turn. Vidal's sources contend that at one time there were three separate groups—the Djore, Kàkàrekre, and Put-Karôt. The engineer Kissenberth listed three separate locations for Dzore, Purukaroto, and Chicris in 1909 (Hartmann 1982, 161). But Vidal states that it was the Djore, rather than the Kàkàrekre faction, that was denominated as "Xikrin." If individual Xikrin keep track of the past in order to reconstruct their personal antecedents, there is no reason to believe that all will agree on a single unified version of events. As is clear from his other accounts of events within the region, Jaguar's story compresses a good deal of time during which these different factions coexisted on a war footing and ranged over a wide swathe of territory between the Araguaia and Xingu (see following) and also diverges from Vidal as to which faction emerged victorious. However, both Vidal's informants and Jaguar believe that remnants of the original groups were eventually reassembled into a single community. Moreover, Jaguar adamantly maintains that Djore, Kàkàrekre, and Purukarôt antecedents can be found among residents of the present-day Bakajá village.

Jaguar tells of the village located near the present day town of Tucumã, called "Roiti Djam" ("Roti Djam" in Vidal 1977), which was inhabited by the Put-Karôt (Purukarôt) according to Vidal (p. 28). Indians engaged in trade with white settlers in this locale. During this period remnants of the Kàkàrekre who had been attacked by a band organized by rubber boss Chico Trajano were said to have joined the Put-Karôt group at Roiti Djam (ibid., 28, 17, fn. 14). Vidal's informants describe trade between Djore and Kàkàrekre factions with non-Indians; the Djore were said to possess shotguns during this period and to have joined with the rubber boss to attack the Kàkàrekre. There followed a time of constant conflict with the Gorotire group, and both Jaguar and Vidal's informants agree that a defensive palisade was constructed around some of the villages occupied during this time.

In other particulars Vidal's account fits in well with that told in the Ba
village. We can feel a degree of certainty regarding the names of villages occu
after the split with the Goroti Kumrēn (True Gorotire) Kayapó faction and
contact with Brazilian settlers was fairly common at this time. Both acco
confirm the friendly relations between the Djore and the Karajá, and both c
that villages were constructed in both savanna and tropical forest habitats. Fi
Vidal is clear that the internecine warfare between the Xikrin and the Gor
became a decisive factor in their decision to shift settlements frequently. More
Vidal's judgment over the essential accurateness of Coudreau's reporting hel
to establish with greater certainty the central place occupied by the nascent s
ment of Conceição do Araguaia in the lives of the Northern Kayapó of this pe

In striking particulars Jaguar's version of events confirms some of the i
mation gathered by the French explorer Henri Coudreau in 1896. The par
are significant because the source of Coudreau's information came by way c
Dominican missionary Frei Gil Vilanova, who was fairly proficient in Kaya
the time and enjoyed very good relations with the Irã'ãmrajre faction c
ancestral Kayapó. The settlement of Conceição do Araguaia was fruit of a
effort of Brazilians, principally ranchers, farmers, and rubber collectors fro
town of Sant'Ana da Barreira and the part of the Irã'ãmrajre faction whc
their own Indian village just outside the town (Ianni 1979, 14). Coudreau
204–5) points to the existence of four different groups of Kayapó: Gor
Irã'ãmrajre, Chicris, and Purucarús.

Jaguar's narrative helps us understand what may have been the outcome
relations between the Purukarôt and the Mekukakĩnhti or Djore. Altl
Coudreau locates the Chicrîs to the northeast of Conceição, and the Pur
(Purukarôt) to the west, this in itself is not evidence of a history of relati
between the two groups. More to the point, the Karajá Indians them
informed Coudreau (ibid., 205) that they had excellent relations with the C
and these Indians could frequently be found in one another's villages.
relates that at one time the Purukarôt occupied a village called Kapôt
rolling savanna not far from the Araguaia River ("Bytire"). From there he c
that the group roamed all the way to what is presently Serra Norte and T
and even as far as the region of São Félix do Xingu.[2] He explained that he
ered São Félix an "old" Brazilian settlement because it was along the water,
the town of Marabá. Other towns such as Serra Norte, Tucumã, Redenç
Conceição do Araguaia he identified as "new" because he claimed that
arrived there long after the Kayapó. He claimed that not only had the I
been living at Conceição do Araguaia before whites but that they had a
helped them to build what is now the Brazilian settlement. The historical

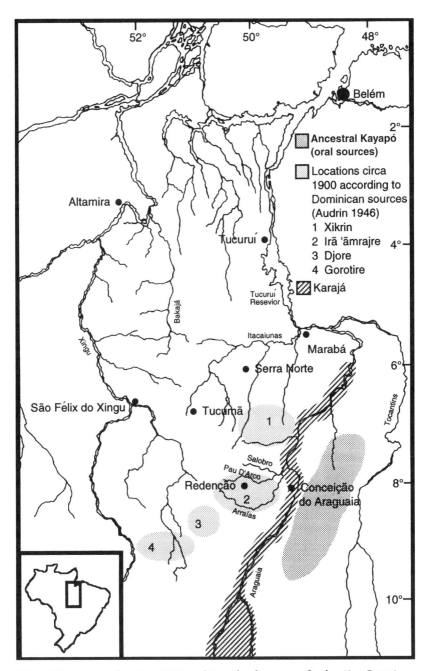

Map 1. The Araguaia frontier c. 1900 overlain with urban areas of today. (Ann Peters)

certainly bear this out. But Jaguar's knowledge of the role of his tribesfolk in founding the settlement implies some kind of contact between those "missionized" Irã'ãmrajre Kayapó and "wild" Kayapó of the Gorotire and Xikrin factions.

While they collaborated with missionaries and the settlement of Conceição do Araguaia, the Irã'ãmrajre maintained contact with kin in other villages. The realization that Conceição do Araguaia became the center of contact for several Kayapó factions turns out to be crucial for understanding the place of the Xikrin in the regional political economy during the rubber boom.

LIFE ON THE WEST BANK OF THE ARAGUAIA

The advantages of savanna living were great for people without firearms: armadillos and land turtles abounded and could be hunted with bare hands. While Jaguar was not sure if fish were plentiful, other easily collected resources such as honey were, and Xikrin ancestors formerly went into the forest only for specific reasons. They considered themselves savanna dwellers. On the savanna, they constructed the village of Kàkàrekre, which was surrounded by a palisade of saplings approximately eight feet high. Defensive precautions were necessary because of attacks by the Gorotire Kayapó, with whom they waged an incessant series of raids and counterraids. The conflict with the Gorotire was to prove decisive in their eventual move to the Bakajá region. However, in the meantime contacts between Xikrin and whites began to occur with increasing frequency.

The question of when Xikrin first encountered Brazilians or non-Indians is not cause for much reflection among Indian villagers. Whites, or *kubẽn kryt,* are simply another species of foreigners *(kubẽn)* with whom the Xikrin have come into contact. Early conflicts or trading relations with whites or mestizos do not form a distinct genre of stories; "foreign affairs" during the early part of Xikrin history encompassed relations with different groups, among whom Brazilians seemed to hold no greater interest than relations with other peoples. As Turner has commented, "The Kayapó . . . possess both 'historical' accounts and 'mythic' accounts of themselves, of other native peoples, and of their contacts with the Brazilians, and in either mode their accounts of the latter show no special forms or features that distinguish them from their accounts of the former" (Turner 1988, 199). On the other hand, while Brazilians may have controlled a broader array of manufactured goods than Xikrin, apparently the latter were successful in obtaining these through "result"-oriented raiding and trading. In other words, Xikrin did not have to contact whites directly to get their goods, and, aside from their goods, whites held no particular fascination.

Of perhaps greater interest than the origin of whites was the origin of the goods themselves. The appearance of such wondrous and useful items as machetes, ax heads, and glass beads was indeed cause for contemplation and is accorded mythological treatment along with other existential and ontological mysteries such as the appearance of war, fire, aspects of nature, and indeed the origin of the Kayapó themselves.

While the analysis of myth is itself almost an independent discipline, it is worthwhile contrasting the relative uniformity of the mythic origin of manufactured goods with the widely varying histories of contacts between different Kayapó groups and whites across the Brazilian frontier in the nineteenth century. Indeed, in a myth shared by many Gê peoples, it is thought that the errant shaman Wakmêkapran gave rise to Brazilians after inventing goods such as knives, axes, and beads.[3] That the Kayapó should assert that they themselves (or at least a dissident of their number) should be responsible for the origin of both Brazilians and their worldly possessions is not as astonishing as one might think. Myths also assert that the origin of many preeminent features of the natural world, such as birds, fish, and Brazil nut trees, were the result of transformations caused by Kayapó activity in the mythic past. On the other hand, natural items such as fire and even the bow and arrow were appropriated from the jaguar in order to establish enduring aspects of Kayapó sociality (Turner 1985). This interplay between the Kayapó and their surroundings, through which both nature and society continue to be formed and reformed, continues to play a prominent role in Kayapó philosophical thought, ritual, and ordinary beliefs and practices, which are reflected in a multitude of ways throughout the course of daily activities. The dependence of the Xikrin on manufactured goods is in no way mitigated by the ultimate origin of the latter in the actions of an antisocial Kayapó outcast who was driven from his village and forced to live by his own devices.

Xikrin versions of their contacts with whites are the stage for presenting the actions of ancestral relatives. Often immensely personal, in that these tales may be unknown to others in the village, they reveal an awareness of the ongoing presence of Brazilians and of a need to develop some policy toward them, less it seems because whites competed for living space or resources than because trading or raiding for goods became part of an economic policy for furthering the Xikrin's own subsistence and military aims. Although histories with whites are not marked as distinctive in oral histories, Xikrin have long been aware of the need to develop special expertise to deal with Euro-Brazilians.

Another curious fact mentioned by Coudreau was that while the Chicris transacted frequently with the Karajá and were on poor terms with the other branches of the Kayapó, they apparently lived in a state of mutual coexistence with Brazilians, each "keeping to their own side." Here it is interesting to hear Jaguar's version of this coexistence, which, according to his father before him, almost led to a "mixing" with Brazilians. The phrase used for "mixing" *(kam aben akà)* applies to dry stuff that mingles with things of another type, as when powdered milk is mixed with sugar, rather than a mixture of liquid substances. This, of course, implies that the Xikrin do not conceive of intermediate phases, analogous to the dilution of liquids, in which gradual acculturation occurs. They believe that a classificatory void lies between themselves and foreigners, and while it is possible for an Indian to adopt Brazilian ways and become a Brazilian, one cannot be only "partly" Indian or partly Brazilian.

In any case, whether referring to the payments whites made for sex with Xikrin girls or the presence of Xikrin among backland Brazilian towns or work parties, mixing with whites was a threat but also had some obvious advantages. Another chief, Bep Pruin, recalls that at one point whites offered an ax head in return for sex with a man's daughter and the offer was eagerly accepted. Others followed suit and offered their own daughters for axes and machetes. "I would have requested at least a firearm in return," Bep Pruin commented archly. At last, others in the group protested this practice. Men were mobilized to remove a Xikrin girl from where she was being held by whites. This led to a series of skirmishes in which both whites and Xikrin attacked one another.

Missionaries were very successful in convincing Indian adepts to cooperate with the river trade between Goiás and Belém. Frei Monte Vito, for example, helped organize the Gê-speaking Apinagé to settle near the Brazilian outpost of Boa Vista and provide a variety of services to navigators who descended the Tocantins and Araguaia Rivers. The French explorer Castelnau, who traveled the Araguaia in 1844, observed:

The [Apinagé] Indians are very industrious, and it is they, with their vast plantations, who feed not only the people of Boa Vista, but also the personnel of the river transport that navigate the Tocantins up to the post of São João. They pride themselves in being excellent rowers, many of them having made the voyage by river up to Belém of Pará. In return for this long trip that lasts anywhere from six to eight months, they receive by way of payment an ordinary shotgun costing some five or six francs. This explains the great number of firearms that one sees in their houses, notwithstanding the fact that they always prefer to do their hunting with bows and arrows. (Castelnau 1949, 348 [my translation])

Along other stretches of the Tocantins, an adventurous breed of private merchants helped to enlist allied Indian communities in the river trade, as exemplified by Pinto de Magalhães, who allied with the Gê-speaking Krahó to advance his commercial fortunes (Magalhães 1852). In contrast, the development of the rubber industry in the vicinity of the nucleus of Conceição do Araguaia obeyed a different logic. The land and labor of indigenous peoples were targeted by an industry that aimed to extract raw material found in the wild.

CONCEIÇÃO DO ARAGUAIA
AND THE RUBBER INDUSTRY

Around Conceição do Araguaia, as in the rest of the Amazon, rubber extraction was organized through the *aviamento* system. The *aviador* furnished the necessary equipment, credit, and foodstuff in return for the right to whatever was produced by the *aviado*. The basic relationship between aviador and aviado extended throughout the different links of the production and marketing process. Natural commodities, primarily different types of rubber, were treated as essentially free resources, access to which depended solely on an ability to physically locate them or to enter into a relationship with whomever controlled them. In his study of the changes in appropriation of land around Conceição do Araguaia, Ianni explains,

The land was abundant and practically free, but the latex trees did not occur in profusion: at times they might be concentrated in a given locale, at times dispersed over vast distances. Communication was difficult and slow, either along rivers or meandering waterways or over dirt roads and paths. Transportation was by means of pack animal or river transport, either by oar or motor. But always communication was slow. Animal power was important. In the transport of goods, motors were employed as well. But the main source of energy was human muscle applied to modest and rudimentary tools used in the extraction of latex and the preparation of rubber to be transported to the embarkation points along rivers and streams. The ax, hatchet, knife, bowl, bucket, basin, and the smoke necessary to coagulate the latex into rubber exhausted the sparse and rudimentary technology employed by rubber tappers in making rubber sheets and balls for transport to Belém and subsequently overseas. Capital was scarce, and normally appeared in the form of script, accounts, or credits and debits. In the interchange between the rubber tapper, rubber boss, and the merchant, everything referred secondhand to money that was itself absent. Industrialized goods circulated as did foodstuff all transported by the merchant to the rubber boss and transferred from him to the rubber tapper in exchange for sheets and balls of rubber. The productive forces were technically and socially organized in the relations of production that linked and submitted the rubber tapper to the rubber boss and him in turn to the merchant and the merchant to the exporter. The system of aviamento was the form assumed by the social and technical organization of the productive forces and the relations of production. In the extractive rubber economy, nature was broadly incorporated into the productive process, whether through the latex trees that were tapped and felled, whether through the roads, paths, or waterways that were used in transport. In the extractive rubber economy, nature was incorporated in the process of reproduction and accumulation of industrial capital in the same trajectory that the work effort of the solitary rubber trapper in the midst of the forest collecting latex linked itself to the effort expended by the factory worker producing items made of rubber. (Ianni 1979, 55 [my translation])

In the area inhabited by ancestors of the Xikrin, most latex was gathered from the tree sap of *Castilloa elastica,* which produced a form of rubber generally inferior to the more familiar *Hevea brasiliensis* (Ianni 1979, 34ff). Unlike this latter species, which could be repeatedly bled for latex, the castilloa tree is destroyed in the process of tapping its latex. In the Xingu or Tapajós region, a rubber tapper could regularly and repeatedly work "rubber avenues," which, if attention was paid to the health of the trees, could sustain production indefinitely. Once its bark was cut to bleed latex, or caucho, as it was commonly known, castilloa was destined to die. The normal process was to slash into the bark at a height between six and eight feet from ground level and allow the latex to collect in holes dug at the base of the tree for a period of a week to ten days. Subsequently, the entire tree would be felled and further cuts made in the upper trunk and large branches for another twenty-four or thirty hours. After this the fallen tree was simply abandoned and the tapper would move on with his pack mules or other supplies in search of other trees (Soares 1928, 45).[4]

The essentially destructive nature of the enterprise should be apparent: It immediately eliminated its raw material source, thus forestalling any further extractive activities in a given area. But its other distinguishing feature derived from the control that export companies exercised over its collection and marketing. As noted, control was exercised through a system known as aviamento. In this mercantile chain each succeeding link was dependent on the previous one for advances in capital and supplies, from the extraction of rubber in the forest to its transport and eventual sale to the export houses located in Belém at the mouth of the Amazon. At all levels of the chain, except perhaps for some of the diversified financial and industrial interests, rubber was not merely an industry but a way of life. Since the rubber tapper needed to survive in the forest, all the necessities of life as well as of the trade proper were supplied by the rubber houses in Belém to those backwoods seringalistas or bosses who controlled a particular area of territory. They, in turn, would supply laborers and their families with life's necessities. These necessities were extremely simple as a rule, consisting of beans, rice, sugar, coffee, salt, jerked meat, lard, and tobacco where rubber tappers did not grow or at least partially produce these. Other common items supplied were a bare minimum of household necessities such as basins, eating utensils, machetes, axes, knives, hammocks, firearms, and ammunition. The rubber tappers themselves worked in a state of constant debt, which they owed to the seringalistas or bosses who controlled the area in which they labored. It was common for a rubber tapper to be further in debt at the end of the rubber season than at its onset due to the quantity of goods advanced to him prior to the harvest season. Once in debt (often incurred in the course of moving from the desperately poor northeastern part of the country), the rubber tapper was obliged to continue working for the same boss and thus suffered a sort of indentured servitude.

WITHIN THE EXTRACTIVE ECONOMY

With the expansion of caucho production around Conceição do Araguaia, the Xikrin found themselves willingly or unwillingly within the system of social relations that comprised the extractive economy of rubber. That is, they played a vital part in the relations that organized production of rubber in the area, whether they were directly involved in the work of rubber tapping, which by both indigenous and nonindigenous accounts at least some Indian men were, or simply continued to live in areas traversed by rubber convoys and tappers.

The price of a gleaming mahogany bed frame on display today in a North Carolina furniture shop hides the costs associated with extracting mahogany illegally from Indian reservations in the Brazilian state of Pará. So, too, the accounts of the export firms that imported rubber at the turn of the century indiscriminately mixed expenses incurred in dealing with indigenous and nonindigenous people—expenses associated with the refinement of raw rubber in the forest included items paid to Indians to permit harvesting or transport in areas of their traditional circulation. Just as the furniture industry has no interest in revealing the extent to which timber stocks originate in illegal operations on Indian reservations, neither did rubber exporters broadcast the extent to which rubber production could never be conducted in accordance with the legal niceties of property ownership, labor laws, or free trade. The public view of rubber spotlighted the extravagant wealth of elites in the urban centers of Manaus and Belém and the worldwide boom in bicycles and, later, automobile tires. Amazonia supplied the global industrial demand for rubber for more than fifty years between 1850 and 1912 (Weinstein 1983). Behind the public face of rubber, however, lay not wage labor and increasingly rationalized production but the aviamento system, which in its turn organized complex cross-cultural transactions. The result was the creation of a class of relatively solitary peasants (known as *caboclos*) dependent on extractivism as a way of life (Ross 1978), and cultural changes to people like the Xikrin who were involved in the trade without losing their collective identity.[5]

To what extent the Xikrin were simply victims of the rubber trade or participants bears consideration. To be in the path of a bulldozer is obviously not the same thing as to assist in the construction of a building. We must pay close attention to the social relations and forces of production organized by the aviamento system—labor, technology, land, resources, money, political power—in order to understand the way indigenous forms of social organization could articulate with the extractive industries. And we must be attentive to indigenous accounts of their own past.

The structure of the aviamento system means, first and foremost, that unlike latter-day wildcat gold prospectors, each link in the chain of production and distribution is closely tied to neighboring links. Although the rubber gatherer's work may be solitary, he is not a free agent but is committed to working for an agent who advances him goods. Although Indians and individual rubber tappers ran across one another, the Xikrin were not primarily dealing with "stray backwoodsmen," as is made clear in Xikrin stories that identify dealings with "chiefs" of the white men. Rubber tapper work was coordinated by a seringalista who "bankrolled" the basically cashless operation with goods he himself received from a merchant who bankrolled him in turn.

Several factors made it advantageous and even sometimes imperative for the seringalista to maintain good relations with the Indians in areas he sought to control. The maintenance of de facto control took priority over legal title. Seringalistas usually set up their operations so as to act as exclusive agents for receiving rubber along a section of a river and its tributaries. This sort of control became more complicated when the rubber tapper was required to be mobile, as was the case with caucho around Conceição do Araguaia. The constant movement involved in the search for rubber and its transport along known trails increased vulnerability to Indian attack and also encouraged the use of Indian labor to act as guides to productive tree sites and to participate in the extraction of rubber itself. From a strictly economic point of view, Indians were not competitors for resources since they had no particular use for caucho.

Indians were powerful economic allies because they successfully restricted access to resources by other seringalista competitors. Thus, far from merely confronting isolated backwoods folk, the Xikrin and other peoples were drawn into long-term relationships with their bosses, the seringalistas. Associated with particular seringalista bosses, the Xikrin had a free hand to raid or trade with other whites they encountered as they saw fit, as long as they did not disrupt the productivity of "their" white man. This explains the coexistence of different sorts of relationships with the wider world revealed in Xikrin accounts of the period.

During the expansion of the rubber trade, convoys moved through the forest over trails first established by Indian peoples. This is not surprising, given that Indians were recruited for these convoys as well. These trails often led through indigenous villages in the interior, a fact lamented by the Dominican fathers because it exposed potential converts to the debased aspects of civilization.

> The trails that led to the forests with *caucho* cross the territory of Indians, being the case that some pass through their villages. Convoy workers and rubber tappers hired young Indians deluding them with ridiculous promises and, at the end of long trips and tough treks in the forest interior, paid them with miserable salaries. Many people exploited the simpleminded and addicted Indian. For only a bottle of rotgut sugarcane rum, for a fistful of salt, some sweets or a few liters of manioc flour, they took from the poor savages new clothes and tools they had received shortly before from the hands of the missionaries. (Audrin 1963, 14 [my translation])

This perspective, of course, reflected the divergent interests of missionaries and extractivists with respect to the indigenous population.

While it is certain that convoys took trails leading through the Kayapó villages on the Arraias and Pau d'Arco Rivers and that alcohol was a prime incentive to assist convoys, there is no specific mention of contact with villages inhabited by the Xikrin. However, according to Frei Gil Vilanova, relations with the Xikrin were not unfriendly. In seeking funds to catechize the Xikrin, Vilanova states that only the distance of their villages from the settlement of Conceição kept them isolated from missionary influence: "The understanding of the language and the friendship of our Indians almost guarantees us the success of this work" (Gallais 1942, 245). While the Xikrin were contacted by missionaries only later, we can look to statements by Xikrin for an indication of the way the rubber trade affected their lives during the rubber boom.

The location of the Kapôt settlement was far from secret to rubber tappers and missionaries. Xikrin relate that their former village of Kapôt ("open grassland") lay six nights sleep from the town of Conceição do Araguaia, or Kuiti Djam, as the town was known. They claim that the town was full of Kayapó at the time, and they could slip in and out unnoticed by whites. Historical descriptions of the early settlement describe a scene in which Karajá, Kayapó, and other indigenous peoples frequented the streets and domiciles of the settlement, which, after all, had been founded as a center for evangelization of Indians. The settlement experienced continued rapid growth, particularly after 1904, as a result of the rubber trade. A full-fledged municipal government was installed by Pará state authorities in January 1910, at which point the town became seat to a judge and a contingent of eighty state police.

According to the Xikrin, their settlement at Kapôt was visited at least once by a rich trader named Miguel, who presented himself as the "chief of the kuben" and who generously distributed useful presents. These included the familiar "manioc flour, rice, machetes, and ax heads." The Xikrin took him to be leader of the kuben in Conceição. Numerous accounts of whites entering their villages during this period further underline the fact that the location of the village was near rubber-tapping activity. The Xikrin were able to observe tappers at work and, on approaching them, would be offered a meal of cooked food (*omrô*). Not all Brazilians received a warm welcome, however. Shortly after constructing the village of Kàkàrekre, two men in a canoe entered the village around sundown and were invited by the Xikrin to share in a meal of sweet potatoes. At the time, Xikrin knew some Portuguese. They called to the men *"amigo—vem"* (come friend). That same night, as they slept, these two were efficiently dispatched by their hosts, who promptly appropriated their supplies. Another tale tells of a man who entered the Xikrin village on foot, head bent, and looking downward under the weight of the burden he carried fastened to the tumpline straining over his forehead. His appearance took village residents by surprise and he eventually continued on his way unmolested. Frikel collected the testimony of a single informant who worked along the Cateté River, well to the west, between 1903 and 1913. While claiming he enjoyed good relations with the Xikrin throughout this period, he also marked 1903 as the year in which hostilities involving Xikrin and rubber collectors broke out (Frikel 1963, 147).

Some Xikrin men were evidently among those who agreed to work with rubber tappers in return for trade goods. One such fellow, remembered as "Paulo," was a classificatory brother of Ngôrārāti, who was chief at the time the Xikrin were officially contacted by the Brazilian Indian Protection Service. Paulo knew white ways well. In fact, he had spent part of his childhood living with a Brazilian couple. While I was not able to learn the events that led to this, a contributing factor may have been that Paulo's parents had been kidnapped by the Gorotire Kayapó and he had become an orphan. He rejoined the Xikrin at the Kàkàrekre village and later was instrumental in convincing his fellows to raid the Gorotire, which they did several times. When villages were raided, parties were raised to pursue the attackers as they retreated. Revenge-minded pursuits of this sort could go on for months. After one raid Paulo was chased by the Gorotire almost up to the place where the Pacajá River flows into the Xingu, well to the north of the present Bakajá village and hundreds of kilometers from both Gorotire and Xikrin settlements. Thus, today's Xikrin claim that while their present village location was far from the perambulations of the Kayapó in former times, it was known to some extent before they moved to the Bakajá region during the 1920s.

Paulo joined the ranks of other Xikrin specialists who "really accompanied whites around" *(kuben o ba djwỳnh)."* A couple of men, Kukrã'êrê and Bem-nhõngri, had not only spent a long time in the company of rubber tappers but had also gone all the way to Belém. They returned from this trip with sugar, coffee, and machetes. Some Xikrin, such as Kakonktire and Brinhõkre, were specialists known for their skill in tracking *kubẽn krɏt* (or European-derived *kubẽn).* They would "really make the kuben appear" *(kubẽn o apoj djwỳnh).* One technique they used involved tying a parakeet feather around a finger as an aid to divine the whereabouts of whites. The Xikrin valued those among their ranks with knowledge of white ways as a valuable community resource.

Particularly belligerent Xikrin developed reputations for ferociousness among neighboring Brazilian populations. The grandson of a man named Bandjy fondly recalls that he was dubbed the Dog Captain (Capitão Cachorro) by Brazilians. The Dog Captain was so called because of the terror he inspired. In the words of the Xikrin, "he heeded no counsel" *(amak kre kêt*—ear hole absent) and was quite successful in capturing and using firearms of Brazilians. He was unafraid to approach Brazilian settlements and make off with goods from the houses.

One older Xikrin compared the relations between rubber workers from Conceição do Araguaia after the turn of the century to relations with mahogany loggers today. He explained that people would go eat with and work for the *kubẽn,* and sometimes *kubẽn* would come to the Xikrin village. What is highlighted in this parallel is the form of contact between the Xikrin and outsiders. The parallel between relations on a frontier backwater a century ago and those of a modern reservation only become clear if we examine in more detail the extractive economy within which the Xikrin began to come to terms both materially and ideologically with the presence of Brazilians.

THE BASIS OF AUTONOMY AND CONNECTION

The Xikrin community is marked on maps drawn by the Dominican missionaries (see Map 1, page 27). Those who entered into this territory expected to meet (if they encountered anybody at all) people who identified themselves as Xikrin. While the Xikrin did not think in terms of property ownership, a collective aspiration to control a certain territory was ascribed to them by outsiders. And, in fact, as a recognized member of the community, any Xikrin could hunt, fish, garden, or collect products from nature within this area. This, of course, was subject to certain local norms of conduct. A man would have the right to continue collecting wild products from the successional growth of trees, bushes, and herbs within the area of a garden plot he had previously cultivated. A certain age group might appropriate a particular location to gather Brazil nuts or other resources during a certain period. Common kinship and residence entitled one to work the resources in a particular area. This is a common characteristic of noncapitalist social relations. As Sider (1986, 28–29) suggests, the autonomy of a community subject to the power of merchant capital lies in its resource base, in the "resources . . . and forms of property (territory) for which membership in a community or collectivity is the precondition for access, and for which the capabilities of the community or collectivity (including the equipment, skills, organization potential, and political power of those who have, or want, access) delineates what can be done with and to the resource."

The structure of merchant capital and resource distribution took the local form of the aviamento system and caucho trees dispersed across the landscape within the social network of relations radiating out from Conceição and its satellite settlements. We need to inquire into the aspects of Xikrin community that permitted both involvement in trade and a concomitant maintenance of community autonomy. And furthermore we need to ask about the countervailing pressures that pushed for a further rapprochement between indigenous peoples and the Brazilian pioneer front on the one hand and the severing of relations between them on the other.

The resource that seringalistas sought to control was latex. In order to gather latex, they had to locate latex-giving trees, control access to them, provide the instruments to work the rubber and usually to transport it as well. In addition, individual rubber tappers had to be compelled to sell their latex to the seringalista who controlled their area rather than to the highest bidder. The needs of the seringalistas were not necessarily best served if native peoples were eliminated from rubber producing areas. In the first place, labor was generally scarce and rubber tappers often had to be induced to emigrate from other areas of Brazil. Although we cannot document the actual proportion of native labor used, we have the testimony of Dominicans and of the Xikrin themselves that Kayapó peoples comprised at least some of the necessary labor.

Due to their expertise in locating resources, Indians were historically essential elements of extractive enterprises in the Amazon. We can assert without much fear of error that a good part of the usefulness of Indian labor to the caucho trade lay in the Indian ability to locate stands of rubber-yielding trees—successful reconnaissance was key to the entire enterprise.

Both Dominicans and historians have described how the "infrastructure" made by indigenous peoples, the trails and the food supplies, allowed rubber tappers to penetrate into the interior forests away from the main waterways. While cattle were the primary focus of settlers who founded Sant'Ana da Barreira and Conceição do Araguaia, the contacts between cattlemen and Kayapó were "eased by the presence of Indians who were fluent speakers of Portuguese and who had been students at the Colégio Isabel founded on the Araguaia by Couto de Magalhães. . . . Indian trails were the first cattle roads, and their villages, spread along the Arraias and Pau d'Arco Rivers, were the primary source of provisions and first points of settlement in the pastures of the interior" (Moreira Neto 1960, 12).[6]

The control exercised by an intact Indian community over a given territory heightened the ability of the seringalista to control the access to resources and the labor force at his disposal. The Indian community helped exclude economic competitors and cow the Brazilian workforce into not striking out on their own. The fact that value was exchanged within the aviamento system in the form of trade goods rather than money also facilitated dealings with indigenous peoples across cultural boundaries.

As in the case of modern-day loggers and Brazil nut gatherers, encroachers on Indian lands were not interested in permanent settlement. In effect, while rubber tappers identified caucho as a resource, the Xikrin did not. The main extractivist activity consisted in felling rubber trees from an impermanent base camp where rubber was coagulated in a form to be transported. After this extraction process the rubber workers moved on.

Given the dispersed inland location of caucho, there was a constant race to find new trees. This form of economic activity pitted rubber gatherers against one another in an effort to find and establish control over certain widely dispersed resources located in unfamiliar terrain. Under these conditions savvy seringalistas, by means of gifts, attempted to use Indians to locate resources and to exclude competitors from the area. This type of arrangement held advantages for both parties. Often the mere presence of the Xikrin or other peoples was enough to frighten competing tappers from certain areas. The seringalistas' key to profitability was to establish de facto control over an area where natural resources were located. Legal title was less important than the ability to exclude competitors.

The peaceful coexistence of Xikrin and the ones they called the "rubberbark folks," *Me Barôktikà* (rubber tappers), was thus more of a kind of selective engagement. Xikrin continued to alternately raid and trade in order to acquire the goods they needed. The status quo was maintained as long as the extractive economy was not disrupted. The knowledge and confidence of the Xikrin grew, as individual men were able to learn more about the customs and habits of the white invaders. This was a result of working for periods in rubber ventures and of the observation of settlements such as Conceição do Araguaia and the makeshift temporary camps in the rubber groves. The presence of villages of Irã'ãmrajre Kayapó ensured that communication between seringalistas and other Kayapó groups was less of a problem than may be supposed. Xikrin accounts of this time claim they already knew some Portuguese, and, by enlisting the aid of Pau d'Arco Kayapó, seringalistas were capable of making trade overtures to any Kayapó group. That the Kayapó were aware of this diplomatic strategy can be gleaned by the way the Gorotire Kayapó made use of Brazilian captives to sue for peace with Brazilians inhabiting small villages between the Araguaia and Xingu during the 1930s (Nimuendajú 1952). They used captured Brazilians to negotiate with Brazilian communities by long-distance shouting across water courses.

The aviamento system was based on the exchange of goods between people with personal ties rather than on wage labor. This was a system that was easily intelligible to the Xikrin. Moreover, the items exchanged gave local Brazilians no advantages over the indigenous natives. While collecting rubber, tappers were forced to live in a fashion similar to Indians, although they relied on purchased food to some extent. Xikrin stories repeatedly mentioned coffee, sugar, and food cooked in Brazilian style. The fact that food seems to have been put on a par with metal tools in the stories of the Xikrin seems inexplicable unless rubber tappers themselves had only a very limited store of tools available. Of course, for the Xikrin, the sharing of cooked food is also a strong sign of amity.

In the context of the local boom in rubber along the Araguaia after 1904, the Xikrin retained their autonomy and their ability to pick up and trek in preparation for villagewide ceremonies. And their combination of hunting and horticulture supported them in ways that were not visibly inferior to those of Brazilians. The white men seemed to have no larger designs on their land than the removal of trees for which the Xikrin had no use anyway. In return for this activity the Xikrin received implements that made their lives easier and that they were able to employ in ways identical to the white man. At no time, however, did everyone have metal tools to work with, and firearms, although possessed in a limited quantity, were even scarcer.

Violent or even fatal conflicts with some whites did not mean a rejection of contact with whites in general. The presence of conflict is not obvious only from the personal stories told but also from the names of some of the Xikrin villages established during this time, such as one settlement dubbed *kubēnaptàràdjà* (place where kuben assembled), in which many *kubēn* were also said to have been killed by Xikrin. Within the rubber areas between the Araguaia and Xingu, violent conflict between Indians and Brazilians was a result of familiarity rather than contact. While the first meetings were generally peaceful, violence escalated over the years, and Xikrin recount that both they and the Brazilians began making runs at one another. Tensions became heightened not only with an influx of new Brazilian migrants to the area but with an accumulation of incidents of abuse— of Indian girls prostituted and shady dealings of rubber tappers. In the end what turned the Xikrin world upside down was heightened warfare with the Gorotire Kayapó and the crash in rubber prices, which succeeded in severing the links that made up the aviamento system.

Fighting between Brazilian non-Indians and the Kayapó seems to have increased after 1909–10. As noted, Vidal (1977, 17) cites a personal communication from Frei Gil Gomes Leitão indicating that the Xikrin were massacred in 1910 by the seringalista Chico Trajano. The Cateté Xikrin explained to Vidal that at the time, the Kàkàrekre village was trading with Brazilians who came by canoe along the Rio Branco. They say that a Xikrin had killed the father of a man named Luis, which led to the subsequent massacre (Vidal 1977, 27). That is, hostilities were the outgrowth of tensions that arose in the course of trade and interaction rather than from first contact; the adversaries knew one another by name.

The decadence of the rubber trade contributed to the escalation of tensions by cutting off the flow of trade goods that oiled diplomacy between seringalistas and indigenous groups. Moreover, the decline in their financial strength made seringalistas more vulnerable militarily. Nimuendajú notes that when he went up the Xingu River in 1915, there were not only thousands of Brazilian riverine inhabitants but the rubber bosses maintained private armies of hundreds of hired guns. In the beginning of 1940 when Nimuendajú undertook his study of the Gorotire, the entire population along the upper Xingu above Altamira amounted to no more than several hundred who wrung out a miserable existence collecting rubber and Brazil nuts (Nimuendajú 1952, 436). It was under these reduced conditions that attacks by the Kayapó became formidable threats against the tiny colonist population remaining in the area. In his brief journey up the Xingu in September 1940, Burris (1941, 25) reports hearing that thirteen rubber workers were killed by Kayapó along the Xingu in a single week, while he personally visited a settlement where two others had been killed.

The population decline with the onset of the rubber bust in Conceição mirrors that of the Xingu River region. In 1911 the population surpassed 15,000, more than 8,000 of whom lived in the countryside extending toward the Xingu. Many small settlements resulted from the opening of a road in 1909 linking the Araguaia and Xingu Rivers. By 1920, however, the total municipal population had declined to 11,000; in 1940 it was further reduced to 4,715 for the entire municipality (Ianni 1979, 62–63). Vidal (1977, 28) reports that the assorted small settlements that existed along the Itacaiúnas between 1890 and 1920 disappeared as the economy shifted toward Brazil nuts and legal title for large holdings of land was gradually established. With the disappearance of populations, the flow of items pumped in through the aviamento system decreased to a trickle and Xikrin found it more difficult to acquire manufactured goods. They stepped up their hostilities against invading Brazilians in large part to acquire a booty of useful items. As one local inhabitant commented, "they only attacked if we had something that interested them, they didn't attack those with nothing" (ibid., 17).

WAR WITH THE GOROTIRE KAYAPÓ

Today's elders at Bakajá recall past conflicts with the Gorotire Kayapó far more vividly than they do skirmishes with rubber tappers. To this day, Xikrin recount the names of their relatives who were killed or captured by their Gorotire foes during the years they first inhabited Kapôt and Kàkàrekre. Subsequently they established several settlements at places called Màdtikre,[7] Pykatingrà, Roiti Djam, and Kubēnaptàràdjà before moving to the Bakajá region. Except for Màdtikre and Kubēnaptàràdjà these settlements were occupied more than once. Settlements were commonly deserted under fear of imminent attack and reoccupied when the danger was felt to subside. The conflicts were incessant and ongoing, filled with raids and counterraids. One man even tells of an aunt who, after being captured by Gorotire warriors, escaped and returned to the Xikrin village only to be recaptured in an ensuing raid.

The fear and hatred of the Gorotire far surpassed that felt by older Xikrin for any other indigenous group or for Brazilian society, of which they knew little. Vidal says that during her first field work in the late 1960s, this loathing amounted to a veritable obsession. An effective, if pithy, threat used to frighten ill-behaved youngsters was to simply bark out the name "Gorotire!" Even through the mid-1980s, the most respected war leader at Bakajá had forged his reputation in battles fought with the Gorotire long ago. The strength of the conflicts with the Gorotire seemed little diminished in spite of the many subsequent armed conflicts with other Indian peoples and Brazilians in the intervening fifty years. Ironically, many Xikrin originally from the Bakajá village now live in the Gorotire village, as we shall see in Chapter 4. However, no battles have been fought with the Gorotire since the 1920s, and the younger generation seems to have little animosity toward their Kayapó brethren and former foes. While uncles and parents of the older generation related tales of loved ones killed or stolen away by Gorotire, the younger generation for the most part has no direct familiarity with the actors involved. In a culture without lineages or deep pedigrees, the current generation sees past rivalries as very distant from their present concerns.

CONCLUSIONS

Ironically, it was probably the *decrease* in the rubber-tapping population and the concomitant decimation of the Pau d'Arco Kayapó most directly integrated into the trade relations centering in Conceição do Araguaia that led the Gorotire after 1910 to pursue raiding much more vigorously than before. This raiding appears to have been caused by greater difficulty in acquiring trade goods and was itself not a cause of the Brazilian depopulation of the region, which Ianni (1979) shows was closely correlated with rubber's decline. When the Catholic mission at Santa Maria Nova was founded in 1859, ties between it and the Gorotire were peaceful, and a number of Kayapó learned Portuguese (Magalhães 1977).[8] Most likely the breakdown of the previously established network of cross-cultural trading ties made vigorous raiding a more attractive option for the Gorotire than it had been in several generations.

While little description can be gathered about the social organization of the Xikrin during this time period, it is clear that Kayapó settlements were scattered over a wide area of central Brazil between the Araguaia and Xingu Rivers. During this period, the Mekrãgnotire probably were established to the west of the Xingu as well (Verswijver 1992). The collective organization of the Xikrin made them attractive allies of seringalistas, less it seems as a labor force than as a military ally who could help patrol a given region. If the dealings with the Pau d'Arco Irã'ãmrajre groups are any indication, chiefs accepted diplomatic overtures and trade goods on behalf of their followers. Individual men were at liberty to leave the group and work more closely with either missionaries or rubber tappers. Caucho was the primary form of rubber gathered in the vicinity of the Xikrin, and the aviamento system apparently provided a flow of goods to the Xikrin. An expressed reason to remain in the area with Brazilians arriving in ever greater numbers was the access to iron tools and firearms, for Xikrin needed firearms in their battles with the Gorotire. With the crash of rubber, the decline in population of the Brazilians, and the augmented attacks of Gorotire armed with firearms, the Xikrin had to make a monumentous decision. They decided to withdraw from the fringes of the frontier and its access to manufactured goods. By such a move they resolved to isolate themselves both from encroaching Brazilian society and from their relentless Gorotire foes.

The move was not simply a geographical one. The stories of the Xikrin reveal the hidden history of the tribal zone. The expansion of the rubber and even the cattle frontier was less an advancing wave than a porous and fitful trickle that tended, in fact, to follow the paths laid out by indigenous peoples. If the history of Conceição do Araguaia is not taken in isolation and the other towns of northern Goiás (today located in the newly formed Brazilian state of Tocantins) are considered as well, we get a fuller picture of the import of indigenous peoples for the scanty settlement of Brazilians that occured during the nineteenth and early twentieth centuries (Fisher 1996). In northern Goiás at this time, the boundary between "domesticated" and "wild" savages was fuzzy. State power was weak and faltering, and missionaries, cattle herders, and extractivists comprised the principal Western outposts in an area where Indians, if not the main reason for venturing onto the backland savanna (as in the case of missionaries), were constantly encountered, traded with, and often relied on as a labor force.

By moving to the region of the Pacajá tributary of the Xingu, the Xikrin were removing themselves from a system of intergroup trade relations and from an ongoing feud. Their place in the impoverished, depopulated post-rubber-boom network of social relations was much less attractive than that which they had enjoyed during the rubber boom, when they were able to both raid and trade and the series of smaller settlements of rubber tappers buffered them from all-out attacks by the Gorotire.

3 | RENOUNCING THE FRONTIER

In the next two chapters we continue to explore the the frontier period and, with the help of Xikrin elders' recall, to describe Xikrin work regimes and organization. The current struggle for livelihood among Xikrin does not only involve their reliance on manufactured goods or the omission and inconstancy of FUNAI administration of their reservation; it is also a struggle to lay claim to the future. Loggers and miners are not the first outsiders whom the Xikrin have had to face, nor are the hardships they face without precedent. In order to grasp the meaning of village events today we must follow the swings and changes of circumstance experienced within the hollow frontier that continue to be part of the legacy transmitted to current generations.

This chapter describes the sojourn into a new territory. The presence of other indigenous groups in the region, all of whom coexisted on a hostile basis, introduced the Xikrin to a regional system in which small endogamous groups treated all other peoples as potential foes. Nonetheless, the Xikrin relished the separation from their former region of settlement because this acted as a buffer against Gorotire raids. For other reasons, they also tended to avoid contact with the impoverished Brazilian settlements in the region. While a number of minuscule clusters of Brazilians dotted the Bakajá and Xingu Rivers, the Xikrin remained distant from these areas, avoiding confrontation with firearms in favor of clandestine forays where they could make off with desired objects. Trade with either indigenous or nonindigenous people appears to no longer have been an option.

The region of the Xingu and Pacajá Rivers and surrounding areas to which the Xikrin migrated have seen successive in-migration and out-migration since the early 1600s, as displacement of peoples and the stimulation of inter-Indian warfare by Europeans unleashed a swell of population movements. The native peoples inhabiting the area along the Xingu River up to the mouth of the Irirí were very different when the first Dutch settlements were founded in 1616 near the town currently known as Porto de Moz and also at present-day Vieiros along the lower Xingu River (Hemming 1978, 223, 580). These Dutch settlements lasted approximately seven years and were supplanted by Jesuit missions along the lower Xingu after the Portuguese and their Indian allies drove the Dutch out of the Amazon. In this area, the Pacajá, Waiãpi, and Juruna peoples were the principal targets of missionization. Attempts after 1650 to either imprison them or transfer them to villages under the direction of Jesuit priests led to the dramatic northward migration of the Waiãpi to what is today the border area between Brazil and French Guiana (Gallois 1986). The Juruna and their allies were successful in repelling European-launched military incursions against them. However, at least some Juruna and Waiãpi consented to join Jesuit-run settlements. At the end of the eighteenth century the remaining Waiãpi were dispersed among the lower Xingu missions of Aricari (Souzel), Pirawiri (Pombal), and Itacuruça (Vieiros) while the Juruna continue to exist to this day along the upper Xingu, although many live outside of demarcated reservations. The extinct Pacajá tribe, target of early slaving expeditions and resettlements, has given its name to two Xingu tributaries (the Bakajá and Pacajá). When the Xikrin entered the area, they confronted very different peoples who had also entered in the wake of its being vacated by prior peoples under the pressure of extractivists and missionaries.

The opportunities and challenges of the new regional situation seem to have had an affect on the organization of Xikrin work. Age grades formed an organizational focus for a large part of the productive process. Meat, for example, was prepared in a collective oven located near the *atykbe* (the men's house on the village outskirts) and then distributed to men who would pass portions on to their female relations. The face of authority was more apparent in the *ngôkonbàri* (gourd-rattle leaders), who led groups in their daily tasks. Settlement patterns were dispersed. While enjoying a common ritual focus that would bring everyone together for the climax of the festivities, during most of the year the population was spread among different settlements. Long treks were an important feature of the yearly economic cycle. Roaming over large stretches of territory, for the thirty or so years between the mid-1920s and the mid-1950s the Xikrin lived in a world that seemed, on the surface, to have existed since time immemorial. Their apparent isolation from the larger world was misleading, however. They were not only conscious of the human foes surrounding them, they also charted the changes, the encroachments, and the diseases that could strike whenever a foreign object made its way into their midst.

Thirty years later the period of isolation from the frontier ended in a way eerily reminiscent of its beginning. Under outside attack by Cateté Xikrin, the village split and there ensued a last frantic period of mobility and raiding against prospectors and rubber tappers who were beginning to filter into the area. These attacks attracted the attention of regional officials and the government Indian agency, the Indian Protection Service. Their efforts led to the "pacification" of the Xikrin in large part because the Bakajá Xikrin were ready to exchange a future of unending flight from well-armed foes for one in which they enjoyed the seeming security of firearms and trade goods.

EXODUS FROM THE FRONTIER

I entitle this chapter "Renouncing the Frontier" to underline the conscious decision-making process involved—this meaning is missing in the notion of flight, which can be unthinking and automatic—since Xikrin made their move with an acute awareness of the drawbacks and advantages involved. Xikrin identify three reasons for their ancestors' move from the village of Kàkàrekre to the Pacajá region. Together they give a good indication of the sorts of pressures experienced by Indian peoples on a frontier: armed threats, disease, and the diminishing of important natural resources.

Fortified with firearms and intent on pursuing their long-standing feud, the Gorotire presented the greatest threat. Migration northward ended the clashes between the two groups. One can speculate that perhaps the Gorotire did indeed attempt to follow the Xikrin northward but lost the trail. Nimuendajú (1952) reports seeing captured Assuriní ornaments among the recently contacted Gorotire in 1939 as evidence of a raid that had occurred a few years earlier. The Assuriní may not have been the initial goal, since they lived adjacent to the area inhabited by the Xikrin. Failing to encounter their traditional foes, the Gorotire war party probably directed its attention to a more accessible target. The area between the Xingu and the Bakajá Rivers was apparently an easier destination for those traveling northward from the upper stretches of the Xingu than the headwaters of the Pacajá, where the Xikrin had established their new village. Bakajá storytellers agree that three large river crossings were necessary between Kàkàrekre and their new village. The crossings presented some hardship for people without watercraft—at least one Xikrin woman died in the attempt.

Another reason offered for the move to the headwaters of the Pacajá was the dearth of annatto *(Bixa orellana)* further to the south. Tellers of this version are relatives of the elder Bep Ngrati who led a small group of men to the land of the "Large Red Strangers," the Kubēnkamrêkti. These people obtained their red hue through the liberal use of red annatto dye on their bodies. Xikrin supposed that large quantities of the plant, which is also essential for good Kayapó grooming (Vidal 1981) and may have qualities as an insect repellent as well (Posey 1979, 29), would be found in proximity to the Kubēnkamrêkti settlement. Thus, according to descendants of Bep Ngrati, the move from Kàkàrekre was not a blind rush in search of a safe haven but a journey with a specific destination to places already traversed by Xikrin trekking parties forearmed with knowledge of the Kubēnkamrêkti presence.

Bep Ngrati's party aimed to go to the Kubēnkamrêkti village and appropriate their massive annatto stock. Whether intended or not, a battle ensued, Xikrin guns put the Kubēnkamrêkti to flight and the abandoned village lay at the mercy of the Xikrin. A messenger sent back to Kàkàrekre urged the rest of the village to come and help harvest the huge corn garden they had captured. Xikrin identify the Kubēnkamrêkti as their present neighbors, the Araweté, and reliance on corn rather than root crops does indeed distinguish these Indians from other people in the region (Viveiros de Castro 1992).

The Xikrin who remained in the Araweté settlement treaded cautiously because they feared retaliatory action. In this tense atmosphere, one man, Katàpkino, fired at long range against a presumed Araweté foe only to discover that he had killed one of his fellows. The victim's relatives were upset at Katàpkino's lack of judgment and indignantly pressed him to explain his "poor eyesight" (which is taken as a sign of stupidity).[1] Rather than face their anger, Katàpkino left and headed back to Kàkàrekre. Shortly afterward another group from Kàkàrekre arrived, led by the chief Ngôrārāti. During the journey north one Xikrin man, Bàtkati, was killed, and Bep Katori's child was also slain although it is not clear by whom.[2]

Apart from these incidents, Xikrin found their new surroundings much to their liking. Besides the natural abundance, there did not seem to be any of the diseases that were becoming common in the area around Rio Branco from where they had come. One man cited disease as reason for the migration, but without stories of specific epidemics this may be based on the generalized observation that the presence of Europeans tend to spread diseases among indigenous peoples. A Bep naming festival was triumphantly celebrated in the new region since the gardens of the vanquished Araweté provided ample supplies for the ceremonial meal. Xikrin guns proved devastating to local game, and an elderly man recalled that meat was stacked shoulder high for the feast culminating the ceremony. A half-dozen decades after the fact, the vision of the resulting feast continues to bring a gleam to the old man's eye. He recalled that the intense heat of the day caused the beeswax helmets worn by him and his formal friend, who assisted him on ceremonial occasions, to melt during the festival climax.

The new land held rich promise, and the Xikrin decided to remain, housed initially in the dwelling constructed by the Araweté themselves. In short order, they performed a Bekwoj festival, as there was still much food to be had from the abundant Araweté plots. After a brief time, infused with a new sense of security since the arrival of Ngôrãrãti and his followers, the Xikrin set out to construct a village of their own in traditional circular form. Members of the generation who lived here (those above sixty-five years) recall the village as much larger than today's village with its 275 people. Several names are used to refer to this location: "Ikiêbêpuru" (garden of the other side), "Kubēnkamrêktinhõpuru" (Araweté's garden), "Kikre poti" (house with open gently sloping roof), or "Memõrõdja djwỹnh" (the place we truly originated). This last name acknowledges that residents of this village gave rise to the group that is today known as the "Bakajá Xikrin."

Most Xikrin have the experience of living their entire lives surrounded by the same array of people, many of whom are kin and all of whose personalities, quirks, and strengths are profoundly familiar. The "settlement" or "the village" is adequate to refer to the nexus of one's social universe; no special name is necessary. To refer to a village by name is inevitably to recall a specific history and a relationship with other places of settlement or people of another village. One's settlement appears to exist as a sort of unmarked form, *krĩn be* (circle of residences). Villages are referred to by name only if you are not living there or are not physically present.

In addition, village names are also indicators of a personal history. A narrator emphasizing the contemporary identity of the present day Bakajá Xikrin may stress the village erected near the Araweté's garden as a place of origin, even though he would not hesitate as well to specify a mythical *memõrõdja*, or village of origin where the jaguar's stolen fire was received. Another narrator wishing to make a contrast between the initial village and the subsequent one in which postholes were dug for houses may refer to architectural type and prefer the *kikre poti* form of designation in contrast to *krĩ mêj* or "beautiful village" that was built subsequently. One problem in reconstructing an understanding of the Xikrin past lay in compiling a list of the several synonyms that could refer to the same settlement. Often informants would simply choose the name they had heard from their own relatives. While the existence of different names for the same place was recognized, there was never any attempt to compile them or reach an agreement as to the most appropriate simply because there is no attempt to produce a single version of history acceptable to all.[3]

OPPORTUNITIES AND COSTS
OF THE NEW REGION

As soon became apparent, the abundance of the new region was not due solely to environmental factors; technology and military prowess contributed as well. The possession of firearms had allowed Xikrin to appropriate the extensive gardens of the Araweté with no casualties to themselves. Firearms were responsible as well, at least in part, for the bountiful game capture. The new technology also had its downside since the inadvertent slaying of a fellow Xikrin was a direct result of the long-distance killing capacity that made it so effective. Once the Araweté crops were consumed and munitions exhausted, the costs of moving to the new region began to be felt more sharply. After the Xikrin had spent a short time at their newly erected settlement of Ikiêbêpuru, reasons to return to the Cateté/Rio Branco region began to assert themselves.

The reasons are a countermotif to those cited for fleeing north in the first place. Not all Kàkàrekre dwellers had made the trip from the Rio Branco region, and apart from an allegiance to these relatives, an investment had been made in their own gardens that exerted a return pull once the easy pickings of the new settlement were exhausted. On the other hand the hostility that erupted when one of their number was accidentally shot was a simmering product of previous factionalism—a constant feature of Kayapó life. Even the bounty of conquest was not enough to quell all long-standing resentments, and staying put now seemed less inviting than returning to familiar lands and relations. Thus it is not surprising that after a period of some years, some villagers of Ikiêbêpuru decided to withdraw from the settlement and return to their kin and gardens farther south.

While they were free of disease and the threat of Gorotire raids, those who remained were cut off from the source of trade goods that had made their initial foray into the Bakajá region so successful. They had to face the hostility of the region's inhabitants, but the fighting prowess of these folks seemed to be little match for the Xikrin. At Ikiêbêpuru the Araweté returned to attack the village in a vain attempt to dislodge the Xikrin usurpers. They were repulsed and driven to the south, and informants recall no Xikrin casualties.

Nonetheless, lack of access to firearms, munitions, and steel tools promised to make subsistence more onerous and to level the playing field between them and other indigenous peoples in the region. Before examining the work organization, settlement patterns, and annual treks that characterized Xikrin life in the Pacajá region, it is worth reflecting on the impact of the breakup of Ikiêbêpuru on the people involved.

Figure 4. In commemoration of Brazilian Independence Day in 1984, Xikrin men perform an "anger dance," simulating that preceding a war raid. My handheld cassette recorder being the only one available, the chief has borrowed it to record the event. (Photo by author)

Village splits like the one between the Bakajá and Kàkàrekre group are recurrent throughout the last 150 years of Kayapó history (Bamberger 1979; Verswijver 1992). Such splits are held to give rise to long-lasting generalized enmities between the two groups. As one Xikrin said, "After a split, people really hate each other." Xikrin believe that any lack of balance can only be resolved by striking a new equilibrium, and the only way to rid oneself of the feeling of hatred left over after a split is by evening the score. Killing an offender returns one's own emotions to a status quo in which no ill feelings are present. Former village mates may expend a tremendous amount of energy in their war effort against one another. While rituals are performed to collectivize the hatred or ill feeling, in fact ill feelings may not be universally felt and it is common for some portion of the village to make peace with the opposing faction now residing in a separate settlement.

Ethnic or group hatred seems not to be easily passed along as a group birthright. Today at Bakajá, the younger generation bears none of the ill will toward other Kayapó villages still in evidence among older residents who have suffered from relatives killed or kidnapped by Gorotire war parties. For the most part moral judgments are reserved for the impact that events have on oneself or one's kin who, according to Xikrin beliefs, are also, in some sense, part of oneself.

The common pattern of fissioning seems well illustrated by the split at Ikiêbê-puru. When the entire circle of houses was occupied, there were five men recognized as chiefs. Among them Ngôrārāti was the one who went around with the *menõrõny,* or bachelors, while the others, Bep Kamêti, Pangri, Bep Karôti, and Bep Tyk were somewhat older. It was generally held that leaders were referred to as *ngôkonbàri* (gourd-rattle leaders) because of the emblem of office they carried. They assembled men in the *atykbe,* an open sided house constructed outside the circle of residences in line with the trajectory of the rising sun.

Old-timers report that it was in the atykbe that bachelors slept and men ate together and spent time adorning one another during the day. Within the atykbe it was customary for the *ngôkonbàri* to be seated in the center surrounded by the bachelors. The bachelors, in their turn, were surrounded by men with children *(mekrare)* and elder *mebêngêt* were strung along the outer periphery. At dusk, the *ngôkonbàri* would leap dramatically out of the circle center and, aggressively challenging the men to perform with bravado, would lead them to the center of the village plaza, the *ngàbe,* where dancing would take place.

Just as a chief would lead his followers on forest expeditions or collective work parties, the separation of people from a village is assumed to require some kind of leadership. Incidents of village fissioning are referred to as actions of chiefs and their followers. Unlike quotidian activities that involve single-sex groups, in the case of splits, chiefs lead groups comprised of both men and women. So it was that Bep Karôti and Bep Kamêti led their followers back to the Cateté region. The group that remained at Ikiêbêpuru was a solid majority of the village. Reflecting on this time, Bakajá Xikrin find it ironic that their brethren at Cateté should receive vastly greater sums of assistance from outside sources today since they were the numerically smaller group until recently. "They were few, and we were many. Now it's all changed," remarked one man bitterly.

After the dissident faction left for their old haunts near the Rio Branco, the remaining Xikrin were left with a circle of houses of which many, having belonged to departed families, were now vacant. The possibility of a rapprochement between the factions seemed distant, and, in any case, common residence reflects kinship and cooperative arrangements. Rather than simply occupying the empty houses, it was decided in typical Kayapó fashion to build a new village on the other side of the Pacajá River where a new and completely occupied circle of residences could be formed.

The new village lay near where a large tree had fallen across the Pacajá, hence the name "Bàtprànõrõ" (tree species/lying).[4] *Bàtprà* bark is mixed with genipap to form the blue-black dye Xikrin use for body paint. The new village circle was built and fully occupied, enabling the residents to "once again close the circle" (*ajte krĩ ojpôk*) and live their ideal of a fully occupied village periphery.

Bàtprànõrõ stands out most vividly in contemporary historical memory as the birthplace of the current leadership generation. Despite much roaming over the next thirty to thirty-five years, Xikrin returned to this location many times. In the mind of many it has assumed prototypical status as a large well-built village, *krĩ mêj,* or what a beautiful village should look like. From Bàtprànõrõ the Xikrin fanned over a wide area to cultivate gardens and to found feeder settlements. During construction of the village, Xikrin clashed with the Parakanã (Akôkàkore), whom they routed, dividing them and driving the different groups toward the southeast, in the direction of the Brazilian settlement of Marabá and toward the headwater region of the Bakajá on its opposite bank.[5] They also fought with the Assuriní (Krãakỳrỳ), pushing them toward the opposite bank of the Bakajá.

The last recorded club duel between feuding Xikrin occurred during the early years of Bàtprànõrõ. While the bachelors watched, men from the "people with children" age grade paired off and took turns striking each other with hard wooden clubs outside the village periphery near the atykbe. This sort of duel, *aben tak,* has been described for other Kayapó villages. While the reason for this particular fight was not clearly recalled today, informants repeatedly assured me that in former times people would "fight about anything." Jealousy over spouses' sexual escapades or failure to hand over a piece of game that belonged to a man as a result of ceremonial privilege could set off skirmishes during which, informants were fond of pointing out, any sort of weapon might be used—clubs, sharp-edged paddles, large heavy bows, or hand-wielded arrows.

The fallout of the duel resulted in the founding of another village close by the headwaters of the Anapu River not far from the Portel River. The village was named for the babassú frames on which feather headdresses are mounted so they may be carried by ritual performers (Kwỳkàkaỳrỳ). After the residents perished in an epidemic, the abandoned site became known as the "Dead Folks' Garden" (Metyknhõpuru).

Xikrin tell of a man, Purore, who passed the night in the village on his way back to Bàtprànõrõ after an excursion down the Anapu River. There he had killed a man washing clothes along the river bank and was toting home his booty. In his wake an epidemic broke out almost immediately; people began dying. In the face of so many lost lives, the village was abandoned. Survivors made their way back to Bàtprànõrõ, but at a snail's pace. They slept in the forest for many nights, able to move only a short way each day because illness, small children, and presumably low morale made travel difficult.

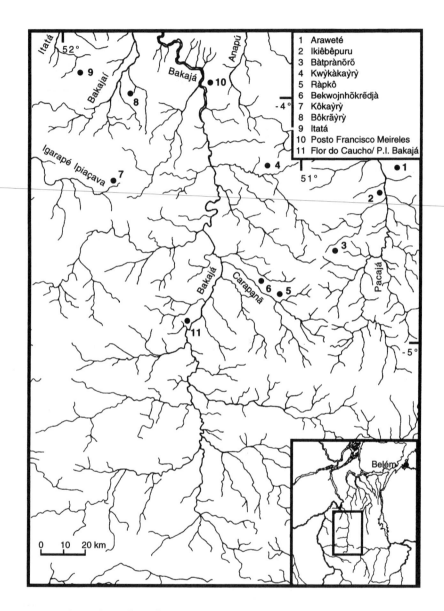

1	Araweté
2	Ikiêbêpuru
3	Bàtprànõrõ
4	Kwỳkàkaỳrỳ
5	Ràpkô
6	Bekwojnhõkrĕdjà
7	Kôkaỳrỳ
8	Bôkrãỳrỳ
9	Itatá
10	Posto Francisco Meireles
11	Flor do Caucho/ P.I. Bakajá

Map 2. Bakajá Xikrin villages from 1926 to present. (Ann Peters)

In the meantime other squabbles in the Bàtprànōrō settlement had resulted in the founding of two new communities by disgruntled residents of the main village. Kwykàkaỳrỳ seems to have been about four hours from Bàtprànōrō traveling NNW while the settlement of Ràpkô was approximately the same travel time, due SSE. A case of wife beating resulted in the founding of yet another village, Bekwojnhōkrēdjà (later called "Krīmêjmadjàrà" after it burnt to the ground), approximately one hour's walk from Ràpkô. Like Kwykàkaỳrỳ, these settlements were made up of babassu palm thatch layered over a lean-to. Unlike the main settlement of Bàtprànōrō, the house frames had no true "legs," that is, no postholes were dug to erect the frame. Composed of relatives and allies of the aggrieved parties, newly formed settlements also appointed their own sets of chiefs. At Bekwojnhōkrēdjà the chiefs were Bep Tūm, Kanhỹm, and Bep Tyk.

While divided into three or four separate settlements, all Bakajá Xikrin continued to unite for the celebration of important ceremonies. The dispersed settlement pattern may actually have made food procurement easier. Hosts provided plentiful food for visiting celebrants. The smaller human population probably meant a higher density of game animals, and hunting must have been easier in proximity to the village than if all the Xikrin had been clustered in a single settlement. When different villages united, the feasting and dancing would continue for several days preceding the ceremonial climax, immediately after which visitors would disperse to their home villages.

Xikrin claim that their village today is smaller than any of these previous villages. The large settlement sizes may explain why the Xikrin appear to have been little subject to attack from the peoples they had displaced upon moving into the Pacajá area. After the initial clashes with the Araweté, Parakanã, and Assuriní, informants could remember only one enemy foray on Bàtprànōrō. The foes were Parakanã archers, who entered the village firing arrows in rapid succession. In spite of being hit so many times that he resembled a pin cushion, one Xikrin elder, Bep Kukonti, survived, and the Xikrin repelled the attack in short order. After mounting a posse to pursue the retreating Parakanã, Xikrin were successful in exacting a heavy toll, killing men, women, and children. Apparently, they took no prisoners. While the Xikrin did not possess firearms during most of their habitation of Bàtprànōrō, their past possession of arms and their larger population in relation to revenge-minded foes must have discouraged attacks.

Another indication of the large size of settlements compared with Amazonian norms was the number of chiefs *(benadjwỳrỳ* and *ngôkonbàri)* that informants were able to recall. In the ancestral village of Kàkàrekre there had been four chiefs who sat facing one another in the center of the atykbe. Bep Pryti was the elder chief, Bep Djai sat facing him, and the two *menōrōny* chiefs were Ngôrārāti and

Bep Karôti (Komre). In the new settlement of Ikiêbêpuru, where most of the population from Kàkàrekre was reunited, five male chiefs coordinated activities, including Ngôrãrãti and Bep Karôti. As mentioned above, part of the population, led by Bep Karôti, returned to the Cateté area, and shortly afterward a new village was established at Bàtprànõrõ. While Ngôrãrãti and Pangri kept their followers at Bàtprànõrõ, Bep Kamêti and Bep Tyk led the split that founded the village of Kwykàkaỳrỳ. Later a new chief, Kukrãnhti, along with Bekàrà, founded the settlement of Krĩmêjmadjàrà. Younger leaders—Bep Tũm, Mereti, Bemnibeti, and Kanhỹm—helped organize the settlement at Ràpkô from followers at both Krĩmêjmadjàrà and Bàtprànõrõ. As the Xikrin say, "at that time there were many chiefs," and, with four separate settlements, an expansion of leadership was necessary in order to organize residents to cooperate in complementary tasks.

For various reasons, daily subsistence was more collective compared to present-day organization, and trekking played a more prominent place in village life. In order to understand why chiefs appeared more prominent, we need to turn to Xikrin accounts of how subsistence was organized during the thirty-year hiatus between the time they fled the cauldron of conflict near the Araguaia rubber frontier and the time armed attacks by the Cateté Xikrin group began their last frantic years of movement prior to contact.

THE ORGANIZATION OF SUBSISTENCE

The Xikrin diet has retained a recognizable continuity in pre- and post-contact periods. Some unappetizing foods have been eliminated, such as young babassú palm trunks, which are hard to chew and "tickle the throat." Other items, notably, sugar, rice, beans, cooking oil, and coffee have been added. Perhaps the most dramatic new addition to the diet is bitter manioc, consumed primarily in the form of manioc flour. However, the sweet potatoes, meat, and palm hearts consumed during the course of an ordinary day represent essentially the same intake as in precontact times.

While there are strong continuities in diet, the manner in which work is organized has been radically altered. The Xikrin continue to occupy much the same ecological niche as they did previously while they have reoriented the way in which food is produced and exchanged. In large part this reorganization has been accomplished in order to channel access to steel tools and other manufactured goods as these enter Xikrin society. Even here one must be sensitive to the period under discussion. While it is certain that Gê peoples were savanna dwellers generations ago, old people in the Bakajá village exhort village mates to be tough today by recalling their past as dwellers of the interior forests, or *atàjx'ã*, who hunted and hauled loads on foot rather than living along the banks of large water courses, where it was common to fish and travel by canoe.

Formerly, socially recognized age was used as a basis for assigning people to groups that pursued subsistence on a daily basis. With rattle leaders acting as coordinators, different age groups of men and women would split up and perform complementary tasks. These included foraging, cultivating, harvesting, hunting, and fishing. Complementary products would be exchanged by different age and gender groups on a daily basis so that each person might enjoy a complete diet. Informants repeatedly stated that while one group might be off collecting Brazil nuts, another would fish, while yet another might be clearing an area for later planting. Unmarried men would often engage in little or no work at all, as they remained in the men's house making themselves beautiful for the collective dancing that occurred on most nights.

Gathered food items such as babassu palm nuts and hearts, fish, honey, and Brazil nuts would be exchanged between age groups. The clearing and planting of gardens was also performed by age groups, while coresident families harvested, cooked, and distributed food crops. The onerous task of clearing gardens without steel tools was a collective task for good reason. Only stone axes *(djwa mêj tekungãrã)* were available, and most small trees were ripped out by the roots, while the thick vines, common in many areas of the forest, were often chewed through. Thus, sheer brute strength performed by masses of helpmates accomplished jobs that could now be handily performed by a single person wielding a steel machete. The advantage of collective clearing of forest lands over individual or even family effort was obvious. However, harvesting of garden produce, unlike that of foraged plants, took the form of coresident family cooperation. The alternation between collective clearing and family harvesting was bridged by age grades in which cooperation between same-sex age mates was coordinated with an exchange between other age grades on the one hand and cross-sex kin on the other hand.

Whether a single large garden area was cleared or a number of smaller plots prepared collectively, garden produce was collected by related women, usually housemates. After the collective clearing of a large area, adult married women would be called on to begin planting the area with manioc stem clippings, and unmarried nubile women would take their turn at this task the following day. Once the area was planted, a chief would parcel out smaller plots for each married couple. For the designating of boundaries there was no shortage of landmarks in a field filled with charred trunks and tree limbs. While stealing from gardens was certainly feared, as the tale of the war between the Djore reveals, unclear boundaries within gardens was never cited as a source of conflict.

The division of plots was made more complicated by the expectation that each couple had rights to several different types of crops, each with different growing times and locations in the gardens. Informants describe a typical garden layout as similar to those of today's gardens. Sweet potatoes sprout in the center, surrounded by sweet manioc. Outside the ring of manioc, crawling and climbing vines, such as squash and yams, were planted, as were bananas. Smaller gardens belonged to one or more couples connected by their desire to cooperate in food production, processing, and exchange.

Regardless of garden size, crops were harvested by groups of female kin and cooked in small earth ovens and fires located near the houses. Once prepared, each woman would share her portion with her children and parents, as well as husband or brothers. Women in turn would receive meat from their male kin.

Unlike garden products, meat preparation was centralized and controlled by elder men. As age grades returned to the atykbe after a hunt, they would deposit meat in a pile to be cooked in an oven or roasted over a fire tended by elders. Once cooked, the meat would be distributed, and, although the hunter and his kin were assured a healthy part of the kill, generosity was enforced by the elders. In most cases the hunter, while not butchering his own game, would have some say in who should receive a piece of the kill. Fights over game were not infrequent according to Xikrin. Not only were past Xikrin held to be much more fierce, but collective cooking served to assure that Xikrin who had inherited rights to certain portions of meat *(õ mry),* a tapir leg or neck, for example, would demand what they considered their rightful allotment. Their requests were not always willingly acceded to. Elders, on the other hand, received portions in return for their necessary role as butcher.

Thus the maintenance of a separate men's earth oven for cooking meat did not ensure that everybody received an equal share. It did prompt some kind of equivalence between the meat hunted by one age group and the natural products, such as fruit or Brazil nuts, collected by other men's age groups for which it was exchanged. Bonds between age mates were stressed, and cooperation between men living in the same household was not very important in daily subsistence. That there was nothing automatic about the distribution process can be seen from Xikrin accounts of the tensions that accompanied meat redistribution. Fights and shouting would break out over the way food was redistributed. Such tensions reveal the moral imperative of equality, that everybody considers himself and herself entitled to a more or less equal share of what the group produces. Rights exercised on the basis of ceremonial inheritance, which seems to give some people rights over the product of others' labor (e.g., the right to claim a particular cut of game, irrespective of its owner), were thus identified as a source of conflict. Every boy's education continues to include admonitions to not fight over the distribution of meat. By taking charge of the butchering, cooking, and distribution of meat, elders thus played a dual role—as peace makers and as food distributors.

To this day, elders play the role of butchers for the community as a whole. In the course of hunting, an elder, even if not a kinsman with whom meat would normally be shared, will be called upon to make the necessary preliminary division of the carcass. Such a partition makes it possible to transport game from the forest. A tapir, for example, would have the stomach and intestines thrown away as well as the heart, unless an elder wanted to prepare and eat these parts normally prohibited to unmarried youth and parents with children. After the carcass has been divided into four body pieces and the head severed, a minimum of four men would be required to carry the meat back to the village. Older people are not subject to the same invisible dangers that afflict adults with younger children or children themselves. They may eat the intestines, heart, neck, and tailbone of "noble" game species, such as white-lipped peccary *(Tayassu albirostris)*, collared peccary or "caititu" *(Tayassu tacaju)*, red brocket deer *(Mazama americana)*, gray brocket deer *(Mazama guazoubira)*, tapir *(Tapirus terrestris)*, large armadillo *(Priodontes giganteus)*, and the sloth (*Choloepus* sp.), although informants disagreed about the advisability of anyone eating this last animal. The intestines and other parts of smaller animals, such as coatimundi *(Nasua nasua)*, would be avoided even by elders. *Mry ni,* or sliced meat, is destined primarily for young people.

A greater understanding of past organization of production can be gained through the description of an exchange between age grades that is practiced only sporadically today. In the past, age grades organized the predominant forms of production and distribution. Known as "collective assembling stuff for each other" *(aben kadjy mỹja o ba)*, groups of men organized according to age comprised opposed, complementary teams of workers. During the course of the workday, young men might go off in search of fish, which they would gather using timbó poison, while older men might busy themselves in the gardens (with or without their wives, depending on a number of factors). Garden products would be used to make steaming banana-leaf wrapped cakes of cornmeal, plantain, or green banana mash, which would be consumed together with fish. Assembling in the atykbe (or the *ngàbe*), older men roasted the young men's catch over a low wooden rack of saplings.

On the occasions I observed such exchanges, men, both young and old, partook lustily of both fish and steaming cakes, and young boys were kept busy bringing drinking water for the group. Simultaneously, women held their own collective meal of vegetable foods. Eventually they received some fish saved by their husbands or kinfolk. Inevitably, in the collective exchanges I observed, some young wives would wait by their own hearth fires rather than with the assembled women. They would often be favored by more attentive young husbands who, upon delivering a choice bit to the object of their affection, would then hurry back to the boisterous group of feasters in the men's house.

By three o'clock in the afternoon, the repast would wind down. Greasy babassu palm fronds lining the floor of the men's house would now be littered with fish skeletons and shredded banana leaves. The palm fronds would glint with a greasy sheen, the result of the many fingers adroitly wiped clean. Men would wander to their houses, many carrying portions of fish or corn cakes wrapped in a bit of banana leaf. Some older men would linger in the men's house where they would be forced to fend off ravenous dogs hungry for the leftovers. Boys would be left with the task of gathering fresh fronds and changing the flooring of the men's sitting place before the evening gathering. Full stomachs and high spirits would be much in evidence along with the generalized feeling of well-being attributed to the smooth functioning of age- and gender-organized groups. While fairly infrequent today, informants agreed that such scenes would be repeated day after day in villages like Bàtprànõrõ.

Age-grade exchanges highlight gender divisions and seem to pit individual male-female relations against the collective esprit de corp of same sex agemates. While individual married couples may collaborate when preparing the vegetable cakes, men exchange food within the context of age grades, and women receive portions through their relations to individual men. The social nature of the exchange between age grades is further emphasized by the collective dancing and singing undertaken the night before the exchange. In one case older men sing while younger men perform a strenuous dance in which they represent schools of fish scattering and then finally being driven together to their doom. The dance steps performed by individuals are more complicated than the usual stomp-dances and a good deal of coordination is required to dance as an ensemble. In this case the choreographic unison of the young men plays off against the stationary singing of the elderly men to mimic and prefigure the exchange that will take place the following day in which the young will leave the village as a group and their elders will remain anchored to their individual garden plots.

In previous times all fishing expeditions demanded a collective orientation. Without fishing line, hooks, or nets, fishing was done exclusively with vegetable poisons. The use of barbasco or timbó vines to stun fish requires complex group coordination. A small stream is dammed, vines are beaten to release fish poisons, and arrows and baskets are used to impale or capture the oxygen-starved fish as they seek to leap the dam. The success of the activity depends not only on co-ordination but on the performance of songs to capture the fish. These "songs for the water" are traditionally highly valued forms of knowledge whose performance privileges were handed from social mentor to protégé.

Lack of firearms also made hunting a more collective endeavor. The effectiveness of hunting fleet, four-legged creatures such as deer, tapir, and pig depended on the use of dogs and group cooperation. The most efficient way to run down game was to force it into shallow waterways where it could be clubbed to death. Game more adept at climbing, could be treed by dogs. The club rather than the bow and arrow appears to have been the weapon of choice for larger game. Bows and arrows were used most effectively for birds. Significantly, other important meat sources such as tortoises can be gathered without the use of any weapon at all. The four different species of armadillos used for food can be captured with pointed digging sticks. Nonetheless, because burrows have multiple entrances that need to be covered and because men tire quickly while digging after the fast-tunneling animal, help from at least two or more men significantly raises the chance of a successful capture. I have seen smaller mammals, such as paca *(Agouti paca)* and rabbits, captured barehanded by groups of men acting in concert.

As stressed, the move to the Pacajá region meant the loss of supply sources for metal tools and firearms. Given the dearth of factory-made tools, the organization of most productive activities according to collective age groups did not merely entail more subsistence efficiency in fishing, hunting, and horticulture, it also ensured collective access to the benefits of the limited steel tools and firearms that were present. While private ownership was recognized in the case of goods captured by virtue of a man's prowess and courage in a raid, the organization of food production and exchange was collective. Clearing gardens or hunting as a group constrained people to enter into exchange relations with other groups for the foodstuffs that would make a complete meal. Under these circumstances were a man to use his steel tool to singly clear a plot for his family alone, he would also be excluded from exchanges that would furnish his family with meat and gathered foods. He would be forced to obtain these items on his own. While the occasional steel tool was privately owned, it was invariably deployed in the productive activities of age groups and kin groups. The benefit of added productivity was shared by all the participants in the owner's group.

Age organization assumed a greater role in daily production than in today's village where most people have steel tools and firearms are relatively plentiful. Far from Brazilian settlements, it was difficult to replenish factory-made items through raids without lengthy expeditions. The presence of these items was so extremely rare that to this day the names of those men who possessed them are passed along orally.

One man remembered that when he was little there was only a single knife in the settlement of Kwỳkàkaỳrỳ. It was normally used to make lip disks and earplugs rather than for clearing brush or butchering game. There was also a single ax. Laughing, he recalls that it steadily got smaller and smaller each time it

Figure 5. Freshly painted unmarried girls' age grade in ritual procession in 1984. During regular work days, age grades often form separate work groups. (Photo by author)

was sharpened, until it was reduced to a mere nub. In the settlement of Bàtprànõrõ, the chief Pôpôkre successfully absconded with a knife, machete, ax, and a puppy from the Brazilian settlement of Marabá. Although the tools continued to belong to him, they were borrowed by work parties, especially those under his direction. While the valor and organizing ability that enabled Pôpôkre to lead a raiding expedition against Marabá were relevant qualifications for chiefly office, there were certainly many other chiefs from this same period who possessed no manufactured goods at all.

TREKS

Werner (1983) points out that Kayapó organize their treks in many ways, and both trip duration and composition of the trekking group may vary widely. Men of different ages, mixed male and female collectivities, groups organized according to men's club affiliation or, assembled in "teams" chosen by parents sponsoring name-ceremony treks on behalf of their children, were all the basis of treks observed by Werner. The pattern of life at the various settlements near the Pacajá cannot be understood if the portion of the year spent trekking is omitted.

Xikrin informants recalled that treks during this period were undertaken by entire settlements. After the gardens were burned and planted, men, women, and children would begin their annual peregrination. Treks were geared to increase the amount of food collected during the months new gardens were not yet ready for harvest. The same basic route was followed year after year and described a large arc toward the Xingu, south toward the Cateté settlement, and back to the headwaters of the Pacajá. While each settlement tended to trek on their own, boys were sent back and forth between groups on a regular basis in order to keep track of each others' whereabouts. In the case of a particularly rich find of food, the groups might come together to share the bounty.

Treks were an important organizational form within the frontier context and played a role in plotting out potential "escape" routes and in researching how other people and resources were distributed in far-flung areas. Xikrin recalled their treks as portions of the year during which they renewed their familiarity with a system of trails that stretched between the Pacajá and the Cateté region. There were no overt military objectives, and contact with other groups, including their Cateté brethren, was generally avoided. The occasional scatter of Brazilian homesteads that dotted the Bakajá region was skirted as well.

One such Brazilian settlement occupied the location of the contemporary Xikrin village. During their treks, Xikrin would ford the Bakajá River several miles downstream from this Brazilian settlement known as "Flor do Caucho" and move quickly into the forest again. For their part, residents of Flor do Caucho must have been aware of the seasonal movement. Informants can still show signs of the trail close by the village that served as the yearly Indian highway toward the south. There is no doubt about the importance of the route since the physical evidence of the overgrown trail and the large depressions in crests of creek banks leaves no doubt that the route was repeatedly traveled by large numbers of people. In contrast, today's hunting trails used by the men are barely visible.

Raids for booty were distinct from treks. For instance, while Xikrin had, on occasion, tried to steal useful items from the settlement of Flor do Caucho, they had not met with much success because of guard dogs and the settlers' general wariness. After two bachelors were killed eating watermelon in one of the Brazilians' garden in the vicinity of the settlement, Xikrin tended to avoid the area altogether. Annual treks, therefore, did not result in any appreciable increase in manufactured goods controlled by the Xikrin. Moreover, in spite of their proximity to Cateté during the further portion of the trek circuit, there was no attempt to trade or petition relatives for desired items. Nor were annual treks used to make warfare on neighboring indigenous peoples.

THE IMPOSSIBILITY OF RETREAT

In the decades following 1930, the Great Depression swept millions into poverty, nations armed themselves for war, World War II enveloped the globe in fire-storms of previously unseen magnitude, revolution convulsed the most popu lous nation on earth, and colonies worldwide clamored for their independence. Perhaps the wartime influx of rubber tappers into the Amazon shook the world of the Xikrin, but their oral history makes no special comment on this period. From the 1930s through the mid-1950s, the Xikrin continued to traverse thousands of forested miles unmolested. Little could they know that the contact and pacification of their Cateté brethren would set off a new chain of events that would propel them into a last-ditch frenzied flight and eventually a resolve to enter into contact with wider Brazilian society.

In 1953 the Brazilian newsweekly *O Cruzeiro* (11 July) published an eyewitness account of the newly contacted "Chikrins" who, it was claimed, had for decades terrorized the entire region between Conceição do Araguaia and Marabá (Ferreira and Ballot 1953). According to Lux Vidal, however, the first press reports regarding Indian-White hostilities in the Cateté region are found to post-date the period around 1940. During this time the Cateté Xikrin evidently became more aggressive in their forays to supply themselves with guns and ammunition.

Meanwhile, within the Bakajá region the persistence of separate villages attested to continuing factional divisions. Witchcraft accusations and the threat of conflict sent one party off to the Cateté village. By chance, this occurred at the time when a part of the Cateté Xikrin population was entering into sustained contact with the Indian post at Las Casas, which housed a dissident faction that had split from the Gorotire Kayapó. After the initial appearance of the Xikrin at the post, the Society for the Protection of Indians (SPI) decided to launch a full-scale attraction effort in order to gather the entire population of Cateté Xikrin under its auspices. Feeling that there were too many Brazilians in the Cateté area, many of the initial Bakajá migrants decided to return to their own territory.

In the meantime, apparently flush with the goods received at contact, and at the urging of the Bakajá dissidents who remained at Cateté, the young Cateté leader Bemoti undertook an expedition in the direction of the Bakajá village.

Although he never actually reached Bàtprànōrō, he did make contact with some Bakajá dwellers along the stream called "ngôjakare." He shot and killed three of them and returned to the Cateté region. At this point Bakajá inhabitants actually launched an expedition to wreak revenge. One man recalls setting off nearly blinded by rage and hate. However, the mission was aborted and the would-be avengers returned to Bakajá shortly thereafter.

After a period of a year or so, Cateté leaders including Bep Karôti and Bemoti once again set off in the direction of Bàtprànōrō, ostensibly to tender a peace offer. Among the party were recent emigrants from Bakajá, including the accused sorcerer, Nhàkrekampin. They were well received and sat with their kinsfolk to eat. Before departing in direction of Cateté they were given two firearms taken from Brazilians. After publicly making their departure, the Cateté group doubled back and launched a surprise attack on a group seated in the *atykmã* region immediately outside the circle of houses. Those killed included Ngreikaro, the chief Pôpôkre, Bemnigrati, and Pyprêktire. Bekati was wounded in the hand, and Topãn was wounded in the hand and thigh. This incident continues to evoke outrage even today. Bakajá residents recall that the Cateté chief, Bep Karôti, placidly shared a meal of corn before committing his calculated assault. The shorthand version of referring to any backstabbing Benedict Arnold–like betrayal has come to be known as *Bep Karôti bay umijã*—Bep Karôti munching on corn.

Much as the insistent raids of the Gorotire a generation before had prompted a move to the Pacajá region, the Cateté attack threatened the very survival of the village. Isolated from the circuits of the extractivist economy Bakajá residents realized that the possession of firearms without the means to acquire ammunition was meaningless. In fact they gave their weapons to the Cateté visitors because they understood that the contacts of the latter at Las Casas would ensure their continuing usefulness. Rather than manufactured technology, Pacajá Xikrin used collective raiding and work parties, usually organized along age-grade lines to supply subsistence needs. They also relied on mobility—dispersing both their settlements and spending months on treks. It was not the attraction of manufactured goods that forced them to leave the comfortable surroundings intimately familiar to a whole generation of Xikrin but the success of the Cateté Xikrin in negotiating contact. As for many indigenous peoples throughout the Americas, contacts with Europeans, trade goods, and disease often wreaked havoc with intermediaries well before face-to-face meetings with Europeans or their descendants.

4 | THE BEGINNINGS OF REDISTRIBUTION

MOBILITY

This chapter title refers to the process whereby Xikrin chiefs became important suppliers of trade goods to others in the community. Although, early on, the Indian service, Brazil nut gatherers, and fur traders sought to use chiefs as a conduit, the Xikrin contributed their own ideas and rationales to the incipient new forms of inequality. While the concept and role of chief was refashioned under the conditions of contact, so too were ideas about what it meant to be a "commoner" or follower.[1] Such relations remain contentious issues today and will be explored throughout the remainder of this volume. To understand the entire trajectory we must follow the movements of the Xikrin after the breakup of Bàtprànõrõ.

The Cateté attack on the Bakajá home village meant that the Bakajá villagers had to move. But where to? The main waterways were not safe. The Xikrin decided to make for the interior forests in the middle of the triangle formed by the Bakajá and the Xingu Rivers. They hoped to avoid both Brazilian settlers and their Cateté pursuers. The danger of pursuit was great because, in the wake of the attack, the village had split, with part of the population making their way toward the Cateté settlement in hopes of a rapprochement. If these ex-Bakajá villagers decided to participate in raids on their former village mates, whatever advantage may have been gained by fighting on terrain unfamiliar to the Cateté attackers would be lost.

The village split took the typical form: a portion of the village circle was abandoned. Generally household residents remained together within contiguous houses, and groups of houses were arrayed against one another. This pattern not only points up the constant factionalism within Xikrin villages but its typical form. Splits leave an incomplete village circle. If in the wake of a split residents desire to patch up differences they may build their new village with a gap along the village circumference—an implicit offer to the opposing faction to complete the circle by returning and constructing houses. This happened at several junctures in Xikrin history. The form of the new village itself thus becomes a giant signboard indicating to would-be attackers the readiness of its occupants to put aside past differences.[2]

Skirting the Brazilian settlements along the Bakajá River, the fleeing Xikrin headed inland along traditional trekking trails. After detouring off the trail, they decided to attack a village of Assuriní Indians. Most of the younger Assuriní fled, but informants tell of the killing of older people as they lay in a large house. The bodies of these slain Assuriní were simply thrown into the bush where they were consumed by vultures.

By expelling the original inhabitants, the Xikrin were able to enjoy the large stores of manioc flour (as yet, unfamiliar to most young Xikrin) and the clusters of annatto pods stored in the houses. There were lots of pets as well, which apparently went unconsumed since many were tabooed species. These included many kinds of monkeys, a falcon, and one large coati.

The Xikrin occupied the large communal house and erected a fence around it against attackers. Afterward they referred to the village location as "Kôkaỳrỳ" or "fenced place." However, the Assuriní, in common with many Tupí peoples, bury their dead under the floor of their houses. One day, so the story goes, a Xikrin dug a hole in the floor of the house in order to store some green bananas for ripening. To his horror he began unearthing human bones. Terrified of living in the midst of what was to them a cemetery, the Xikrin fled. The threats of returning Assuriní spirits searching for contact with their living relatives was thought to pose a tangible danger. This preoccupation reveals much about the Xikrin's own relationship with their deceased, who are removed from the village and thrown off the track by various ruses to ensure that they do not find their way back to the households where they lived.

Moving northward, Xikrin set up camp along the Bakajá River. The new site was simply a place where gardens had been planted, presumably by the Assuriní. The site was notable for the large number of bottle gourds *(ngôkon)* growing there. There were many babassú palms as well, and the spot was referred to as the place of the palm hearts (Bôkrãỳrỳ). For a period of years, the Xikrin constructed no real villages and hence no real gardens.

In effect, the regional equilibrium whereby the Xikrin's presence was largely known and avoided by regional Brazilians and neighboring Indian peoples was broken when the Xikrin were forced outside the familiar routes of yearly trekking circuits. Deciding that the clearing of gardens would leave them more vulnerable to attack, the Xikrin subsisted on wild foods and also attempted to expropriate the gardens of neighboring Indian peoples when possible. Previously, regionals had avoided Xikrin territory, but now rubber tappers, prospectors, and Brazil nut gatherers found themselves targets of Xikrin ambushes. One Xikrin commentator characterized this period as the time when they "really went around killing kubën." The Brazilian daily published in Rio de Janeiro, *O Globo,* hysterically reported in its 1 November 1957 edition that the state of Pará's entire Brazil nut and rubber harvest was threatened by the Kayapó. A year later, the *Folha do Norte* news daily continued to feature stories reporting attacks on rubber workers along the Xingu by Kayapó. While more than one Kayapó group was almost certainly involved, Xikrin recall numerous clashes that date from this period.

Referring to my field notes I find only six cases of confirmed deaths among Brazilians as a result of Xikrin attacks. Not all men participated in every attack and quite possibly this is an underestimate since few men today are of an age to have participated. The Xikrin did reacquire firearms as a result of these raids and it seems that even a few incidents were sufficient to create widespread alarm within the Altamira region among a population that largely sought to make a living through activities such as rubber and Brazil nut gathering and gold prospecting. The Altamira population had its own reason to play up the Kayapó threat, having years before lured another Kayapó band with promises of friendship, only to kill them as they slept (Nimuendajú 1952).

Ironically, Xikrin access to steel tools and firearms increased as a result of their raids, but this did little to make their lives easier. In the context of an economy oriented primarily toward wild products, steel tools did not appreciably diminish the work involved—scouting, climbing, gathering—as it would have in the case of horticultural labor in which the bulk of work entailed forest clearing. On the other hand, collective hunting in which bands of men drove animals such as deer and tapir toward flooded depressions where they could be clubbed to death without the use of firearms continued to prove quite effective. The party of Brazilians who made first contact with the Xikrin reported that they enjoyed an abundance of meat of all kinds (Corró, personal communication).

In many ways, the new move paralleled the previous migration from the Cateté region. But rather than seeking to avoid contact with other indigenous peoples, they aggressively sought them out and attacked them, with the aim of taking over their stored food and gardens. They also expanded their attacks against extractivist workers. In both cases the military precision and ferocity of the attack rather than any advantage in weaponry secured the Xikrin victory.

However, after occupying the Assuriní village, the Xikrin set about building a palisade in order to fend off any counterattacks—indicating that they hardly felt secure in their position.

THE ECONOMIC CONTEXT OF CONTACT

In response to the disruption of the Altamira extractivist economy, Francisco Meireles, veteran scout of many contact campaigns of the Society for the Protection of Indians, was enlisted to "pacify" the Xikrin. With Meireles in Altamira, the threatened violent vigilante action by the mayor and townspeople against the Xikrin settled into a standoff. Meireles proclaimed that any attack on the Xikrin "is the sole responsibility of prospectors, rubber tappers, and Brazil nut gatherers themselves, since they have been warned by me that they should not have invaded the wild Indian territories" (*O Globo* 31 October 1959).

Despite being an official emissary of the SPI, Meireles had difficulty receiving the needed support and supplies from the central administration and finally vowed to set off on his own if necessary, with or without the assistance. The *Jornal do Comercio* noted in its 17 November 1959 edition that "Inspector Meireles, despite the lack of SPI resources, will try to approach the [Xikrin] village, thus avoiding an armed confrontation with its unpredictable consequences." At the time, the "city" of Altamira boasted five streets and two thousand inhabitants (*O Globo* 30 October 1959). In the enormous region comprised by the municipalities of Altamira and São Félix do Xingu, there were only 12,090 Brazilian residents in 1960 (Diniz 1963). Among a population that made a living largely by collecting forest resources, the presence of hundreds of armed natives of unpredictable movements did indeed pose a sizable threat.

Although the Gorotire Kayapó were contacted in 1937, other Kayapó villages—Kubēnkrākêjn, Metyktire, Mekrāgnoti, Kôkrajmoro, Bay, Cateté Xikrin, and Kararaô—were only contacted in the 1950s. The Bakajá Xikrin were the last of a succession of pacification expeditions that sought to make the region safe for extractivist activity. So much so that in 1958 the Indian Protection Service signed an agreement with the Superintendência do Plano de Valorização Econômica da Amazônia (SPVEA), the agency charged with Amazonian development, in which the agency agreed to fund pacification programs aimed at the Kayapó.

In addition to some young SPI employees, the party that Meireles assembled included Kayapó from the previously contacted Gorotire, Mekrāgnoti, Kôkrajmoro, and Cateté villages. One of the first acts of the SPI when contacting Kayapó groups during the 1950s was to recruit young men to serve as guides in further contact operations with uncontacted Kayapó. To this day, the Xikrin easily recite the names of other Kayapó involved in their contact. These included three men from Cateté who were quite familiar with the recent history of the Bakajá group.

As they trailed the Xikrin, members of the Meireles party would enter abandoned Indian campsites shouting the name of the Xikrin leader, Ngôrãrãti (Corró, personal communication). As a result of the previous conversations with Cateté men that postdated this group's contact with the settlement at Posto de las Casas, Bakajá Xikrin apparently knew what to expect from the SPI party. When they finally came face to face with the Xikrin, Corró, a new SPI employee at the time, recalled that one hulking man stepped out from behind a tree trunk, pointed to himself, and said "Não mata, eu bom" ("Don't kill, I good"). Ngôrãrãti was among the seventy-three Xikrin at the campsite. Dogs were as numerous as Indians. These must have been quite effective as hunters since every successive campsite tracked by SPI pursuers gave evidence of tapir, deer, wild pig, and other large game remains. Although few in number, the remaining Xikrin were not experiencing any deprivation of food and Corró was impressed with their health and vitality.

Within minutes after meeting the contact party, the Xikrin demanded to borrow their firearms! This was a bit unnerving for the SPI party, but the Xikrin claimed that they merely wanted to go hunting in order to bring back game for a celebratory feast. The request represented an admirable bit of diplomatic probing on the part of the Bakajá Xikrin meant to gauge the real intentions of the SPI. The SPI party had been traveling for weeks through uncharted forest and although it included fluent Kayapó speakers, these were also members of groups with whom the Bakajá Xikrin were on an unfriendly footing. Having been involved in a frantic pursuit on foot through the bush, the SPI had no large stores of gifts to offer to indicate their peaceful intentions. In the end, Aibi, the Gorotire Kayapó among the contact party, lobbied in favor of the Xikrin request, and the Xikrin returned shortly before dark loaded down with game. The use of firearms also demonstrated that although "uncontacted," Xikrin were not unfamiliar with the technology wielded by outsiders and, in addition, used it to show hospitality to their SPI pursuers. The Xikrin were prepared to enter into contact with wider Brazilian society and were striving to do so on their own terms.

SETTLEMENT AND FLIGHT

The aims of the SPI were twofold. They sought to stop the Xikrin raids on extractivists and to forestall any vigilante action on the part of officials of Altamira against the Xikrin. The SPI planned to settle the Xikrin along the lower reaches of the Bakajá River, allowing them to be easily reached by water from Altamira. The Xikrin agreed because they were told that resettlement would mean not only an end to their fear of reprisals from the Cateté but also the receipt of many presents from the SPI. Approximately 120 Xikrin relocated to the site of the future Indian post, dubbed "Francisco Meireles," located at the site of the present village of Trincheira (Anonymous n.d.).

After a few short weeks with the SPI employees many Xikrin perished in a devastating epidemic that they called "mekwỳtyk" (black feces disease). The remnants of the population fled the Indian post and headed for the site of the last large precontact settlement of Bàtprànõrõ. Only about forty Xikrin remained at the post, and that number diminished even further as some of the men were drawn into the extractive trades or into work for the SPI. The few remaining Xikrin at Posto Meireles were used as a buffer against Assuriní attacks against extractivists along the Bakajá River and began working closely with the fur and pelt traders (Corró, personal communication; Cotrim 1971). Bemnoypa, his brother Kanhỹm, his sister Ngreikaro, and their parents formed the core of a group that worked closely with extractivists. In 1986 this same group of close kin comprised the nucleus of a group that split from the main Xikrin settlement in order to return to the site of Posto Francisco Meireles, today renamed "Trincheira."

Grim conditions faced those who fled the epidemic at the Indian post. Survivors were sick, weak, and hungry. They foraged on whatever plant foods were available and watched the more vulnerable elderly and children succumb. One dramatic incident, oft retold, illustrates the precariousness of their existence. Upon his return to the Bàtprànõrõ village one man was so enfeebled that he was attacked and killed by a jaguar, as he lay too weak to defend himself inside his very own shelter! The chief Ngôrãrãti was among the victims of this period. Demoralized and confused, the group rebuffed all attempts to convince them to return to Posto Francisco Meireles.

One of the scouts hired by the SPI to go after the fleeing Xikrin was a young man, Mauré, whose mother had been a white Brazilian and whose father was Kayapó. He pursued the survivors to their old haunts, but was unsuccessful in convincing them to return to Posto Meireles. Returning himself, he married Kôkprĩn, the daughter of Ngreikaro, and, following Kayapó custom, upon marriage, became a resident in his mother-in-law's house. An energetic advocate of the extractivist industries within the group, Mauré was to play a large role in later developments as a leader of the dissident Trincheira faction.

To reestablish the trust between the SPI and the Xikrin, a pair of brothers, Afonso and "Kamiranga" Alves began a large garden near the old village site of Ràpkô, within hailing distance of the fugitive Xikrin. At the same time, several young Xikrin living at Posto Francisco Meireles were commissioned to begin clearing gardens and a space for houses at the site of the former Brazilian settlement "Flor do Caucho." Finally, in 1965, after several years of effort, Kamiranga and Afonso, both fluent Kayapó speakers, were successful in convincing the refugee Xikrin to transfer to the Flor do Caucho site along the Bakajá River, where they were rejoined by the Xikrin of Posto Francisco Meireles. They were lured to the site with the promise of extensive goods and assurances that they would remain far from the location of the former epidemic.

As is frequent in the case of native peoples (Cook 1998; Davis 1977) the post-contact epidemic had taken its toll. A census taken in 1971 revealed that only 57 of the total population of 107 had been alive at the time of the initial contact and move to Posto Francisco Meireles (Fernandes 1971). This represents a survival rate of less than 50 percent from the count of 120 reported at Posto Meireles. If we add the population lost in the defection to the Cateté village and the subsequent period of flight, the group assembled in 1971, a decade after official contact, was only a small portion, perhaps 10 percent, of the once large village many hundred strong at Bàtprànõrõ.

In recalling their transfer to the Flor do Caucho site, one man recalled that the SPI had assembled an opulent display of presents. For the Xikrin, the offerings were an indication of the affection in which they were held by the SPI. To this day, there is a vivid image of hammocks, mosquito nets, flashlights, and flip-flops ostentatiously arrayed for distribution. The SPI purchased revolvers for all the men. Ammunition arrived in a wooden crate the size of a large suitcase. Although the revolvers proved to be ineffective hunting weapons ("You'd shoot an animal and it would just walk away," remembered one man), the gifts of trade goods were greatly appreciated.

The delivery of goods inaugurated a period of close collaboration with fur traders, among whom were SPI staffers. Xikrin men worked as *gateiros* or fur hunters and trappers and traded pelts for more goods. Veteran traders taught the Xikrin how to trap jaguar and ocelot without damaging their pelts. Informants recalled that they would also trade other skins such as wild pig.

The mid-1960s was a time of great turmoil and controversy for the SPI. In the aftermath of scandals involving massive internal corruption, the agency was abolished in 1967, and a new agency, the National Indian Foundation (FUNAI) was established the following year. The national shake-up had remarkably little impact along the Bakajá. While aid from the Indian agency stopped, the goods from the fur trade continued unabated to supply the mainstay of Xikrin supplies.

However, the death of the main middleman in the fur trade was an event of greater significance. He was known to the Xikrin as "Oliveira." SPI records list a man named Oliveira as the navigator and engine mechanic at Posto Francisco Meireles. Apparently, Oliveira stayed on, continuing as an SPI employee as well as a middleman in the fur trade. Some Xikrin men still refer to Oliveira as "chief" *(benadjwỳrỳ)*. After years of coordinating fur trading among the Xikrin, Oliveira was gunned down in the streets of Altamira. The story of his shooting is still told, and the similarity between war stories and hunting stories is evident. Xikrin know which parts of the body were rent with bullets and the make of the weapon; the specifics of the death throes are avidly imitated. Despite his evident corruption as an SPI employee involved in fur trading, his demise left the Xikrin without trade goods, and they felt his loss keenly. It may be a mistake to judge Oliveira too harshly for his role in the fur trade. Maybury-Lewis's (1968) description of a SPI employee at the remote Xerente Indian Post, who went for long stretches without being paid, reminds us that often government employees in the bush had to survive by their wits rather than by their paycheck.

After Oliveira, Afonso Alves was returned to administer the post and did so only with great difficulty because he had, according to the Xikrin, insufficient goods to offer. As so often happens to Brazilian Indians, once the scouting wing of the Indian agency responsible for establishing contact turns the group over to the agency's administrative wing, gifts available for distribution dwindle rapidly. Xikrin tell of starting to clear a landing strip for small aircraft at this time. The work ground to a halt shortly after it became evident that Afonso had only a few cans of sardines to distribute. Unfortunately for him, a boat load of goods, including arms destined for the Xikrin, sunk on the way to the village, and its entire cargo was lost. On top of it all, fur trading was outlawed in the face of international revulsion regarding the slaughter of endangered species and Xikrin were forced to look elsewhere for ways to attract trade goods.

The organization employed by the FUNAI and Xikrin was patterned after the norm of the aviamento system. Families of Xikrin were outfitted much as were Brazilian *gateiros,* who were advanced hammocks, ammunition, salt, coffee, and the like before entering into the forest for extended periods to trap furs. These items would be subsequently be deducted from the payment made after the furs were delivered. Xikrin would travel in groups of several households—women, children, and the elderly included. Their peregrinations could last for months at a time, as they tended traps, foraged, and hunted. Xikrin recall this time with enthusiasm. Groups would number around twenty persons and men were tied together through bonds of friendship as often as kinship, while women were often related to one another. In effect, such parties constituted two or three cooperating households that were not bound by the strictures of structured village life.

These small groups ranged over large stretches of territory in all directions.

Every man had at least a pistol by this time and Xikrin were unafraid of attacks by Indians who lacked firearms. Base camps were set up for the collection of furs to the north and south of the Flor do Caucho village site. These camps were organized by subchiefs appointed jointly by the Xikrin chief Mereti and the trader. It was in this capacity that several chiefs were appointed—Jaguar and his brother Snake (both classificatory sons of Mereti), Kanhỹm, and Mauré, the scout who had been hired to contact fleeing Xikrin. Jaguar and Snake dealt with skins collected from the north, building a compound near the former Kôkaỳrỳ settlement, and Mauré and Kanhỹm were stationed to the south near the stream known as "Goiaba." I was able to observe this division of followers in action in 1985 when the Brazil nut harvest was organized along the same spatial and organizational divisions. These divisions, in turn, prefigured the split resulting in separate villages of Bakajá and Trincheira.

For the first time, Xikrin chiefs were known as *kubẽnnhôbenadjwỳrỳ*, or "whitemen's chiefs." They acted as intermediaries, collecting pelts and apportioning merchandise. Whitemen's chiefs were organizationally necessary because the wide-ranging movements of small household groups precluded frequent returns to the central village to trade. Existence within small mobile groups was very satisfactory, and the existing wildcat population virtually guaranteed success in acquiring trade goods. The main chief, Mereti, was himself elderly and tended to remain in the centrally located village, where he could consult with SPI and later FUNAI officials and fur traders.

As they were constantly moving over an area of land the size of a small New England state, Xikrin groups came into conflict with neighboring indigenous peoples. In one case a party of seven Xikrin men attacked a village of the Araweté near the Rio Branco to the south of the Bakajá village. They succeeded in killing four and took two teenage girls captive. They also took large quantities of black beads and arrows from Araweté houses. This was not the only clash with neighboring peoples during this time. A FUNAI scout recalled that in 1966, the Xikrin were goaded by fur trappers into attacking and burning the Assuriní village in order to make the area safe against Assuriní attacks (Cotrim 1971). Xikrin took advantage of the raid to stock themselves with useful items. The missionary Lukesch (1976, 13) reports visiting the Flor do Caucho village in 1967 and encountering Assuriní bows, arrows, hammocks, baskets, and beads. Corró in a personal interview conducted in 1987 claimed that the regional population in Altamira feared Assuriní attacks along the Bakajá up to this point. Still other Xikrin remember several clashes with Parakanã groups that lasted until 1977 (cf. Caron 1971, 318, on previous conflict between Xikrin and Parakanã). The final confrontation with neighboring Indian peoples occurred during this year.

Xikrin firearms and clubs killed seventeen Parakanã after a Xikrin man had been wounded in the leg by a Parakanã arrow in the vicinity of the Bakajá village. While the Araweté captives had escaped, in 1984 there were still two Parakanã women captives in the village, one of whom moved to the Cateté Xikrin village in 1985 along with her adoptive family.

The Xikrin did not consider clashes with non-Kayapó to be tests of their military prowess since firearms won the day so decisively in every case. Superior weaponry freed the Xikrin of any fear of neighboring tribes for the first time in their history. The orientation toward fur trapping also tended to lessen the amount of time people spent together in the main village. Moreover, we must remember that the population was severely diminished, and by absenting themselves from the village, Xikrin claimed to be freeing themselves from the sadness stimulated by longing for departed kin.

In the Xikrin mind there is a close association between collective singing, dancing, and preparation for ritual and the waves of longing occasioned by the festivities. Not only are spirits of the deceased attracted to ritual activity, but they are drawn to the site of their former residences along the village circle as well. Families in mourning often leave their houses temporarily to avoid their own sadness and contact with a spirit. Given these factors, it is little wonder that village life experienced a considerable decompression as people sought to take maximal advantage of the fur boom and enjoy the abundant game and the dominance over their enemies provided by the new acquisition of firearms.

The Xikrin regard this period as a "golden age," and, while this seems difficult to believe after undergoing the deaths and the disorientation of contact, at least one other South American anthropologist has also found that the period of fur trapping was considered something of a golden age by recently contacted indigenous peoples who had also experienced devastating losses (Kensinger 1995, 266). Without referring to the extensive deaths and the dislocation that preceded them, Xikrin point to the perambulations during fur-trapping expeditions and the large number of goods they received as nearly ideal. This is somewhat puzzling only if we forget Xikrin history. The productivity of steel tools and the fire power of new weaponry allowed them to work with their near kinsfolk and friends and to avoid the pressures of village life for long periods. The fur trade paid well (at least according to their expectations at the time) and they felt fairly compensated for their effort. Gone was the fear of armed assaults from either the Cateté or Gorotire Kayapó. Firearms gave them military advantage over other Indian peoples in the region. As undisputed masters of their domain, they roamed widely in small family groups, and the constraint of collective work under the direction of chiefs was still in the future, as we will see.

The main village, in which all families would reassemble, was constructed as two rows of houses, running parallel to the Bakajá River and built in regional Brazilian style, facing each other across a street. By 1971 an airstrip had been constructed that allowed the village to be reached in approximately an hour's flight time from Altamira. In 1972 this Bakajá village was visited by Englishmen Edwin Brooks and Francis Huxley, Indian rights activists from the Aborigines Protection Society (APS). Although their impressions were based on a short visit of an hour or so in the village, the visitors believed that the Xikrin appeared acculturated compared to other groups they had witnessed in their tour of many endangered Indian peoples. A photo of a dance performed in honor of the visitors comprises the frontispiece of the resulting APS report *Tribes of the Amazon Basin in Brazil 1972*. The picture's caption reads: "The motley clothing, with its combination of traditional head-dress and manufactured oddments, undermines the dignity of the chief and the pride of the dancers. More generally, it hints at the way in which National Integration can result in the 'ethnicide' of tribal man" (Brooks et al. 1973).

That the Xikrin, after less than a decade of sporadic contact, primarily with SPI officials and fur traders, could have appeared "acculturated" seems primarily due to their embracing of material goods received from traders. Brooks et al. give conflicting village population figures (94 on p. 79, and 127 on p. 165) but agree that the Xikrin looked quite healthy and vigorous. Moreover, an on-site FUNAI employee insisted that they "had no real problems" (Brooks et al., 79). We have seen that from the Xikrin point of view this time was a culmination of a period of years in which they actually saw their sense of security increase as a result of the trade goods and the newly established peaceable relations with Brazilians and other Kayapó groups. Far from undermining the dignity of the chief, the influx of trade goods ("manufactured oddments" in the words of APS) was becoming the basis of a new sort of redistributive power in which chiefs and local extractivist representatives served as intermediaries.

BRAZIL NUTS

In 1970 Brazil's military president, Médici, launched the Program of National Integration (PIN) of the Amazon, which included the construction of the Transamazonian highway along with other initiatives designed to enhance production and the integration of the region more fully into national life. Unlike many other indigenous peoples, the Xikrin did not appear greatly affected by the building of the highway. On the heels of the collapse of the fur trade in 1972, when it was made illegal, the policy of the newly formed FUNAI was to have a much greater impact.

Along with an enhanced infrastructure for its Indian post, the FUNAI sought to institutionalize a practice long in place in other indigenous areas: the extraction of Brazil nuts organized according to the aviamento system. After more than ten years of contact, the Xikrin were no longer seen by regional authorities as a threat to local prospecting, rubber, and Brazil nut industries. While previously the small population of Altamira and its reliance on the extractivist industries made it essential to deal with potential Xikrin disruptions either through armed violence or subventions aimed at satisfying the Xikrin's limited desire for trade goods, it was now possible to contemplate a "normalizing" of relations. In short, this meant an establishment of exclusive FUNAI administration over Indian post affairs rather than a power-sharing arrangement with local fur traders. In addition, Xikrin labor was now to be used to underwrite the costs of running the Indian post itself through their collection of Brazil nuts. Assured of the status quo, the FUNAI sought to turn the Xikrin into a self-financing and dependent community.

In effect, this simply meant that the Xikrin were initiated into a system that had been in existence since the rubber boom in Amazonia, a system still widely practiced on Indian posts. In the early 1960s the Brazilian anthropologist Edson Soares Diniz had observed the operation of the "general store economy" *(economia de barracão)*, through which trade goods were advanced to extractivist workers without any money changing hands among the Gorotire Kayapó.

In this way the employee in charge of the Indian Post agreed to sell part or all of the Brazil nut harvest . . . beforehand in order to obtain credit. As a result of this, given the circumstances of an "agreement" based on future payment, the capitalist [merchant] imposes his will, furnishing only a part of the merchandise representing the value of the harvest. By virtue of this, Indians recruited as "laborers" suffer what could be called official exploitation because, besides being poorly paid, they acquire merchandise at inflated prices. In this specific case, the Post employee is exploited by the financier to whom he has promised the sale of the harvest and ends up blamed for the inadequate payments. (Diniz 1963 [my translation])

Nonetheless, Diniz claimed that the Gorotire Kayapó were forced to engage in the Brazil nut and cumaru seed *(Dipteryx* sp.) trade year after year since it remained the only avenue through which they could obtain needed goods. Diniz's (1963) description emphasizes the importance of this trade on a regional level since it not only constituted a point of interaction between the Gorotire and Brazilian society but it attracted a continual influx of Kayapó from other villages to Gorotire, whose population was approximately 250 in the early 1960s.

What is clear from accounts such as those of Diniz (1963) and Caron (1971), as well as interviews with Indian agency old-timers from the Altamira region, is that the SPI and later the FUNAI were not able to avoid contact between Indians under their "administration" and extractivist bosses. Rather they were forced to collude or compete with extractivists for influence over the Indian populations formally under their jurisdiction. Under the PIN, which saw a great increase in the reach of government agencies concerned with development within the Amazon region, the FUNAI sought to consolidate its position and become the exclusive intermediary between Indian populations and the outside world. The building of airstrips was one element in this strategy since, at the time, the Indian Agency had a virtual monopoly of air transport in the region. This explains why in village after village Kayapó peoples had to be paid (and well, by going standards) in order to construct landing strips at the behest of the FUNAI or missionaries. The building up of FUNAI infrastructure did not merely represent an increase of services to indigenous communities but also represented the breaking of previous ties with other regionals. Caron (1971, 78) recounts buying 2,500 shells factory direct in order to recompense Cateté for construction of a landing strip.

By the early 1970s all of the Kayapó groups were heavily involved in the collection of Brazil nuts. River boats laden with nuts from many Kayapó villages, in addition to those of the Xikrin, were deposited with the FUNAI in Altamira, whose storehouse occupied half a city block. After taking competing bids, the FUNAI would send truckload after truckload rumbling down the newly constructed Transamazon highway in the direction of Belém at the Amazon's mouth, whence they would be shipped overseas. For a period of years FUNAI was successful in selling everything that the Indians under its jurisdiction managed to transport to Altamira from their respective reservations. This is no longer the case and, for the Xikrin and other Kayapó, the boom in Brazil nut exports was fleeting.

Today the Brazil nut harvest is a time of great anxiety. The work is invariably onerous and marketability suffers unpredictable swings from year to year. During years when nuts are plentiful and easily harvested, prices tend to be low. High prices, on the other hand, generally occurred during years of low supply. But prices are determined by the supply in the Amazon as a whole along with overseas demand, both of which remain mysteries from the vantage point of the reservation. Collecting Brazil nuts is, thus, always a calculated gamble and Xikrin often complain of having collected Brazil nuts *kaigo* (for nothing) in the recent past. Moreover, unsold nuts are not available for consumption, having been shipped from the reservation so that potential buyers can assess their quantity and quality.

From the late 1960s until the middle 1970s, Brazil nut collecting satisfied expectations, and older Xikrin men were able to acquire firearms. In recent times, a man may find that an entire season of collecting—two or three months' effort—may yield only a double foam mattress, or a flashlight and a canvas backpack.

Although Brazil nuts no longer figure prominently in the administration and financing of the reservation activities, the conditions under which the Xikrin labor today hark back some thirty years. Collecting is exhausting and dangerous and requires extended periods away from the village during the rainy months. The occupational hazards involve not only getting hit by cannonball-sized falling Brazil nuts, but also being injured when hacking open thousands of these hard shells under extremely slippery conditions. Rarely does a season go by without someone suffering a severe cut.

Brazil nuts are carried back to camp in large baskets secured to the back by means of both a tumpline stretching across the forehead and shoulder straps so as to ensure the weight is distributed as evenly as possible. Squeezing into narrow openings through drenched vine thickets while carrying bulky loads of forty-five to sixty-five pounds for periods up to four hours requires superhuman effort. The terrain is often broken by ravines, gullies, and the inevitable layer of water over the trail. Whether or not one falls, suffers painful ant bites, or impales one's leg on a protruding branch, the work is truly draining and must be repeated day after rain-soaked day, since harvest time coincides with the rainy season. According to going rates in the region, a single day's collecting may bring only a can of cooking oil or a couple of kilos of sugar, if it can be sold at all.

If Brazil nuts were king in the early 1970s, they would be dethroned only a few years later in a manner reminiscent of all extractive products. Prices dropped and indigenous extractivists found themselves cut off from the market. No longer were Brazil nuts from all over southern Pará channeled to the FUNAI warehouse in Altamira, since this was no longer economically feasible. The FUNAI began to use its space for other purposes. In the village, Xikrin men began to receive many fewer trade goods for the same work performed a few years earlier. The delivery of fewer goods meant dissatisfaction with the FUNAI and with the chiefs as well.

Discontentment with the chiefs stemmed from both the quantity of goods received and how the chiefs chose to distribute the goods within the village. Xikrin had begun to engage in a number of new extractivist activities since contact, and the fallout was considerable. Extractivism carried with it a host of consequences, from the orchestration of sedentarism and mobility to coincide with the needs of the harvest, and the oversight, mediation, and coordination of the chiefs. These changes, in turn, stoked further reaction. The present struggle for livelihood on the reservation seems to have developed its particular dynamic in the course of the fur trading interregnum during which the Xikrin were only tenuously under the administration of the Indian agency. This period provided the Xikrin not only with new goods but with a new vision of social relations in which the autonomy of small groups of self-reliant kin was ensured through the redistributional efforts of the chiefs who collaborated with extractivists and the Indian agency.

5 | THE QUIET REVOLUTION

Overt continuity in Xikrin subsistence since contact masks shifts in organization and emphasis that go to the heart of subsistence strategy and involve changed relations with the outside world as well as between coresident villagers and chiefs. The move toward greater household autonomy appears against a backdrop of greater dependency on manufactured goods for subsistence production. The pursuit of life's necessities—food and shelter—begins to entail previously unknown conflicts. The tensions of frontier life within a traditional community worm their way into daily activities so that these take on an unfamiliar feel. Incremental changes and pragmatic, rather than programmatic, decisions have led to a quiet revolution in the way work is performed and social labor organized.

NATURAL SETTING

A brief overview of the environment, climate, and seasonal patterns of the Bakajá region forms a necessary prologue to the following discussion of subsistence. The vegetation around the Bakajá settlement is dominated by liana forests, or *matas de cipo,* which are widespread throughout the Itacaiúnas Basin and the greater part of the Transamazon highway between Marabá and Altamira. These are forests with relatively low trees, which may or may not be entangled with a profusion of lianas, where babassu palms *(Orbignya phalerata)* are frequent, and where Brazil nuts *(Betholletia excelsa)* and babassú often exist in close association (Pires 1978, 609–12). This low upland forest covers 10 to 15 percent of the Amazon Basin, particularly south of the Amazon between the Tocantins and Madeira Rivers. Soil type and vegetation are not reliably correlated in the Amazon, and the area around the village presents a mosaic of soils. Of particular interest are the black soils that Smith (1980; also see Balée 1989) speculates are of anthropogenic origin. The Xikrin tend to choose these black sandy soils for their garden plots. Average temperature varies more during the course of a daily cycle than over the course of the year. The annual mean temperature is twenty-five degrees centigrade.

By far the most dramatic climatic variation is rainfall, for in this part of the Amazon there is an accentuated division of the year into wet and dry seasons. The Xikrin divide the annual cycle into two seasons. These seasons are not of equal length. The dry season only lasts from the beginning of June to mid-October, when ten to twenty millimeters of rain per month is common, and most of the approximately 175 rainy days each year occur between November and May. Water levels take time to build up as rains flow down through the catchment area. Normally annual rainfall averages around 2,100 millimeters (Ministerio das Minas e Energia 1984–86). Even after the rains have stopped, it may take several weeks for the water to begin receding.

As might be expected, the timing of horticultural practices, clearing, planting, and harvesting are pegged to the alternating seasons. The wet and dry seasons are marked by more than the presence or absence of rain, however. Given the relatively flat relief of the landscape, even a slight increase of rainfall causes streams and rivers to overflow their banks and flood the surrounding forest. Gullies become streams; hollows become lakes. Cracked, hardened earth transforms into a muddy morass.

The rainy season tends to affect the entire Amazonian economy, not just indigenous peoples. Logging is halted since trucks may no longer be able to travel makeshift forest roads and tree bases may be inundated. Depending on the lay of the land, gold prospecting slows. Pumps that suffice to remove water from beds during the dry season are overwhelmed, and prospecting sites may be flooded. Prospectors leave the mining camps.

Hunting and fishing are affected as well. Fish move out of the main channels and "forage" in the flooded forest for fruits and other edibles. Dispersed in this fashion they are much more difficult to catch with hook and line. Smaller waterways, which could be dammed to form pools where fish could be caught with fish poisons, seep away in all directions into the surrounding forest. Not only are game animals harder to track through waterlogged trails, but, according to the Xikrin, they tend to be less active during the rains. Some wild foods, such as Brazil nuts, become plentiful, and these are harvested for both trade and immediate consumption. In short, the rainy season tends to comprise a hiatus of several months in activities tied to the extractivist economy, and it imposes a rhythm on subsistence activities as well.

HORTICULTURE

Today Xikrin continue to produce the great bulk of their own food through slash-and-burn horticulture, hunting, fishing, and the collecting of wild plants. The characteristic form of Kayapó gardens has been described by Flowers et al. (1982). Garden plots consist of circular openings cleared in the forest planted with sweet potatoes, bitter and sweet manioc, maize, bananas, plantains, yams (*Dioscorea* spp), papayas, squashes, and watermelon. Xikrin supplement their garden produce with fresh game, fish, gathered delicacies such as wild legumes, wild cacao, palm fruits, including assaí, bacaba, inajá, babassu, and honey. Increasingly coffee, sugar, imported rice, and pasta are consumed, but these are still luxury items for most people, though not for the principal chief.

Bitter manioc *(Manihot esculenta)* and sweet potatoes *(Ipomea batatas)* comprise the main vegetable staples. The former may be eaten only after processed into grape-nuts-like pellets known as *farinha* or "manioc flour." The complex process has been well described for both indigenous and nonindigenous Amazonia (Murphy and Murphy 1985; Smith 1982). Bitter manioc was never a traditional staple among the Kayapó peoples until quite recently. Although both bitter and sweet varieties belong to the same botanical species, "bitter" manioc is distinguished from its "sweet" counterpart by the presence of elevated prussic acid levels (hydrogen cyanide—HCN), which must be removed during the farinha making process.

While farinha has been the staple of most peoples of the indigenous Tupí tradition, the Xikrin did not adopt this food because of its indigenous origins. Farinha has become a staple in the Xikrin diet because it could be efficiently produced with Western technology and because it serves the needs of a more sedentary population involved in the extractive industries better than do sweet potatoes, maize, and even sweet manioc—these being the traditional fare of Gê-speaking peoples. It was not environmental imperatives that made bitter manioc attractive but the political economy of frontier life in which Western technology became available. New sorts of subsistence insecurities resulting from increased sedentarism, epidemics, and the uncertain terms of relations with the outside world made bitter manioc preferable to the existing staples.

Xikrin first learned to make farinha using large metal toasting griddles. They grate tubers on metal graters rather than on Tupi-style wooden boards embedded with piranha teeth. Xikrin graters are either purchased or crafted by punching out protuberances in a metal sheet or a flattened metal can. A mechanical grinder (dubbed a *caititu,* or "wild pig" in Amazon parlance) powered by a gasoline motor is by far the most efficient means of grinding manioc currently

Figure 6. Husband and wife preparing manioc pulp for toasting by the Bakajá river in 1995. The press is on the right. (Photo by author)

employed, however. Whether grated or ground, the resulting mash is strained through metal-mesh sieves onto plastic tarps or into old canoes. Metal axes and machetes are always used to cut the large amount of firewood needed to keep the griddle temperature hot during the long toasting process. Canoe paddles serve as giant spatulas for the constant stirring needed to uniformly toast the farinha.

The press, which makes use of time-tested principles of pressure and counter-pressure modeled on Tupí technology, is the only part of the operation that does not involve western technology. The Xikrin utilize a boxlike press lined with woven babassú mats quite similar to those used by small farmers along Brazil's Transamazon highway (see picture in Smith 1982, 69 for comparison).

Farinha is easily portable and stores well, and bitter manioc is a useful food reserve. Its usefulness in this regard is due primarily to its slower rate of maturation and its resistance to spoilage when left in the ground—up to three to four years in some cases. Bitter manioc is preferred over other cultigens for the same reason extractivists have favored this foodstuff for centuries: It effectively nourishes expeditions in the pursuit of caucho rubber, animal pelts, gold, sarsaparilla, and other marketable items. In contrast to expeditions for commercial collecting organized by extractivists, Gê peoples have traditionally organized their treks according to seasonal or ritual criteria and pass through areas where food is readily available, hence they have had no need for bitter manioc.

The second advantage of bitter manioc resides in its convenience for life conducted from a FUNAI post. In sedentary circumstances, a crop that can be harvested year-round, such as bitter manioc, is advantageous during the slack seasons when garden produce and game are less available. The beginning of the rainy season is one such time; newly planted corn and sweet potatoes have not yet matured and high waters make fishing and hunting more difficult. In past epochs, Gê peoples would abandon their villages in times of seasonal food scarcity and the months of September, October, and November were the time of the year's longest trek.

All Kayapó peoples have shifted toward a reliance on bitter manioc since contact made Western goods available. In the early 1960s, Joan Turner (1967, 88) found that manioc was the major food crop among the Gorotire Kayapó, who were officially contacted in the late 1930s. In the case of the more recently contacted Mekrãgnoti Kayapó, Werner (1984, 156) reports that they did not rely heavily on bitter manioc until after 1966 when they acquired the equipment necessary to make farinha in quantity. Although they began planting the crop only in 1960, in succeeding years its importance had grown so that by 1982 it made up 38 percent of the garden-derived calories in their diet (Flowers et al. 1982, 209). Even this estimate of Kayapó bitter manioc consumption shows a difference between Gê, for whom it is a new dietary addition, and other indigenous peoples who traditionally focused on this crop. The Kuikuru people present an extreme example of bitter manioc dependence as their forty-six varieties of *Manihot esculenta* comprise some 80 to 85 percent of their diet (Carneiro 1983).

The reliance on manufactured goods and technology in farinha production entails both a reliance on chiefs for basic input and fewer obligations incurred to other households. While households are matri-uxorilocal and generally structured around a group of related women and their in-marrying husbands, household autonomy in matters of production does not result in greater female control over the production process. Instead farinha manufacture forces both men and women to conform to the rhythm of activity orchestrated by the chief. However, female kin continue to act independently of menfolk in other sorts of subsistence activities to be discussed shortly.

Sieves, tarps, sacks, axes, and machetes used in farinha processing are shared freely among residents of the same household who, after all, also freely share food. A household survey, which we will consider at greater length in the next chapter, reveals that manufactured items are considered essential but that the sharing of these items between households is quite awkward—people will often do without rather than impose on a neighbor and the concept of "shame" or "reserve" *(piaàm)* was often invoked to explain this. Manufactured goods exchanged between households represent only 3 percent of Western manufactured goods found in peoples' homes. The griddle, motorized grinder, and hut are considered property of the "community." However, the chief has a good deal of influence since he is responsible for its maintenance and owns essential supplies, notably gasoline and oil. While the chief often delegates the FUNAI post employee to service and fuel the motor, he retains the key to the storeroom and has final say over its use.

When farinha is made from manioc harvested from domestic plots, a household incurs no obligations to other households. Since women are forbidden to undertake the extensive toasting necessary, some households require additional male labor for this process. Labor needed for this chore may be had by simply compensating the workman with a portion of the farinha he helped toast.

While farinha is both produced and consumed within households, chiefs disperse needed fuel and lubricants for the grinder. This fact obliges both men and women to conform to the organization and tempo of chief-directed activities. While households obviously base part of their production decisions on their own needs, they must take the chief's desires and organizational initiatives into account. Although workaday life usually proceeds as if there existed a shared underlying consensus, the potentially coercive nature of infrastructure ownership and the unequal distribution of goods surface from time to time to reveal the constraints under which Xikrin labor.

In theory, all village residents have access to land, water, wild plant resources, as well as game and fish. In practice, the conditions under which Xikrin make their living are heavily constrained by other factors of production. Those individuals who do not conform may have their supplies "cut off" by chiefs or suffer from lack of reciprocal labor help, with an attendant increase in the difficulty of procuring subsistence for the entire household.

Control over implements of production, such as manioc griddles, shotgun shells, and motors, is not equal, and the inability of commoners to directly acquire these items exercises a strong influence over the disposition of all male and much female labor. Whatever the situation may have been in the past, there is no question that material inequalities are at odds with indigenous conceptions regarding the traditional basis for social inequalities between men and women, elder and junior, or chiefs and commoners. A new dynamic has been unleashed that no amount of symbolic reworking can tame and reconceptualize in terms of traditional distinctions.

Within the village, individuals have no access to cash, wage labor, or vendors. Imported goods needed to make gardens and produce manioc are acquired only by "working for" chiefs. "Working for a chief" *(me benadjwỳrỳ apêj)* signifies regular participation in the public activities of a men's club led by a chief. These regular acts symbolize political allegiance and support. A Kayapó man does not exchange his work or labor power for a wage or goods. Rather, goods change hands within the context of preexisting social relationships and chiefs distribute them as tokens of friendship. No strict measure of productivity or labor time governs the quality or amount of goods distributed by chiefs to any individual. Participation in a men's club is the only way to acquire the trade goods necessary for production by men, both for themselves and for others in their households. On the other hand, greater household autonomy frees males from reciprocal obligations to males of other households. Thus bitter manioc processing can be seen as a form of "household production," but the apparent autonomy of each household in this regard is illusory. It is predicated on yet other seemingly collective activities that unite people of different households under chiefly leadership. Although this leadership is overtly noncoercive, its authority, derived from being the sole furnisher of the needed means of production, lurks not far beneath the surface.

We can evaluate some of the significance of the present organization of farinha production by contrasting it with other forms of horticultural production. Such forms can be gleaned from Xikrin history, such as the age-grade-based production discussed in the last chapter, or from field observations. In contrast with bitter manioc, Xikrin women control all aspects of sweet potato production. In the mid-1980s sweet potatoes were consumed almost daily and rivaled manioc consumption. In 1995 sweet potato consumption appeared to be decreasing, largely because other forms of "fast food," such as rice, beans, and even pasta, were more readily available.

Sweet potatoes along with sweet manioc are traditional crops of Gê-speaking peoples. Few peoples around the world depend on sweet potatoes for the bulk of their diet, with notable exceptions occurring in the highlands of Papua New Guinea and Irian Jaya (Hipsley and Kirk 1955). Nonetheless, sweet potatoes produce, on average, more edible energy per hectare per day than other major tropical food crops (Norman et al. 1984).

Since sweet potatoes are invariably consumed either the same day or the morning after they are unearthed, harvesting and cooking must be undertaken almost daily. Xikrin varieties are much smaller than the sweet potatoes commonly available in North American markets, and a fairly large number of potatoes are needed to make up a meal. Groups of two to five women normally leave together for the garden of one of the group members. Members are usually close relatives, mothers and sisters, who take turns visiting each other's gardens. Since only married women or older women with lovers possess gardens, food exchanges are conceived of as reciprocal exchanges between married women, even if younger siblings or widows lend a hand. As a group, women harvest an area to which they return several times over the course of the following months to collect the tubercles that have grown to harvestable size in the interim. Thus, unlike manioc, which is entirely uprooted, individual sweet potatoes are harvested without damaging the parent vine so that multiple harvests from a single plant are possible up to a period of two years.

A typical situation of reciprocal cooperation reveals the conditions under which sweet potatoes can occupy a greater place in the diet than bitter manioc. An exemplary arrangement would involve a group of four women each visiting one another's three producing plots once a month and harvesting one half of the growing area. This would provide twenty-four days of fresh sweet potatoes out of every month for each woman and her family. However, even if both short-growing and long-growing varieties were planted and matured at different rates, such an intensive consumption of sweet potatoes would not be possible during the entire year. Maize, sweet manioc, bananas, plantains, squash, and yams would pick up the slack. Nonetheless, while the example cited here was common during my 1984–85 field stay, the everyday consumption of sweet potatoes was less frequent in 1994–95.

The technical requirements for sweet potato cultivation and harvesting are quite simple. New gardens are planted with slips from older plants, and each plant has a recognizable origin. A woman can readily explain that the "black" variety came from her sister at the Cateté Xikrin village, while the "round head" variety came from her own mother, for example. Only a digging stick, or nowadays more commonly a machete, is used to unearth tubercles for consumption. Harvested sweet potatoes are carried in baskets made by men from babassu palm fronds or from canelike strips fashioned from small vines. The most common mode of preparing sweet potatoes is either by roasting them alone or along with meat and sweet manioc in an earth oven. Although steel axes are used to cut firewood, sweet potatoes illustrate both traditional food production techniques and patterns of sharing centered around hearths in which several nuclear families, usually grouped in a common residence or longhouse, both produce and share food among themselves. The very name for house (*kikre, ki*—earth oven, *kre*—hole) refers to the depression in which the earth oven is constructed rather than to the aspects of the dwelling that would serve to enclose a family or protect them from the elements.

CONTRASTING LOGICS OF PRODUCTION

Although both earth ovens and manioc toasting appear to be typical Amazonian food preparation techniques, in important ways they may be seen as the opposite of each other. Earth ovens are constructed by cooperating people who intend to consume food immediately upon its preparation. When female relatives take turns working on ovens at one anothers' homes, the earth oven is but one step in a process of ongoing reciprocity. The choice of whom to cooperate with lies entirely in the hands of the women involved. One male informant admitted that his wife's companions decided which garden they would harvest and where they would cook the food, and, while he might certainly comment on the portion he received, he merely ate what was provided.

The composition of groups of cooperating women is quite stable and a group may continue more or less unchanged for years. Nonetheless, the maturation of a sister or a daughter, the death of a relative, or some simmering resentment can cause group composition to shift. In general, both the stability and changes reflect female perspectives on the desirability of maintaining a certain set of relationships, and these relationships form the basis for the composition of matri-uxorilocal extended family residences.

Although both bitter manioc and sweet potatoes are planted in domestic gardens, only bitter manioc is cultivated in gardens sponsored by chief-led men's clubs, which, if not monocropped, always contain many fewer species and varieties than domestic plots. Nonetheless, gardening, along with hunting and Brazil nut collecting, comprise the bulk of men's club activities. While different crop requirements do not directly determine the organization of subsistence, the organization for processing and consuming crops highlights the diverse sets of relationships involved in production and exchange. The immediate and ongoing reciprocity embodied in sweet potatoes contrasts with the storageable manioc flour associated with chief-managed redistribution of trade goods and hierarchical control of access to processing technology.

When members of a household produce what they need to live, the organization and division of labor within a household may appear identical to the organization of production. Anthropologists have often interpreted household formation as the expression of a postmarital residence rule (in the Kayapó case, a husband relocating to the household of his wife's mothers and sisters and their husbands after marriage). In the Xikrin case, the networks of relations involved in different kinds of crop production tend to pull families in different ways, particularly when, as is often the case, relations are complicated. We can take the example of the young bride who married a widower living in his elderly father's house (i.e., viri-patrilocally) along with the children from his first wife and two of her own. She continues to frequent her mother's house and works in the gardens together with her mother and sisters. However, the manioc flour she and her children consume is made by her husband and his grown teenage son. The bride's nuclear family does not share the chores of manioc toasting either with her family of origin or with her husband's sister and her three grown daughters and their husbands who live (according to uxorilocal fashion) in the adjacent household.

While many other examples could be cited, all would lead to a similar conclusion. Despite their coexistence in domestic garden plots, sweet potatoes and bitter manioc cultivation and consumption reveal different strategies for cultivating the social ties, gardening partners, and tools needed to eat well. From one perspective, the emergence of different subsistence strategies appears as a breakdown in matri-uxorilocal household organization. There is a notable tendency for young men to refuse to live with their wife's parents, and neolocal residence of young couples is an increasingly common option (although the tendency is to situate the residence near the wife's mother's homestead). There is also a tendency to father children without marrying the mother. This reflects the increased clout of young men who are mobile and may have greater access to trade goods outside the village. Especially when young men forge close associations with chiefs, the increased access to trade goods, food, and influence gives them a way to sustain themselves independently of domestic ties. A later chapter looks at this process taken a step further as chiefs build their personal retinues. Female labor, production, and reproduction of children, on the other hand, remain locked into household forms of reciprocity from which they cannot be pried loose by means of trade good values.

BRAZIL NUTS AND THE LOGIC OF EXTRACTIVISM

The pursuit of natural commodities, even edible ones, is at odds with subsistence requirements. Prior to the Brazil nut harvest of 1986, all the men and women of Jaguar's faction harvested bitter manioc with the intent of making the farinha for the men's Brazil nut collecting expedition. All the men and women of Jaguar's faction took part and divided into gender and age cohorts to perform the required tasks. Women led the way to the large garden and pointed out where the manioc had been planted. This was necessary because the full extent of the cleared patch had not been planted nor had it been weeded for the seventeen months since planting. Even to an experienced eye, amid the low green tangle of vegetation, it was difficult to pick out the places that manioc grew. Men and women divided into separate work groups to harvest the tubers. Peeling took place on the margins of the garden, and individual men and women carried only the tubers they had peeled. In the meantime, bachelors had gathered firewood and taken off for an inland *igarapé,* or stream, where, by beating timbó poison, they were able to capture several baskets full of bony but succulent small fish to feed the entire work party. While men carefully fed tubers into the motorized grater, adult women with children were sieving, soaking, and decanting the resulting mass to extract the tapioca. Single women (female counterparts to the bachelors) went back and forth to the river, toting the large amounts of water required. The next day, adult men took turns toasting the flour. They produced approximately two hundred kilograms, which were deposited in the chief's storage room, minus the quantity consumed hot as men snatched fistfuls from sacks and griddle while work was underway. Just before departing for their expedition in search of Brazil nuts, each male "worker" reported to the chief's house for a share of flour to sustain him during his time away.

When I accompanied the Brazil nut harvest the previous year, in 1985, I was surprised at the vehemence with which the Xikrin claimed that they simply could not undertake such a task without a hefty store of farinha. At the time I thought it a ploy to encourage the FUNAI post employee to buy manioc flour in order to induce reluctant Xikrin to undertake collecting. Some manioc flour was sent from FUNAI stores, and shortly afterward I accompanied a group of seventeen men to the *vinte e seis* Brazil nut grove. There we set up a palm-thatched camp shelter, hung our hammocks, and set out daily, over the course of several weeks, in search of Brazil nuts. Foodstuffs sent by women—bananas, sweet potatoes, papayas—had to be consumed during the first couple of days. For the rest of the time, we subsisted on manioc flour and game that was often recooked so as not to spoil over the two- or three-day period in which it was consumed. By the end of the third day we all found ourselves gnawing on desiccated morsels of meat almost too dry to swallow. Despair over dinner turned to relief with the arrival of freshly discovered palm heart shoots, whose tender tips provided the spongy moist flesh we savored as a welcome counterpoint to the parched game leftovers.

During an earnest collective meeting when setting up camp, it was decided that the first order of the next day's business was to hunt. While stalking their prey, Xikrin men reasoned, they could also scout out the location and quantity of Brazil nut trees to which they could later return. After sleeping on this decision, men left early the following morning, singly heading in different directions. By about 2:00 P.M., the first men returned from the forest. To a man, each staggered in under the weight of an overflowing basket of fresh-cut Brazil nuts. Once in camp, men awaited the arrival of each of their fellows expectantly and with growing consternation as they saw their chances of eating well that night dwindling further with each basket-laden returnee.

Our unfulfilled desire for meat that evening throws the contradictory principles of extractivist and traditional forms of organization into sharp relief. It is not merely that it is hard to track animals and gather substantial quantities of Brazil nuts at the same time. Whereas sharing food brings people together, gathering Brazil nuts separates nuclear families and their members from one another. Each Xikrin collector is credited with the number of boxes of Brazil nuts he collects. While the final determination of his share of goods rests with the chief, he will make every effort to be rewarded for the zeal of his effort, shown by the number of boxes he has gathered. Xikrin have no distinct terms for numbers above four, so each man retains a single nut to represent each box he has collected as evidence of his labor.

The Brazil nut harvest, like a simulated game-theory dilemma, reveals each Xikrin to be a rational actor in pursuit of his own self-interest. Each headed for the Brazil nut groves that day because there was no point in subsidizing the collecting activities of another by foregoing his own collecting to supply another with meat. It can be argued, however, that this self-interest did not emerge spontaneously from a basic human propensity to accumulate for oneself at the expense of others. It was the product of the rise of both bitter manioc consumption and dependence on Brazil nut collecting under the sponsorship of the chief. Under other circumstances to successfully bag game could mean prestige from age mates, success in attracting lovers, or the approval of family or in-laws. Not only does the extractive activity create anxiety and doubt because of market fluctuations but it brings home the truth that each man is competing against his fellows for a limited resource.

HUNTING

The use of firearms and the development of a sedentary lifestyle on reservations have appreciably altered hunting organization. Basic hunting trends can be seen to parallel the emphasis on bitter manioc. These entail hunting game from blinds for use within single households and the formation of large hunting expeditions whose activities are made possible by imported technology under the chief's control. These changes stem both from the manner in which weaponry and ammunition is procured and the decrease of game in the vicinity of the village after some three decades in the same location.

If anything, men spent more time hunting in 1994–95 than they had in the 1980s. Every three days or so, an entire men's club would pile into one of the chief's large canoes and take off either upriver or downriver. Such trips were sponsored by the chief who supplied fuel, motor, and canoe, and male participants were followers of a specific chief. Most larger game that would be widely shared, such as tapirs, were captured in these expeditions, since larger game is now scarce in the vicinity of the village. Hunting trips could be planned to accomplish other objectives as well. The progress of mahogany loggers in a particular area of the reserve might be reconnoitered or men might gauge the potential Brazil nut harvest in a certain known grove.

As with bitter manioc, however, successful long-distance trips require chief sponsorship, and hunting parties are composed of men who follow a chief rather than hunting partners chosen from among friends or kin. Meat continues to be shared throughout the household, and household members are aware that their collective well-being depends on at least one male member continuing in the good graces of the sponsoring chief.

The other radical change in hunting becomes apparent after dark. On nights without moonlight, or when the moon rises late, many men retire to fruit tree locations or their family gardens within a couple of hours hike from the village. There they will wait in blinds or on raised platforms in hopes of killing some small prey foraging for food. This is tiresome, uncomfortable work. Clouds of mosquitoes and tiny biting *pium* insects swarm to anyone remaining motionless in the pitch dark for long periods of time. Aside from the obvious need for flashlights, an unexpected result of this new type of hunting is a need for long trousers, long-sleeved shirts, and hats and boots. Only properly garbed can one contemplate such an undertaking. The technique of hunting from blinds has always been familiar to the Xikrin but they simply did not feel compelled to do it until recently. The physical discomfort, fear of nocturnal spirits, and its unsociable nature were enough to make other sorts of hunting preferable.

When examined in relation to one another, blind and canoe hunting can be seen as symmetrical options. Consider a man concerned with provisioning his family. Chief-sponsored canoe trips are more productive than setting out from the village on foot because hunting parties head for places where game is more plentiful and allow meat to be returned to one's family on the same day. As participants in larger hunting expeditions, male labor gets locked into a particular rhythm. Gardening and other affairs such as manioc processing must be tended to on days when individuals are not hunting. If one does not participate in the collective outings or get enough meat, it is much more difficult to recruit a companion, or preferably several companions, to hunt during noncollective hunt days. Previously thought to be too unpleasant, nighttime blind hunting becomes a viable option, or at least is seen as a necessity in cases of household meat shortages, since this proves more productive than the efforts of a solitary hunter on foot during the day.

It is no small irony that in the face of a sedentary lifestyle and population growth, Xikrin can only continue to maintain the centrality of hunting as a masculine obsession through the use of a Western technology that demands the constant input of fuel, ammunition, and firearms, which the Xikrin must obtain through dealings with the wider world.

Although men continue to hunt approximately one out of every three days, experimentation with techniques such as traps and guns rigged with trip wires were actively being pursued by some individuals. The success of any of these techniques might well change the situation described.

FISHING

As with gardening and hunting, the pursuit of fish may be seen to have both a more traditional and a more "modern" aspect. Fishing in the smaller streams and pools of the inland forest continues to be surrounded by traditional songs and ceremonial activity. As we have seen, this was the only type of fishing prior to contact. In these areas, the presence of water is often seasonal and watercourses are susceptible to damming so that vegetable poisons can be used to harvest fish. Dietary prescriptions and prohibitions are prominently associated with species found in these areas. Inland fishing is usually an all-day affair that is undertaken in a group, particularly by age grades.

The Xikrin have only adopted canoes and water travel since contact and this has expanded the possibilities for fishing. In the main watercourses where canoe travel is possible, fish are larger and procured with either bow and arrow or hook and line. This fishing is also seasonal, being much more productive during dry-season months, when water flow recedes out of the forests back into the main channels. Fishing in the main watercourses may be confined to a few hours in the morning or afternoon, while the rest of the day is spent in other pursuits. The Bakajá River in the vicinity of the Xikrin village continues to yield fish, but fishing can be notably more productive as one moves away from the village in either direction. Men usually paddle in small canoes they have built themselves to locations removed from the village.

Such fishing usually involves hooks and weighted lines of different sizes, depending on the species most likely to be encountered. Tiny hooks are needed to catch bait fish, or a man might stock up on a supply of white fleshy larvae that bore into babassu palm kernels for this purpose. Different sized hooks will be used for piranha *(Pygocentrus piraya)*, fidalgo (sp.?), surubim *(Pseudoplatystoma fasciatum)*, or pirarara *(Phractocephalus hemiliopterus)* species. Even when the same sized hook is used, different techniques are employed. While one might use the same size hook to catch tucunaré *(Cichla ocellaris)* and piranha, for the former one throws the line a long ways off and rapidly retracts it along the surface, while for the latter it is often effective to beat noisily on the water surface with a stick while dropping the hook downward. If possible, a man will take several sizes of line and hooks to improve his chances.

In some areas the fishing continues to be so productive that one can repeatedly throw a line into the water and pull out fish after fish. During one three-day trip at the height of the dry season in late August 1984, four youths, a young boy, and an elderly man returned to the village with eighty-one kilograms of fish and thirteen kilograms of tracajá *(Podocnemis cayennensis)* turtle eggs. Although these 150 fish were returned to the village, perhaps half as many were consumed during the trip along with fifteen or so turtle eggs per person per day. A large pirarara weighing some thirteen kilograms had been left behind after a bit was used for bait. At least four hundred turtle eggs were collected during the course of the three days by digging up the exposed sandy margins of the Bakajá River where tracajá turtles lay their eggs.

Fish such as surubim and tucunaré, from the main channels, are highly desirable food items in Amazonia. The introduction of drying and salting preservation techniques along with motorized river transportation present the possibility of commercializing such fishing for the first time. On a few occasions, when gold prospecting operations along the reservation border were most active during the late 1980s and early 1990s, Xikrin were able to sell salted fish to the mining camp with FUNAI acting as a go-between. Such commercialization is not a dependable source of income for many reasons, but an abundant catch on occasions when salt and motorized water transportation are available and rivers navigable continues to be one of the few occasions in the 1990s when collecting can yield a satisfactory cash return.

GATHERING

Attentive readers will no doubt anticipate that insofar as the collecting of natural products is concerned, a distinction can be made in the practice of gathering marketable items, such as Brazil nuts and pelts, and gathering for subsistence purposes. Many wild fruits are collected in small quantities, including cacau *(Theobroma cacao)*, bacaba *(Oenocarpus distichus)*, ingá *(Inga* spp.), açaí *(Euturpe oleracea)*, inajá *(Maximiliana maripa)*, hog plum *(Spondias mombim)*, frutão (Sapotaceae family), piqui *(Caryocar brasiliense)*, and many others. Genipap fruit *(Genipa americana)* is in constant demand because it yields a dye used for body painting. Many plants are sought out for medicinal purposes, usually as the need arises. Wild honey is considered a delicacy worthy of considerable effort, and lately FUNAI employees have been touting it as an item of potentially great commercial value. However, the energy involved in finding accessible hives and extracting the honey makes this impracticable in most cases. Items used in ritual, such as eggshells, adhesives, inner bark, and the like, are also collected as needed.

Gathered food supplements other subsistence activities and is normally carried out as an adjunct to these activities. On the way to a garden, a man might opt for a route through a moist depression where palms yielding bacaba fruit are likely to grow. Parents might insist that instead of lolling around watching them make a canoe or clear a garden, their children should get busy and look for wild cacau or ingá. In contrast to collecting in the context of extractivist activities such as Brazil nut harvesting, this collecting adds variability and refreshment to the game and cultivated crops that make up the bulk of the diet. Formerly, according to the Xikrin, collected foods made up a much larger proportion of their diet, particularly during the early part of the rainy season.

There is no longer any area of subsistence that can be considered purely traditional; nor have Xikrin abandoned a lifestyle based on hunting, horticulture, and collecting. Subsistence, in addition to producing life's necessities, continues to be the means by which central values and roles are performed. Yet, the tasks associated with making a living also incorporate technology, organization, and the work regimes needed to articulate with people beyond the village. Forms of domestic and political authority in the village are shaped by the demands of producing within the context of ongoing community life as well as the constraints imposed by the Indian agency and the dependency of production on manufactured imports. We will see that reliance on Western implements is itself shaped by Xikrin organization and values, which determine how implements are incorporated and circulate within the community.

Although activities such as sweet potato exchange and the rituals and songs preceding fish-poisoning expeditions hearken back to traditions that preceded reliance on manufactured goods, it would be a mistake to assume that chief-sponsored activities dependent on heavy use of manufactured imports represent accommodations with dependency while other modalities of subsistence represent pure traditional forms. Rather, the emphasis on individual, nuclear-family self-sufficiency and on chief-sponsored activities has developed out of previous organizational forms with no apparent break from tradition. The justification for nuclear-family self-sufficiency is rooted in the idea that family members share a single physical substance (1). This understanding interacts with sociological realities, such as population growth, changes in extended family residence norms, greater dependence on chiefs than on kin for necessary means of production, and so on, to produce a practical orientation to the world that can always rely on "tradition" for its justification. Social forms continually develop in relation to new pressures and opportunities. The efforts to strengthen the possibilities for autonomous production of individual nuclear families that have reshaped relations within the domestic sphere are no less a product of recent history than is the role of the chief in redistributing Western manufactured goods.

6 | INCONSTANT GOODS

Nowhere would indigenous dependency seem so salient as in the administration of the Xikrin reservation itself. Brazilian indigenous peoples are subject to the rules and regulations of a bureaucracy, the National Indian Foundation, whose administrative practices seem to vary capriciously with each area under its jurisdiction. As a federal agency, FUNAI's clout increases or diminishes depending on the responsiveness of the government to human rights, issues of national sovereignty, military concerns over security, or large landowning and mining interests. Within this complex political context, the FUNAI is legally responsible for demarcating and defending reservation borders and maintaining the viability of native societies in its charge. Given the pressures, which today include vigorous lobbying from indigenous groups as well, the job of the FUNAI president is certainly one of the least secure posts in any administration.

Lack of personnel training and budgetary constraints often make it impossible for the FUNAI to make a thoughtful assessment of community needs and to engage in long-term planning. If residents of one reservation cause a stir in their bid for a schoolteacher, more than likely an off-the-cuff decision will be made to divert funds or personnel from a less vocal constituency. I was flabbergasted to find, for example, that despite a predictable occurrence of one or two medical emergencies each year requiring air evacuation to Altamira, such contingencies were never figured into the budget. Money had to be diverted from other sources as administrators scrambled to locate funds in time to save the patient's life.

Well aware of the FUNAI proclivity to direct grease toward squeaky wheels, the Xikrin watch anxiously for signs of unequal treatment meted out to different indigenous groups under the regional FUNAI administration in Altamira. They know that what one group receives is more than likely taken from resources originally earmarked for another. Unfortunately, they find ample reason to feel short-changed, since the posts of other Kayapó villages and neighboring reservations seem to be better staffed and to receive more frequent communication and visits from administrators.

Relations between the Xikrin and the FUNAI can be seen as a decades-long embrace in which cooperation alternates with confrontation. Some Xikrin have close personal relations with individual employees of the agency, extending back to the very moment of contact. At different times in Xikrin history, FUNAI has appeared as a rescuer, an executioner, a generous benefactor, a stingy overseer, a channel to the outside world, and the main roadblock to engaging with the wider world on terms of their own choosing. It would be hard to overstate the influence, for better or worse, that employees of the FUNAI have exercised over the Xikrin view of Brazilian society. But we must not overstate this influence either, for the social relations and movements of people and products associated with extractivism stamp their character both on the reservation and FUNAI alike. The covenant, whereby FUNAI assures health, education, and subsistence within demarcated reservation boundaries, may go unmet and Xikrin left to their own devices within the extractivst frontier.

Medical attention is the last unsullied area of the initial contact covenant, and FUNAI administrators use this as a club when faced with Xikrin criticism of agency shortcomings. Indeed, queuing up for treatment and, especially, medica-tion—aspirin and Bengay ointment are ubiquitous—each morning and evening at the dispensary is as much a routine as any other aspect of village life. The dis-pensary freely supplies dozens of different medications, from vitamins to anti-malarials. Xikrin regard such attention as essential, and the FUNAI's experience in dealing with all segments of the community, including men, women, and chil-dren, is vastly superior to the alternatives offered by mining and logging firms.

During my field stay in 1994, a dispute over logging on the reservation prompted FUNAI employees to withdraw from the reservation, and loggers, sensing an opportunity, quickly sent a nurse from Tucumã to take over the FUNAI dispensary. As a direct result of her ministrations, after a short week, a noticeable number of Xikrin began softly lobbying chiefs for the return of the Indian agency. After a three-day visit by a logger-sponsored dentist, the lobbying effort gained greatly in strength and volume, and a FUNAI health attendant was summoned within a month.

In this chapter we examine the role played by FUNAI in furnishing the trade goods discussed in the previous chapter. In the process we glimpse some of the complexity that Xikrin must face in dealing with a vacillating government bureaucracy and competing extractivist firms as well as with other outsiders. The maintenance and supply of the Indian post facility is essential to FUNAI's ability to fulfill its administrative mission. In order to assure the basic functionality of a productive infrastructure—health, communication, and transport—both the Xikrin and the FUNAI find it necessary to collaborate with outsiders. This connection with the outside is accomplished by means of Xikrin organization and institutions and creates its own stress and growing inequities. Public statements of any of the parties involved—chiefs, commoners, FUNAI employees and administrators, miners, loggers—tell only part of the story. However, an inventory of goods of Western manufacture documents a process about which even the participants are only partially aware. The inventory shows that dependency on the FUNAI is not what it seems at first glance. Extractivist cycles and Xikrin institutions and values along with the growing power of chiefs play a fundamental part in determining subsistence effort. After first describing the Indian post we turn our attention to how the Xikrin have come in possession of trade goods and how these circulate into and through the village.

THE INDIAN POST

Referred to as the Indian Post, "P. I. Bakajá" lies directly adjacent to the Xikrin village, between its houses and the Bakajá River. FUNAI buildings contain space for a dispensary, and living quarters for a medical attendant, a post director, and a teacher, although all of these positions are rarely staffed. The shortwave radio occupies another building, which is also used to store a few sparse items, such as extra roofing panels. Built with funds from the Companhia Vale do Rio Doce, a new dispensary was in the process of completion in the summer of 1995. Overgrown with weeds, an abandoned cement shower house sits slightly apart from the rest of the settlement. The unused facility was funded by a renowned natural cosmetics retailer, the Body Shop, and is a perfect illustration of how aid directed toward indigenous communities may be ineffectual without meaningful consultation.[1] The resources invested in a project of no interest to the Xikrin could surely have been better directed to pressing community needs.

A cement-floored structure serves as a manioc processing center. Housed within are fireplaces for manioc toasting, a motorized grinder, and areas for sieving and decanting manioc pulp. Since the FUNAI-built schoolhouse was pronounced structurally unsound a couple of years ago, the Xikrin got to work building a spacious thatched-roof building for use as a school. With this effort they hoped to attract a FUNAI-funded schoolteacher. So far their efforts have not borne fruit and, as of my 1995 visit, it had been several years since schooling had been available in the village. Finally, there is a well, a structure housing a large motor, and a tightly padlocked storage shed holding precious reserves of gasoline and oil.

The large motor serves diverse purposes. It generates electricity to recharge the automobile batteries used to operate the shortwave radio and it generates the electricity used for grinding manioc tubers and electric lights. Because of the limited fuel supply, operation was restricted to a few hours each day, usually during early evening when the Indian agency personnel would make use of the electric lighting fixtures that had been wired to their residence at the post. More recently the four Xikrin residences closest to the generator receive electrical power at night in the form of a single naked low-watt lightbulb. The nonoperational floodlight in the central plaza, seen in Figure 3, reveals the ambition to illuminate nighttime performances. However, a much larger motor would be needed to supply light to all houses, let alone stadium-style lighting. Although the current setup, in which a single low-watt bulb is strung from a house ceiling, allows for little visibility, Xikrin consider it a big advance over the oil lamps and fires that are in use in most of their residences.

I was surprised that the Xikrin claimed it was they, rather than the FUNAI, who purchased the motor from funds supplied by gold and timber interests. Yet, when asked, the director of the FUNAI post admitted as much. Although he opposes Xikrin dealings with loggers and miners, the very infrastructure on which he depends in the discharge of his work obligation for the FUNAI, such as regular administrative reports via shortwave transmission, has been furnished "extralegally" by the extractivists in return for access to reserve resources. Although the origin of the first generating motor, purchased in 1983, is murky, when it fell into disrepair its successor was purchased in 1987 with money from mining interests. When this second motor was taken to Altamira for repairs and never returned, the current motor was purchased with money supplied by mahogany-logger operatives. When this motor broke in July 1995, the Xikrin sent word to the logging camp, and loggers sent a mechanic out to the Bakajá village within a few days to restore it to working order. Beyond generating the electricity needed for radio transmission and nighttime lighting, the motor is also used to pump water to the houses of FUNAI employees. While the existence of a generator/motor is significant for understanding Xikrin subsistence, of equal importance is the fact that the Xikrin consider, not without reason, that they have "donated" the motor to the FUNAI so that the Indian Agency can properly coordinate its assistance to the village.

Pollutants have been building since the late 1970s, when gold placer deposits were found on the headwaters of the Bakajá and Aguas Claras Rivers. Even during my first field trip in 1984, the Xikrin reported that the water was sometimes discolored, fish yields were declining, and even that some malformed fish had been spotted. The unregulated release of toxins, particularly mercury, into the waterways by wildcat mining operations has had tragic results in the Amazon (Cleary 1990), including other Kayapó villages (Ferrari et al. 1993; Gonçalves, Aguinaldo et al. 1992). Although the mining sites that are responsible for polluting the Bakajá are outside reservation borders, drainage systems do not respect such arbitrary human creations. Use of the single well already in existence suggests that the construction of wells and the further use of pumps and gasoline will increase worktime and the need for factory-made inputs.

SURVEY RESULTS: PROVISIONING THE VILLAGE

By the time of my fieldwork in the mid-1990s, nearly a decade had passed during which the FUNAI had failed to provide subsistence supplies and had begun a policy of de facto reliance on extractive firms to pay for the costs of running the reservation. The simplest explanation for Xikrin acceptance of logging and mining, then, was that the FUNAI, having been for some years the principal source of needed manufactured goods, no longer served that role. The offers of goods in return for natural resources made by extractivist industries were accepted because the Xikrin felt they had no other realistic option. Despite their knowledge that extractivists would cheat and would steal from them, the Xikrin were in no position to resist the offered inducements.

Xikrin chiefs were interested in knowing what aggregate demand for trade goods existed in order to more effectively negotiate with logging and mining firms. As I too was interested in this, I proposed a village-wide survey in order to more fully understand the role of the FUNAI and the effect of the extractivist cycles on village life. A survey of manufactured goods would prove to be a way to document how extractivist fluctuations reverberated within the village political economy and would provide a deeper understanding of the ways in which Xikrin interacted with the outside world.

I developed the survey methodology and questionnaire in consultation with Xikrin chiefs and other adult men. While the general idea was approved by this small group, it was up to me to get support for a survey of each household interior. I was helped by the usual biting humor of Cleared Path at this point. I had somewhat awkwardly explained the idea of a survey as "looking at all the stuff" *(mỳja kuni omũ)*. Cleared Path observed tartly that, given their current poverty, I was really going to be seeing all the stuff they did not have *(mỳja kêt omũ)*! In the end, "looking for what is lacking" caught on as a general term for the survey and actually made it clearer that I was doing the survey to assess community needs rather than for any sinister objective. In the end, I visited twenty-four households, which included the entire village population with the exception of a single four-person family attached to a larger household.

I decided on the household as a survey unit because, within the household, subsistence items (those that most interested me) were shared freely. Thus my definition of household does not conform to the number of actual dwellings, since sharing could occur between dwellings and, in three cases of large houses, did not extend to all members under the same roof. If one man in the household had a firearm, for example, he would lend it to a coresident male. In some households each item was clearly identified with an individual owner, while in other households important goods, such as guns, were referred to by a restricted collective pronoun with the meaning "our (small group)." This was the case, for example, when Cleared Path used the joint possessive *(baranhõ)* to refer to "our guns," belonging to him and his father-in-law. In other houses, sons-in-law would erect internal partitions to separate their family space and possessions from that of others.

As will be made clear, the survey understates the degree of material inequality because I was not fully able to survey the dominant chief's possessions. To do so would have required an uncomfortably long time canvassing all his belongings and prying into suitcases and storage rooms. Clearly, the matter of inequality was sensitive enough that I did not feel in a position to insist on a complete accounting in this case. For other houses, I did not pry into closed containers, but people were often forthcoming and dragged them out of their own accord. In the end I surveyed a total of 1,624 items along with the circumstances in which they were acquired. The resulting picture tells us much about Xikrin's vulnerability to loggers and miners and the risk to the reservation's natural-resource base.

The survey shows the limited number of sources for manufactured items: other Kayapó villages, covillagers, the FUNAI, anthropologists, the Companhia Vale do Rio Doce, and, most prominently, assorted chiefs, loggers, and miners. Even many of the items originating from a chief could be further identified as material turned over from a particular logging or mining outfit and subsequently redistributed by a chief. Clearly the Xikrin must look beyond the FUNAI for the vast majority of their manufactured goods. The census reveals that extractivism accounts for an astonishing 75 percent of goods found in houses, while FUNAI contributions amount to a mere 13 percent. If all mining and logging stopped today, the Xikrin would be hard-pressed to replace these sources.

While the FUNAI presents an imposing facade to anthropologists and closely regulates their activities, it is a somewhat empty shell for those in its charge.

Table 1

Source of 1624 Manufactured Goods in Xikrin Households

Source of Manufactures	Percent in houses
FUNAI	13
Chiefs	20
Loggers	24
Miners	18
Purchases	11
Other Kayapó villages	6
Villagers outside household	3
Miscellaneous non-Kayapó	2
Anthropologist	2
Companhia do Vale Rio Doce	1

Nonetheless, because of the various administrative practices mentioned, caution must be used in extending the findings on the Bakajá reservation to other reservation areas. Forty percent of the goods received from the FUNAI was compensation for collecting natural products, most commonly Brazil nuts, but also honey and salted fish. In such cases, the FUNAI helped transport the product into town and broker the sale to extractivist middlemen. In this manner a Xikrin man might receive items of modest value—a hammock, a foam rubber mattress, or a flashlight. On occasion, after extraordinary effort, a more expensive item, such as a tape recorder or radio, might be procured. During the 1960s and 1970s, when Brazil nuts were more valuable, eleven of the current guns in use were received as payment.

By convention, a portion of "income" resulting from the Brazil nut harvest is turned over to the chief who redistributes this in a manner serving his own political interests. Thus FUNAI post administrators are involved in dividing up the goods between chiefs and commoners, usually to the chagrin of both sides, each angling for a greater share. While the chief receives his "share" without having to work, the FUNAI post director tries to ensure that each man receives an amount roughly proportionate to the number of boxes of Brazil nuts he collected.

Many tools, pots, and even badly damaged mosquito nets were originally given twenty or even thirty years ago by the Indian agency when Xikrin were regularly courted with presents in return for their submission to agency authority. Thus 35 percent of FUNAI-donated items were considered to have been given for the asking, when the agency was still "generous." These are quite old, a decade or more, being precisely dated by the name of the Indian post director at the time they were received. Some machete blades now approach the size of penknives, and mosquito nets and suitcases continue to be used although they are in tatters.

The remaining 25 percent of goods coming from the FUNAI were not received in the village at all, but during the course of medical visits to Belém and Altamira. Family members accompanied patients whenever possible, and whatever goods they received in town would generally be put to use right away, since the accommodations at the FUNAI lodgings consisted of little more than an empty room in which to sling a hammock.

If the Xikrin had relied solely on what they received from the FUNAI, they would have been unable to maintain their level of subsistence. In effect, they were left with no choice but to seek other sources of Western manufactured goods. In the remaining chapters, readers will learn more about the means through which extractivists and Xikrin cross tracks and negotiate or battle over access to resources. In order to understand these interactions, we must focus on Xikrin ideas and institutions since it is within this context that indigenous people gain access to the goods they require.

The economy of rural Pará presents few opportunities for Xikrin to engage in wage labor; they are reluctant to engage in such labor in any case, preferring to deal with known individuals in transactions that can be interpreted as straightforward exchanges of favors. Proud and secure in their social standing, they refuse the fast-paced labor and the humiliations to which impoverished peons are routinely subjected in rural areas. In one case, the large cattle farm in the vicinity of the Trincheira village sought to hire Xikrin to clear pasture. After a single day's effort, Xikrin found the work too tiring and hot. Each man received a single machete in payment and retired from the field. By and large, in the context of their own collective organizations, Xikrin do not judge farm labor for outsiders as an acceptable alternative to extractive pursuits.

Opportunities for individual entrepreneurship are rare, although not totally lacking. Better deals are usually achieved through collective efforts, as we will see in the next two chapters. One man sold salted fish to the local *regatão,* or itinerant merchant plying his trade by boat along the margins of the Xingu River. In selling independently, rather than through a deal brokered by the FUNAI, the man sought to gauge whether a better return could be obtained in this manner. He learned that it was actually much easier, and as lucrative, to continue dealing with the FUNAI. In the early 1980s several Xikrin experimented with rubber tapping in order to acquire goods, but they felt poorly compensated.

Xikrin do not routinely have access to cash. Even chiefs and their deputies do not usually engage in cash purchases. Invariably goods are advanced by local merchants after a check for creditworthiness from extractivist patrons. Nevertheless, Xikrin do demand some cash for personal use from extractivists and the FUNAI, or they may occasionally sell an item on the street during the course of visits to neighboring cities.

Although, as previously noted, full data about the origins of goods were not available from the house of the principal chief, of purchases noted in other houses, 50 percent were by underchiefs or by the two men who accompanied the chiefs to town as interpreters. Of the remainder, purchases by commoners who received money from loggers accounted for 17 percent and an additional 12 percent by those who received money from the sale of Brazil nuts, salted fish, or, in one case, honey, mediated through the auspices of the FUNAI. In the remaining cases, without knowing the source of the money used for purchases, goods were acquired during visits to Tucumã and Altamira, and in a select handful of cases, in either Marabá or Belém.

When individuals are sent (usually in groups of three or four) to work at the local prospecting area along the Manezão creek, they are sanctioned by the chief, and, in addition to the work they perform, they must reconnoiter the comings and goings on behalf of the Xikrin community. Their earnings are turned over to the chief by the prospector boss and they are given a nominal sum with which to acquire a few items on their own. Female Land Turtle, for example, worked for one month at the mining camp under the direction of Nonato. In return he received cloth for a woman's dress, shorts, and a hammock. As we shall see, familiarity with the mining operation was later key to the success of a raid against it. Because of their knowledge of the locale and its population, men who worked at the camp were successful in obtaining firearms and other items of value on returning to the familiar site of the raid. Female Land Turtle, for example, acquired a .38 carbine in this manner.

Female Land Tortoise's story as a delegated prospector's helper who worked for a limited period under the aegis of the chief can be contrasted with the story of a young man who struck out on his own and attempted to find work as an individual in various mining and logging camps. Surubim's story not only adds a human dimension to the itemizing of goods in the survey, but illustrates the kind of reminiscing that was often associated with the process of enumerating household items. His experience shows that the royal road to material advantage does not lie in hard individual work but in ties of kinship and favor by the chief. Poor in relations and on the outs with the chief, Surubim occupies a residence, which he shares with his wife and their five children, that is almost bare of possessions despite his many years of sporadic short-term labor outside the village. He lists the names of eight different bosses for whom he claims he had unearthed much gold and scouted many mahogany trees. He was first driven away from the village by the overwhelming desolation that assailed him in the aftermath of his first wife's death from malaria. After working for several prospecting teams, he returned to the village and remarried. As an orphan with no parents of his own to whom he could turn for help, he was also unable to rely much on his father-in-law for support because the older man was himself relatively impoverished (and reputedly slow-witted as well). His sister and brother-in-law are industrious, and he shares food and some work with both them and his in-laws. He longs for the past, when his father was alive. His father was feared for his unbridled fierceness, and Surubim claims that since his death whites have had much less fear of reprisals for encroaching on Xikrin lands. His father took him into the depths of the forest to teach him about the healing properties of plants and the habits of animals. Before setting off, he would sharply box Surubim's ears to "open them up," thus ensuring that his mind would be receptive to the knowledge he received.

A good hunter and fisherman himself, Surubim sorely feels the lack of his own firearm and appears to have few prospects of acquiring one. At one time, he did receive a gun from a mining boss, Oscar, who acted as his patron in the dog-eat-dog world of the mining camp. But Oscar himself fell victim to violence, and after he was killed in a gunfight, Surubim hurriedly escaped, leaving behind all his possessions, including the gun. He returned to the Bakajá village empty-handed, but later left again. Without the sponsorship of their chiefs or mining overbosses, Indians are easily taken advantage of. What few goods, usually clothes, Surubim acquired during his stays soon wore out. Recently, he managed to steal a pistol from the nearby logging camp. In response, the logging boss contacted the Xikrin chief, who put out the word that the pistol had best be returned. In pressuring him to return the pistol, Jaguar promised Surubim a new gun of his own, but at the time of my survey, the gun had not materialized and Surubim had little hope that he would ever see it.

When I interviewed Surubim, he had resolved to no longer work alongside other followers of Jaguar in chief-sponsored projects. He had little choice but to throw his lot in with other chiefs, however. I had observed over the years that he had been a fairly diligent participant in many collective work parties. But his claim that he had little to show for this effort was borne out by the survey. Of the twenty-four items counted in his house, he had received only a suitcase and a knapsack from the principal chief, Jaguar. His new chief, Raimundo, had already given him another knapsack and a shirt in return for having planted bananas and manioc. By Xikrin standards, Surubim and his family were not well off. He was

Figure 7. A Xikrin man with hoe, machete, rifle, and tobacco prepares to work his garden plot in 1994. (Photo by author)

poorly positioned within village circuits of kinship-based reciprocity and he was alienated from the chief. Fortunately, the collective action of the men's organization allowed him to bypass these impediments and obtain needed goods directly from outside sources. Ten of the twenty-four items in his house, or slightly more than 40 percent of the Western goods that he owned, had been stolen in raids on the mining camp and two separate logging camps. In addition, he had held onto two pairs of sneakers and some clothing from his time in the mining camp, and he had received a hammock and mosquito net from the FUNAI in return for collecting Brazil nuts.

Even with the relatively large quantity of goods possessed by his brother-in-law, Surubim faces the risk of not having ammunition or fishing line on any given day.

The raid on the mining camp, sanctioned and organized by Jaguar, was an extremely important event. Unwilling to give him any of his own goods, Jaguar, as a practical leader, realized that to let men such as Surubim become desperately dissatisfied with the current village alignments could jeopardize his own hold on the chieftaincy. By sanctioning and leading the raid on the mining camp and thereby mobilizing village men for collective action, he reinforced his own effectiveness as an intermediary to extractivist firms and the FUNAI. Riding a wave of popularity and a reputation for fierceness, Jaguar was able to maintain his policy of targeting his redistribution of goods to selected followers without having to worry about the malcontents who did not enjoy his favor. He also provided less well-off families with an opportunity to provision themselves with stolen booty, thus dampening some of the demand expressed for redistributed goods. While this may have taken some of the edge off existing dissatisfaction, many Xikrin were still privately disgruntled over the growing material inequality between chiefs and commoners.

OTHER SOURCES OF GOODS

Xikrin receive almost twice as many manufactured goods from relatives in other villages as from extrahousehold kin within the same village. Every household at Bakajá has kin living in another Kayapó village such as Cateté, Gorotire, Kikretũm, or Kôkrajmoro. Goods from kin in these villages range from ceremonial beads to items designed to stand out as distinctive. The only Bakajá woman with a tape recorder received this from a male relative in the Kayapó village of Gorotire. A glass bowl is another gift of extravillage kin, notable, if a bit impractical, in a community where cooking conditions demand metal utensils. In general such gifts assert the relative opulence of other Kayapó villages in comparison with Bakajá and also the generosity shown by social mentors and parents toward their junior, subordinate relatives. Overall, Bakajá Xikrin claim that other villages are much wealthier, and extravillage giving seems to confirm that opinion. Such gifts have the effect of boosting the reputation of other villages and consequently of their leaders, who are seen as responsible for the relative wealth of their villages. Such giving can therefore be somewhat threatening to leaders of Bakajá, since it leaves people wondering why such items are not forthcoming within their own village.

Such transactions may help sway collective opinion toward logging, since gifts originate, along with the mahogany boom, in the Kayapó heartland in the deep south of the state of Pará. Southerly Kayapó were instrumental in encouraging their Xikrin brethren to accept logging, and logging companies have acquired expertise in these areas that helps them in approaching the Xikrin. Bakajá leaders fear the emigration of the community's young men to better-off Kayapó villages and feel compelled to play the same games with extractivists who have enabled other villages to attract desired goods.

Bakajá residents sometimes collectively play the role of satellites to the metropole of richer villages. In 1985 I hitched a ride from Bakajá to Tucumã via the Cateté Xikrin village, during which I was forced to endure an hour kneeling amidst a mound of live, squirming tortoises trussed and ready for consumption at a Cateté ceremonial! The Bakajá residents had graciously responded to appeals from their relatives to help in feast preparations threatened by a dearth of game on the Cateté reservation. In return, these sent their poorer relatives manufactured items such as cigarettes. Natural productions from the periphery were thereby exchanged for the manufactured goods of the more "advanced" indigenous village. On another occasion in 1984, Bakajá women were mobilized to press babassú palm oil to be sent to the Kayapó village of Kôkrajmoro in return for manufactured goods.

THE VALE DO RIO DOCE COMPANY

The other significant source of outside supplies was the partially government-owned Vale do Rio Doce Company (CVRD). Although the Bakajá Xikrin are not as close as the Cateté Xikrin to the Serra dos Carajás, where the recently privatized CVRD built the world's largest iron ore and bauxite mine, they were marginally included along with the Cateté village in a program of assistance to native communities affected by the expansion of mining and the transportation of mineral wealth. As the aid from CVRD is channeled through the FUNAI superintendency located in Altamira, much of it is earmarked for larger expenditures that ostensibly contribute to the well-being of the village as a whole. As previously mentioned, the dispensary constructed at the Bakajá village in the summer of 1995 was funded by the CVRD, as were the annual fuel supplies. In the past the CVRD has also helped provision Brazil nut expeditions. Since the FUNAI had stopped supplying unremunerated goods to the village for about a decade, Xikrin suspect that the CVRD is the source of any supplies arriving for general distribution. During my last field stay, I did observe a box of metal tool heads—rakes and scythes—arrive on the aircraft with the visiting FUNAI administrator, who made a big show of handing them out to individual adult men since there were not enough for everybody. *"Vale?"* the men intoned, pointing to the tools. "Yeah," the administrator replied none too exuberantly. Drawing me aside, an underchief commented, "See, they [the FUNAI] are afraid of the Indians [Xikrin]; they would never show up without something to appease them." The implication is that the FUNAI simply uses CVRD-supplied goods to keep face in their dealings with the community.

ANTHROPOLOGISTS

Xikrin cited myself and a University of São Paulo student, Clarice Cohn, as donors of twenty-four household items, fifteen of which were beads. In most cases these beads had been given to the chief, Jaguar, who handed them over to other commoners. During the course of my work, I had given away many more items, but most of these were either consumed or not the sort of things one would find hanging on a wall or lying on the floor of a Xikrin hut. Ammunition, fishing line, and lead weights do not last forever. Other donated materials, such as mosquito nets or machetes, helped to confirm the reliability of the survey, in that I was able to recall giving an item to a certain person and then was able to locate it again in his or her house (rather than someone else's house).

ACCESS TO TOOLS AND TRADE GOODS

The growing gap between chiefs and commoners has come to be reflected in differences between commoner households regarding access to manufactured goods. The survey revealed that while goods are freely shared within households, they are rarely exchanged (3 percent of all manufactured items) or loaned between households. In this sense manufactured items are treated quite differently from labor, food, and specialized instruction in traditional knowledge, which is often exchanged between households.

Only four firearms were passed from father to son, for example, and this was done before the son left his house to get married (with a single exception). Within a household, acquiring a firearm meant rights of use, but not of exclusive use, should others in the household need to hunt.

Over 25 percent of the items given between houses were from a single individual, who is both a newcomer in the community and an interpreter for the chief. Since he resides in his own house with his wife and children, any goods given from his fairly ample stocks necessarily consist of interhousehold giving. In one case, this man offered clothing to another for helping him with his garden. If this sort of transaction becomes common it would represent a new trend since—although food, including manufactured food, is offered to those helping to clear gardens—clothing, money, or other manufactured items have not been exchanged in this manner.

Clearly the fact that Xikrin continue to identify themselves in terms of their kinship ties extending through at least several village households does not mean that such ties are the basis for widespread exchange of imported goods. The restriction of tools of production to a single household underlines the fact that in many respects Xikrin see households as units of production rather than as building blocks for larger productive enterprises formed by extended kinship or communal networks.

This pattern of confinement, by which manufactured goods are restricted to individual households, alerts us to the fact that the Xikrin's insecurity regarding the availability of manufactured goods is not solely the result of externally imposed domination. In contrast to the Xikrin, among many indigenous peoples, durable factory-made goods are not treated as a separate class of goods but are treated similarly to goods of indigenous manufacture. This situation is well illustrated by Ramos (1996, 138) in describing the Sanumá Yanomami in the Brazilian state of Roraima:

When the Sanumá go to town to sell their gold dust, they follow the rules of the market laid down by whites. . . . They receive cash for their gold and spend it on objects desired by the community: salt, clothing, shotguns, at times, even manioc flour. Once they arrive in the Indian village, however, these objects enter immediately into the ongoing chain of exchanges, not in a mercantile mode, but in the spirit of the gift. (My translation)

The Sanumá example helps us to see that the social organization of different indigenous peoples is a crucial variable in setting the parameters within which different peoples maintain the continuity of their traditions within a larger nation-state. Indigenous social organization, which is never wholly imposed through external domination, is an active element in constituting the stresses that domination imposes on daily life. Xikrin responses to new conditions under which subsistence is produced have, for better or worse, created a situation whereby kinship relations are ineffective in ameliorating inequalities between households resulting from redistributive choices made by chiefs. The sight of a relative with fewer machetes or pots does not seem to move a Xikrin to offer these as presents if he or she happens to possess more than can immediately be used. The political maneuvers that mark Xikrin life are equally shaped by the 85 percent of manufactured goods they receive directly or indirectly from extractivist firms and the fact that these goods rarely circulate beyond households.

INEQUALITY BETWEEN CHIEFS
AND COMMONERS

The survey turned up ample evidence of the accumulation of goods by chiefs. As important, the survey reveals distance in the potential for control and accumulation between the principal chief and underchiefs. I will refer to Jaguar as the principal chief and other leaders of somewhat lesser stature as underchiefs.[2] All Xikrin recognize that the chief Jaguar is without peer, but they are equally adamant that he cannot exercise unlimited influence and must share the spotlight with other village chiefs. In some ways the survey results break down in the case of the house of the principal chief. There were simply too many goods to count comfortably. The amount of time spent in the house would have been inconveniently long and the public scrutiny of the chief's goods too great. It was unthinkable that I should publicly go through all of the goods in Jaguar's house while he kept them carefully concealed from the rest of the villagers, with the exception of his wife. Instead of getting the full accounting of the origin of goods, with the chief's permission I was given a tour by his son-in-law on an occasion when the village was almost empty. This enabled me to get an overview of his possessions, but certainly nothing like the detailed account offered in other houses. In addition the chief's house had a great many more locked spaces such as suitcases, bags, and a small storage area that I could not investigate. There was also a qualitative difference in the number and types of goods stockpiled. Large areas within and outside the house were devoted to storing the accumulated goods and provisions. Not only was it obvious that the chief and his family were incapable of consuming all of the stored goods themselves, but it was also clear that there were prominent stores of foodstuffs that were simply nonexistent in other houses.

Aside from accumulated apparatuses for production, such as motors, the principal chief's house was clearly marked by the existence of a cement floor in the sleeping area. All the other houses, with the exception of one of the chief's lieutenants and translators who knew how to pour concrete, had floors of beaten earth. Jaguar slept on a foam rubber mattress over a plank base, which also set him apart from all but one other household. Another significant item that distinguishes both the principal chief and the underchiefs from commoners is their ownership of at least one bank account and the identification papers necessary to open such an account.[3] The FUNAI assisted chiefs in applying to the proper government agencies for papers, and both the FUNAI and extractive firms helped open the accounts. Several of the chiefs had separate accounts in different towns, although none were sufficiently numerate to specify the amount of their savings. When Jaguar showed me the minuscule amounts of cash deposited, I was

Table 2
Comparison of Possessions of Chiefs, Underchiefs, and Commoners

Principal chief (1)	Sub-chiefs (5) & Interpreters (2)	Commoners (269)
stereo	stereo (3)	stereo (1)
tape recorder	tape recorder (4)	tape recorder (8)
cement floor	cement floor (1)	
identification papers	identification papers	
bank accounts	bank accounts	1 had small account
Prosdocimo multishop		
H40 freezer		
medical supplies		
2 large canoe motors	3 canoe motors	2 canoe motors (1 broken)
9 sacks of rice, beans,	2 underchiefs and 1 interpreter	
Brazil nuts, manioc flour,	had small stores (less than	
and cases of other food	a case) of cooking oil,	
items such as spaghetti	crackers, and salt	
and cooking oil		
5 suitcases + 1 bag of clothes	3 suitcases (2)	4 suitcases (1)
	2 suitcases (3)	2 suitcases (8)
	1 suitcase (1)	1 suitcase (9)
VCR		
gas stove		
2 "americano" hunting dogs		
4 new firearms		
laborer (1 or 2)		
personal retainers (3)		
does not work on collective	does "collective" work	does "collective" work
projects		

shocked since this represented the cash received in return for the harvest of mahogany on the reservation. Although the price per cubic meter of mahogany amounts to hundreds of dollars, six different deposit slips for sums paid over the course of three years (1992, 1993, and 1994) totaled only $6,556.00.[4] The final deposit on 27 June 1994 was for a paltry $7.85. In the next chapter, the reader will get an idea of how far cash goes in the inflated Amazonian economy. It is sufficient to note here that this quantity of cash represents more a symbolic value than any recognized purchasing power, since there is no clear understanding of currency. Extractivist firms made small cash payments because these were demanded by the chief, but commodities redistributed in the village comprised the overwhelming portion of their "payments" to the chiefs. Several hours after discussing bank deposits with Jaguar, another chief approached me with his deposit slip for a bank at Serra Norte, in the vicinity of the Carajás Project of the CVRD. The total amounted to less than $40.

Finally, the chief Jaguar had a large stock of medicines kept under lock and key. He was not able to use and administer these himself, and they may have been kept primarily for reasons of prestige. However, if the dispensary ran out of specific medicines, Jaguar would allow the medical attendant to draw from his personal stock, especially to administer to the health needs of Jaguar's own family. The store of medicines may have represented a real difference in life expectancy between a chief's family and that of a commoner's.

Chiefs had more things, but they shared the same general living conditions as commoners. Any goods of an exceptional character, such as the large propane-cooled freezer, were supposedly held for the benefit of the community as a whole. In fact, items such as the freezer and the VCR (neither of which was operational), both supplied by logging companies, were the closest things to luxury items since they marked the principal chief as having access to possessions typical of a middle-class Brazilian family. The results of the survey of the chief's house, in any case, show types of items comparable to those found in other houses. In all cases the extractivist industries and the FUNAI were the original sources of most important goods. I regard my inability to question the principal chief in depth regarding the quantity and origin of his goods as similar to the difficulties of many ethnographers in documenting the extent of privilege and power in other societies. Nonetheless, I was able to interview extensively all of the under-chiefs regarding their possessions, and I had extensive contact with the principal chief, as well, regarding his redistribution of goods and the amount of money that he received from extractive firms.

Despite their differences in possessions, the lifestyle of chiefs and commoners was similar. All gardened and gathered wild foods; all men hunted and all women prepared food. If chiefs were to enjoy possessions and experiences free of the demands of kin for a share, this could only be accomplished during sojourns away from the village where their comportment could not be generally observed by commoners.

CONCLUSIONS

Unexpected results of the survey reveal basic facts that have to be taken into account in any analysis of the involvement of the Xikrin with predatory extractivist firms. The first fact is the overwhelming dependence of the Xikrin on these firms for basic subsistence goods—the basic tools needed to make a living based on the traditional activities of hunting, cultivating, fishing, and gathering. Despite appearances to the contrary, the FUNAI has contributed an increasingly smaller proportion to the material well-being of the Xikrin in the last ten years, and frequent agency omissions have left a vacuum in the oversight of reservation administration that extractive firms and the Xikrin themselves have sought to fill to some extent.

The second major surprise is the degree to which manufactured items do not follow the same circuits as other sorts of exchanges of goods and services between houses. Instead, we find that each commoner household remains self-contained with respect to outside trade goods once these have arrived in the village. This is in contrast to what we would expect based on the Xikrin's claim to live in a village of kinsfolk and their frequent collective mobilizations for work, ritual, or socializing in the village plaza. Some shortages of vital goods, such as shotguns, are not the result of an absolute lack but of an unequal distribution of trade goods among different households. We cannot therefore deduce the aggregate trade-good requirements for a community by looking at population size alone, even if we parcel population according to gender and age. The functioning of the Xikrin political economy determines in the final analysis how imported goods will be distributed within the population. In the preceding chapter we have seen how the political economy shapes the tempo and organization of work within the community. In the following chapter we learn more about the logic and organization that governs the circulation of imported food and trade goods through the social forms Xikrin have created.

7 | INFLATION, FOOD, AND THE NEW ECONOMY

In the last chapter we saw that chiefs control significantly more goods than commoners and that the unequal distribution of goods imposes real constraints on how most Xikrin expend their labor. Chiefs are the conduit for the vast majority of needed goods into the village and Xikrin men must establish a good relationship with at least one chief with access to surplus goods in order to assure the viability of their own households. This particular pattern of redistribution is primarily related to two factors: the distinction Xikrin make between the public/collective and the domestic/kinship domain, and the existing repertoire of social relations on the frontier, which favors collective means to acquire needed goods and offers few opportunities for individual strategies. In addition, there is a large quantity of imported goods that we have not yet discussed, namely food and drink. An understanding of the place of food in the circulation and exchange of goods will help us better understand how the material wealth controlled by chiefs will likely lead to the inception of social forms that will tend to widen rather than narrow the power gap between chiefs and commoners and make reservation resources more vulnerable to predation by extractivist firms.

In Chapter 5 we discussed the way in which households organized themselves to produce major garden staples. Once we realize that a man can only count on consuming the cultivars from his own domestic plots, the decision to work alongside other men in clearing a collective garden sponsored by a chief can be understood as based less on a desire to eat manioc flour the following year than on a desire to acquire shotgun shells from the chief's storehouse in the coming weeks. Although he is producing food that may be appropriated by the chief, the appropriation is grudgingly accepted because a man does nondomestic garden work primarily as an investment in a relationship with the chief, who is the sole provider of goods necessary for domestic food production. Domestic gardens supply the needs of a household, while chief-sponsored public gardens are often contentious and the eventual distribution of the harvest uncertain.

The additional food produced by a collective garden does not seem to add to overall security. In fact, the effect may be the opposite, since it may cut into effort devoted to domestic gardens. Nevertheless, collective gardens have an important political function. Horticulture adheres to the natural rhythms of the crop cycle. Unlike a hunting or fishing trip, which may be over in a day, horticultural cycles require long periods of cooperation. Chiefs make good use of these since the initiation of a garden by a men's club or age grade implies an ongoing unity of effort for a period that may exceed a year. Additionally, chiefs draw parallels between work done for them and that expended on domestic labor. Chiefs cast themselves in the same role as a male household head who would invite his sons and sons-in-law to help him slash his garden plot. Whether sponsored by an older man or a chief, such a call for help never relies on authority alone but also on good cheer and hospitality, often in the form of coffee (with plenty of sugar!) and crackers generously distributed throughout the workday.

In chief-sponsored efforts, the labor contributions of commoners are reciprocated at each step of the production cycle with manufactured goods and food. On days of collective work, a Xikrin male may receive a meal, a machete, or even promises of future goods. While he may relinquish direct control over the product of his labor, since the end product will be retained by the chief for later redistribution, he does not cease to agitate for some portion on future occasions. In other words, receipt of an item from the chief is understood as a token of relationship and, in reaffirming the relationship, creates expectations for future transactions. "Payment" of a machete, then, is not a payment that cancels any further claims a commoner will have on the harvest. Instead, from the perspective of a commoner, the chief has merely initiated the first step in a cycle of production that includes tending, harvesting, and processing, as well as saving seed and clipping material for future production. From a chief's point of view, he has gained future claims on the political loyalties of male followers and (hopefully) their wives as well.

Performance of group activities such as hunting, fishing, gardening, and collecting appears to be geared more toward putting a collective face on chief-led men's clubs or age grades than toward efficiencies of scale or other technical requirements of the production process. While sometimes such activities reveal a rousing esprit de corps, at other times the veiled coerciveness becomes apparent. People may grumble about whom the chief has delegated to oversee the work. Xikrin familiar with work outside the community may derisively refer to him with the Portuguese term *gerente,* or "manager." At base, although the form of activity is collective, each man or women participates in order to assure the viability of his or her own domestic production.

This may explain why such "collective" work is often staged to show individual effort. Many times I have observed an entire group troop en masse to a garden for the purpose of fabricating manioc flour for the chief's stores. Although production transforms the harvest from a single garden into a single mixture of flour, the labor of each individual is carefully differentiated. Each laborer will harvest, peel, transport, and wash his or her own pile of tubers to the point where passerbys will stubbornly refuse to pick up tubers their fellow was unable to carry and add them to their not-quite-filled carrying basket. The point of the activity is to demonstrate individual zeal, in return for which one may receive goods from the chief. What is actually produced may be beside the point.

"Collective" activity under chief sponsorship, then, can be seen as a particular form of labor control. Undoubtedly, fishing and hunting chances are improved on chief-sponsored expeditions because of the use of motorized canoes. In these cases, the addition of fuel, motors, and large canoes diminishes individual effort. Garden work is much less welcome in this regard because of the ongoing obligation involved; it is not seen by the Xikrin as being an unmitigated collective good from which all equally benefit. The "false" collectivity of chief-sponsored production is tied to the growing inequality between chiefs and commoners. Activities of this nature do more than underline the superior status of the chief. Besides serving as a pretext for the redistribution of manufactured goods, they also help ensure the possibility of the collective mobilization of men's clubs and age grades to project Xikrin power beyond the village and to influence the terms of transactions between Xikrin and the extractive industries and the FUNAI.

Chief sponsorship of collective gardens proves to be less about subsistence and more about legitimating political allegiances through a mimicking of household authority. A moral discourse framed in terms of honor and shame, widely used to express obligations toward kin, also is used to express a chief's obligation to provide food and goods to his followers. The rhythms of domestic cultivation find their parallel in the never-ending cycle of horticultural production sponsored by the chief, which allows the tempo of chief-commoner exchanges to be drawn out over time. I have seen disaffected men stay with a particular chief through the harvest, as an earlier departure would mean forfeiting the effort he has made in preceding stages of the agricultural cycle.

Despite chiefs' efforts to maintain allegiance, the composition of men's club may change, as men opt to work for other chiefs or even leave the community for other Kayapó settlements or for stints in the outside world. For a chief, maintenance of a men's club under his leadership is achieved only with constant gifts and (of almost equal importance) success in barring access by his followers to other sources of goods. Under these circumstances, household autonomy and female-oriented production are crucial for men. A cohesive bloc of female kin, who produce bountiful food with fewer manufactured inputs and who can support a greater number of spouses and sons, allows certain households to diversify ties with different chiefs and retain a greater degree of independence from the collective work regime that chiefs try to impose.

CHIEFLY QUALIFICATIONS

Within the reservation system, imported trade goods are required both as means of production and as tokens of relationship between chiefs and followers. The maintenance of the chief's authority is crucial precisely because, under assault from squatters and extractivists, and in the face of FUNAI neglect, strong chiefs are needed to leverage goods from the outside world and preserve the integrity of reservation boundaries.

On the boom-bust frontier, Xikrin access to trade goods depends on using collective forms of organization to establish ties with outsiders who are capable of serving as a conduit for goods. Chiefs use these forms to project their power onto a wider social field. Such forms underwrite the chief's legitimacy and are used to indicate village cohesion, collect natural commodities, intimidate outsiders, stage raids, and, in the case of other Kayapó communities, even stage demonstrations in Brazilian cities. While such forms are the means whereby Xikrin intervene in the world beyond the reservation, they can only be established by means of relationships constructed according to Xikrin values. Central among these is a well-established cultural consensus regarding chiefly virtues. Natural commodities are taken off of reservations for sale, but Xikrin insist on treating chiefs as party to ongoing transactions in which manufactured goods reaffirm a relationship governed by traditional morality. One reason the chief may be called on to perform the role of intercultural mediator is precisely because traditional expectations may act as a check on his power and influence.

Vidal (1977, 146) reports that Cateté Xikrin claimed that chiefs, together with song leaders and orators, served as administrators in the village. Although a chief should possess many desirable qualities, what distinguishes a chief from the other types of leaders is his generosity: the notion that he must readily and fairly distribute trade goods that are channeled to him. Verswijver (1992, 68–70) discusses Kayapó ideas regarding desirable chief qualities. These include abilities as a healer, shaman, orator, ceremonial specialist, scout, and leader of collective activities. These diverse talents may coalesce in one person who would come close to matching the chiefly ideal. In the overwhelming majority of cases, however, no single person displays ability in all these areas, and leadership roles are distributed among different individuals with specialized talents and expertise. This tends to act as a check on authority since no single person attains preeminence in all the leadership roles considered necessary for collective village life.

The Kayapo term *benadjwỳrỳ*, often translated as "chief," refers to one who has the knowledge and performance skills to deliver the ceremonial chant *(ben)* on the different occasions when it is required. Unlike some other Gê peoples, such as the Suyá (Seeger 1981), who differentiate between political and ritual leaders, Kayapó chiefs are expected to play leadership roles in both contexts. Xikrin like to say there is a *ben* for "everything," by which they mean that there are innumerable ben, each appropriate for a particular occasion. Verswijver (1992, 68) states that the "performance of the ben is one of the basic ritual functions discharged by a chief." In fact, Werner (1980, 91) noticed that many different people, male and female, are called *benadjwỳrỳ*, "the one who truly delivers the ben," although they wield little influence.[1] The term may even be used for important figures beyond the village; logging bosses, the FUNAI president, and even the president of Brazil may all be referred to as such.

Ethnographers agree that ideals governing chiefly succession are not ironclad. Verswijver (1992, 71) states that "[n]o formal rule exists for the establishment of the succession of Kayapó chiefs." Vidal (1977, 150) holds that chiefly succession occurs within "the same [nuclear] family," between father and oldest son or between older son and younger son; however, she found the concept of patrilineal descent strange—since patrilineal ideology seemed nowhere else in evidence—and prefers to refer to such a descent pattern as a "tendency."

While concurring that no rules dictate leadership succession, Werner (1980, 276) points out that chiefly descendants have a greater chance than others of becoming chiefs themselves. In attempting to explain how chiefly filiation may result in greater influence, Werner uses path analysis to sort out the relative weight of different variables. He concludes that "knowledge of civilized ways" best explains leadership inheritance. Since chiefs have to play the role of culture brokers and since outsiders tend to focus their attention and become familiar with particular chiefly families, chiefs' sons have a built-in advantage in garnering outsider loyalty and trade goods (ibid., 297).

The lack of clear succession rules and the diverse qualifications that may legitimately be invoked to justify a chiefly position point out some of the ambiguities inherent in the office. Chiefs themselves claim that their position is contingent on approval of their followers. Followers' loyalty must be continually earned through demonstrated forcefulness, administrative competence, and generosity. The ineptness of rivals may also be a significant factor in retaining one's position.

Given these characteristics of chiefly office, Xikrin political economy suffers from a built-in inflationary need for foreign manufactured goods, since what ordinary Xikrin produce within the public realm must be reciprocated with a flow of goods from the chiefs. Within the Xikrin system of values, the chief is not able to transform what commoners produce into a source of income for himself that may be used to purchase goods. The chief made several unsuccessful efforts in 1984 and 1985 to have his followers grow corn and rice by the airstrip, for eventual sale in Altamira. However, this initiative failed when individuals refused to watch over the crop to prevent predation by birds. The small amount of harvested corn was not dried in a timely fashion and was attacked by mildew.

Through their foot-dragging, Xikrin commoners enforced the notion that the continual production of subsistence goods by commoners engaged in horticulture must be answered with a counterflow of different kinds of chiefly goods. Xikrin ideology holds that chiefs should supply goods to loyal followers and redistribute the harvest of collective gardens on the occasions of common activities—such as Brazil nut expeditions—and collective work, such as clearing the airstrip. Chiefs are not authorized to appropriate what commoners produce either in the domestic sphere or in the public sphere. All chiefs must maintain their own domestic garden plots in order to eat, although they may get retainers to work these (see next chapter). By defining chiefs, in their role as chiefs, as *producers of trade goods*, Xikrin commoners blur the distinction between redistribution and reciprocity, as they insist on the separation of the domestic and public spheres, and the analogous character of domestic and public authority.[2] That is, chiefs are only permitted to collect garden products for later redistribution (a public coordinating role) if they offer both generosity and hospitality, as would a kinsperson soliciting aid or the head of a household mobilizing help on his domestic plot. When such transactions involve chiefs, trade goods (and food) are the culturally mandated currency of this type of exchange.

In order to preserve their office, chiefs are adept at stockpiling goods, as shown in the results of the survey. Nevertheless, trade goods decline in value because there are only so many machetes, knives, spools of fishing line, and shotgun shells a household can consume. Recently, chiefs have been distributing in increasing amounts imported food items such as dried beans, pasta, and coffee. Under this exchange regime, there is never a balance of village input and output or a posited equivalence between what is produced and what is consumed and circulated.

Such a system of production may be relatively stable when extractive industries compete actively for reservation resources. While firms are removing resources with monetary value from the reservation, these resources (e.g., timber, gold) have no value within the circuits of exchange of domestic networks or the public sphere. Firms pump goods to the chiefs while removing "free" or unowned goods within the system of Kayapó valuation. It is the externalities of firms' activities—e.g., the noise, disruption of animal habitats, and pollution— that may eventually cause serious damage to the reservation ecosystem and Xikrin subsistence rather than the removal of resources of little or no value in Xikrin circuits of production.

The good times on a Kayapó reservation occur when demand for extractive products is high, a situation with parallels in the relative prosperity a dependent nation-state has when its primary exports are in high demand (cf. Evans 1979). However, during periods of collapse, Xikrin suffer from both a lack of needed supplies as well as a disappointment with what is seen as impotent political leadership. It is precisely under these conditions that the need for strong leadership is reinforced and Xikrin aggressively seek to engage the next extractive boom.

FOOD AND THE OBLIGATIONS OF RECIPROCITY

To this point we have provided evidence for the dependency of Xikrin subsistence on imported manufactured goods and the role of the chief in making these accessible to most commoners. Research findings indicate that the preservation of Xikrin social forms and the fleeting nature of the extractivist fronts themselves have resulted in what might be called a chronic state of disarticulation, in which flows of goods and labor regimes outside the community are not institutionalized. In fact, the nature of this disarticulation is a great frustration to most Xikrin, who see little sense behind their contacts with the outside world. They are, for the time being, resigned to the unpredictable and aleatory character of such contacts.

Under these circumstances, it might seem logical that the Xikrin would attempt to stockpile large amounts of tools and equipment that might see them through times of downturn in extractivism or lean times for the FUNAI. However, if one asks (as I often did) what trade goods were most coveted, the list almost always began with food items. Xikrin do not invoke the Western distinction between utilitarian goods and luxury items to make the case for the indispensability of a particular item. The refusal to distinguish between "capital goods" and "luxury" or "consumer" items puts us on notice that we are not dealing with an industrial-consumer mentality in which the purchasing of goods is an expression of individuality and consumption is a primary avenue for expression of self-identity. Another proof of this contention lies in the universal agreement over which goods were considered essential. The exercise of eliciting what people considered essential imported goods rapidly became monotonous, as identical lists were voiced by person after person. Even if an individual had no use for a certain item such as salt (common in a population in which most elderly people had not acquired a taste for salted foods), he or she was well aware that others used this and thus considered it essential to the well-being of the community. No hierarchy of individual preferences seemed to be expressed through consumer choice.

Among the Xikrin, as in any society, the flow of goods expresses social relationships. The emphasis on imported food items forces us to ask about the role of giving and receiving food among the Xikrin. The serving of food, more than the dancing and singing, is what stands out as a vivid memory in collective celebrations. The father of a child honored in a naming ceremony will comment on the quantity of game served at the ceremony's culmination rather than on the lustiness of the singing and dancing. Invariably, the Xikrin raconteur becomes as animated as any French gourmet when recalling a memorable meal. Ongoing food exchanges pave the way for marriage between two households, although these are not strictly required. A child's parents indulge the child's social mentor and name-giver with favors of food, and children are taught that they should be generous in giving food to their own parents and mentors when they grow up. The tasks most often performed by age groupings involve food collection or processing. During certain ceremonies, men and women exchange food with one another. Women who cook on the same earth oven take turns exchanging food and working in one another's gardens.

If food circulates, it is not the only item that circulates. People perform acts for one another and in exchange for food. Specialized knowledge circulates, as do names, ritual roles, and some special prerogatives, such as the right to specific cuts of meat. To describe the Xikrin system of exchanges would take us far afield. Suffice it to state that cooked food is never exchanged for material goods but only for labor and certain acts performed on one's behalf or on the behalf of one's child. Food is never measured in terms of the equivalence of the value of non-food items. Rather, its sufficiency is measured purely in terms of its ability to satisfy the hunger of the recipient.

The redistribution of food by the chief to his followers reaffirms Xikrin notions of sociality. Unlike other gifts, food does not allow the donor the upper hand. Cooperation in return for food can only take the form of an ungrudging accession to the wishes of the giver. This is because there can never be any absolute amount of equivalency by which food can be measured. Xikrin refuse to measure tit for tat in matters of comestibles. The response to a gift of food is always in proportion to the subjective measure of satisfaction it brings to the receiver. In theory, when the gift is food, one can never say "I knock you down with generosity" in the manner of a New Guinea big man or a Kwakiutl chief. Cooperation is seen as simply a natural consequence of the feeling of well-being induced by food. When people labor, sing, or dance in exchange for a meal, they profess to do so out of a sense of the well-being that their performance is meant to express and spread. Dancers may balk at performing when too little food is supplied for a ceremony. However, their performance does not acknowledge a gift received but rather the internal state of satisfaction felt by all when social roles are well performed.

The fact that food is always rather high up on the list of goods desired by both chiefs and populace does not stem from an irreversible corruption of the Xikrin value system. It is precisely because it is not experienced as coercive that gifts of food encourage people to cooperate with their chiefs. Absolute quantity may be less important than variety—smaller quantities of soda pop, crackers, breads, and candies may satisfy the receiver as effectively as larger quantities of items such as manioc flour, which can be produced in the village. The marginal utility of additional trade goods such as machetes, fishing line, or T-shirts decreases rapidly in a society where these items must be consumed through household labor. Such items may not be traded between households or converted into other forms of value. In contrast, within the Xikrin system of values, food does not decline in value with each successive gift, and each act of giving is interpreted as an act of generosity rather than a goad to future return.

Whereas a limited number of imported tools would seem to fulfill requirements for subsistence, a limited number of such items does not fulfill the organizational requirements to maintain followers within the ongoing cooperating groups marshaled by chiefs. Imported food items fulfill these requirements as they are (1) accessible only through chiefs, (2) in constant demand, and (3) part of noncoercive transactions that (4) create the ongoing basis for a felt community of sentiment.

The fourth point must be explained by the close association between food and sociality and the role of collective feedings and ritual meals in Xikrin thought. The Xikrin believe that the feeling of generalized well-being that results from the consumption of large quantities of food is actually instrumental in creating community. Collective activities are successful if they generate intense common emotions within the village as a whole that are analogous to those thought to naturally emerge through the creation of physical ties between nuclear family members. Thus, in an article on the creation of community among the Xikrin I have written, "Healthy emotions . . . are more than a metaphor. . . . While everyone is not joined through social relationship to all others in the village, all participants in a community share a living ideal regarding common participation in activities that create common sentiments. The social significance of these sentiments is that they are indices, or monitors, of particular social/physical states which social action seeks to achieve" (Fisher 1998). By feeding people successfully, chiefs assert their ability to create a community of sentiment. In doing so they reveal that political affairs are not subsidiary to the "real" life of the village but actually make collective life possible.

Contrary to preconceived notions about self-sufficient forest people, imported food is not merely a luxury or a political tool used to maintain loyalty in the hands of chiefs. Imported food not produced directly is the counterpart of tools acquired but never produced. Such food permits the Xikrin to act out the culturally necessary fiction that chiefs are the linchpins of reciprocity in the recreation of community, thus ideologically recasting redistribution as a transaction analogous to that found in the domain of kinship.

This is reinforced when chiefs act not only as political leaders but as well when they use their acquired wealth and influence to act as ritual sponsors. In contrast to commoners, who may have only one or two children recognized in ceremonies, chiefs' children are all honored in name-confirmation ceremonies. A chief's position and influence allow him to bear the costs of ceremonial sponsorship with less hardship than commoners and to spread the wealth around in the process. As in a trend found in dependent communities the world over, Xikrin commoners encourage wealthier chiefs to sponsor community ceremonial activities in which wealth, often injected from the outside, gets converted into prestige within the community.

The expectations created by the Xikrin social organization put chiefs in a position where they must supply goods to commoners but simultaneously are deauthorized from converting surplus produced by commoners into the means of social control. Chiefs maintain their influence through control of the tempo and organization of work rather than through the appropriation of the product. The survey results in the previous chapter show that the unequal wealth garnered by chiefs is composed almost exclusively of trade goods. Currently, chiefs maintain their organizational authority over men's clubs and age grades by acting as intermediaries with outsiders. Contacts with the FUNAI take place at the Indian post or the regional administration centers, but miners and loggers often must actively court chiefly cooperation.

Typically, extractive firms transported chiefs to town in rented aircraft. In town, owners or their underlings would lodge chiefs in a hotel, escort them to nightclubs, and, in at least some cases, hire prostitutes. They also introduced the chiefs to merchants (often in league with the firms themselves) who would allow the chiefs to buy on credit. Not only the principal chief but also the underchiefs would receive lines of credit. The use of dubious accounting procedures to calculate the tab run up by each certainly contributed to the large debts accrued. One of the chief's interpreters responsible for monitoring such matters reported that as of July 1995 (when Brazilian currency—reais or "R"—held rough parity with U.S. dollars), the Xikrin debt in the town of Tucumã amounted to either R 44,000 or R 48,000 (he was unsure of the exact total). He itemized the debt owed various merchants and repairmen: R 22,000 was owed to a supermarket, R 14,000 to a clothing store, R 800 to an arms repair shop, R 600 to a chainsaw repair shop, and R 1600 to a shop that repairs radios and tape recorders. It should be noted that this debt does not include money owed in other towns, such as Altamira and Repartimento. There is also no way to tell what sort of value was received for these sums. The interpreter showed me some items he had purchased—a case of biscuits, soup, soap, and cooking oil, and ten kilograms of sugar—for which he was charged R 600, about U.S. $600! This money was to be conveniently deducted by the logging firm from timber earnings and turned over directly to the Supermarket Alvorado in Tucumã. While lack of basic familiarity with the value of cash is clearly hurting the Xikrin and proving a boon for local merchants, this is not the whole story.

The sums owed are still not unmanageable, given the available untapped natural resources. But the conflation of the community and its leaders in dealings with the outside world allows debts contracted by chiefs to be held in the name of the community as a whole. Xikrin commoners, however, are not willing to work to pay off the debt that they feel (accurately enough) was run up by their chiefs with little benefit to themselves. In this case, extractivist firms have a great interest in refusing to differentiate debts contracted to buy supplies for redistribution from those incurred in the course of recreational activities or accommodations in town. By the same token, chiefs realize that debt held in the name of the community must be settled because, in the absence of assistance from the FUNAI, provision of needed subsistence goods depends on extension of further credit. Some merchants have already refused to sell more to the Xikrin until old debts are settled. If chiefs are to preserve their own position then they must assure a continued flow of goods into the village. Their means of raising cash is limited by the lack of coercive social mechanisms. Xikrin chiefs cannot force commoners to work, and, even if they could, it is not clear that they could produce much more for sale than they do currently through the annual Brazil nut harvest. The only available alternative appears to be the sale of reservation re-sources. Political necessities of the chieftaincy thus in some sense align chiefs with extractivist firms regarding the expediency of removing reserve resources.

Put briefly, Xikrin have a greater autonomy in subsistence matters than chiefs do in matters relating to the retention of their chiefly status and prerogatives. From the outside, debt hands extractive firms a powerful tool for forcing the Xikrin to open up their reservation resources for exploitation, because, from the perspective within the village, it is the chiefs rather than the community that have largely incurred the outstanding debt. Chiefs thus stand ready, by virtue of the political necessities of Xikrin social organization, to sell off resources that "have no owner" according to traditional values. In all hierarchical societies, when the more powerful contract debts, there are social mechanisms by which these burdens can be shifted to the less powerful. The irony of the environmen-tal destruction facing the Xikrin reserve is that it is produced, in part, by the insis-tence of the Xikrin to not accord their leaders the power of coercion and exploitation through which they could be compelled to produce goods for sale. At the same time, they demand that chiefs must act in the public sphere to simu-late reciprocal household transactions through the use of manufactured goods.

Any attempt to explain natural resource use solely in terms of ecological con-straints runs aground on the complex social mechanisms whereby humans access resources. Xikrin notions of ownership and the cultural schema by which age grades and men's clubs operate within the frontier political economy are part of the equation, and market mechanisms of credit and indebtedness play their part as well. The need for shotguns, mechanical grinders, and canoe motors for tradi-tional living in sedentary villages introduce new needs for chiefly coordination in the production process. Chiefs are in a position in which they must be attentive to the relative strengths and wealth of potential allies, switching their allegiances between firms or government agencies according to their assessment of the situ-ation. These factors are no less crucial than demography, subsistence techniques, and the existing resource base for determining how humans interact with their environment. Use of a political ecological approach to analyze patterns of resource use entails description of human-environment interactions as a social activity. Such activity is subject to all of the causalities and constraints of social life, as well as to those of the ecological systems of which they form a part.

8 | THE SPREAD OF CHIEFLY POWER

Unlike other regions and epochs in the Amazon, extractivist firms on the Bakajá reservation today do not seek to exploit Indian labor for their own ends; Xikrin do not work as peons. Nor do these firms seek the products of Indian labor as they might those of a rubber tapper. Moreover, the resources sought by firms were never collectively or individually owned or controlled by the Xikrin; neither mahogany nor gold are given any value in Xikrin society. For their part, extractivist firms have no interest in taking possession of Indian land on a permanent basis. Firms seek only to appropriate natural items that are foreign to the Xikrin repertoire of values.

Because different cultural systems—Xikrin and Brazilian extractivist—value different things as productive input and output, we cannot narrowly focus on control over any of the factors of production (land, social labor, or even capital, in the form of tools) to understand the basis of the relationship between the Xikrin and contemporary logging or mining industries. Mahogany logging is not a productive activity for the Xikrin, and subsistence farming and hunting are not productive activities for extractivists. Indians, loggers, and miners are basically engaged in pursuits that have no necessary relationship to one another, except their temporary overlap in space. While externalities generated by logging firms—pollution and disruption of animal habitats—increase the subsistence efforts of the Xikrin, with an equitable set of social relationships and sustainable harvesting practices, there is reason to believe that logging and Xikrin subsistence might coexist in a given area. Indeed, some activists and agronomy experts are attempting to implement sustainable harvesting of mahogany within the sister Xikrin reserve of Cateté to supplement rather than displace a traditional subsistence economy (Giannini 1996). Given the potential pitfalls, it remains to be seen whether this innovation will prove viable.

Even when FUNAI acts as an intermediary, extractivists continue to hold a monopoly over the realization of the cash value for natural products within the reservation. Xikrin have no mechanisms on their own to turn mahogany into desired trade goods. Xikrin need what extractivists provide because firms have access to tools and other manufactured goods while Indians do not. The Xikrin need for manufactured goods for the re-creation of political relations and subsistence continues to be the key to understanding the relationship between the Xikrin and extractivists. Although they dominate the region, extractivist firms are not intrinsically necessary to the Xikrin but could be replaced by any other supplier, the FUNAI being an obvious option.

It is precisely the administrative and financial weakness of the FUNAI that today provides the main opportunity for extractivists. Within the reservation, whose very existence depends on the legal authority of the Brazilian state, it is the enactment of laws and the always selective enforcement of those laws that determine the possibilities for extractivist firms to function. The reservation system has created enclaves of space, both literal and metaphorical, for the Xikrin to produce both their physical needs and their social relations. This has led to areas of natural value that have not been exposed to the depletive pressures of the market. Minerals and forest products standing relatively untouched within Indian reservations are a magnet for profiteers. But the same government power brought to bear for the creation of the reservations is often handcuffed when it comes to defending the integrity of the reservations against the forces that would undermine their very viability. Without effectively confronting the fury unleashed by predatory extractivism, the Brazilian government and its Indian agency may be setting aside reservations of land and resources for Indian peoples that exist only on paper. The result of reservations with undefended borders could be massive profit taking by extractivists, leaving behind Indian peoples to survive as they can on the devastated remnants of a wounded and depleted ecosystem.

In the case of logging, Xikrin have no mode of calculating the value drained from their reservation. This is true despite attempts to hire independent "measurers" *(medidores)* to audit the quantity and quality of timber extracted. While it is difficult to ascertain whether or not medidores hired by Xikrin are colluding with loggers, it is almost certain that they never get a chance to measure all of the timber extracted from the reservation. Even when they do arrive at estimates, the innumeracy of the Xikrin prevents them from fully understanding the quantity of wood involved. More important, even if the cash value were understood, there is no means of translating this into a value commensurate with any Xikrin measure.

Indeed, there is something mystical about the transaction from the Xikrin point of view that is enforced by the predatory scrambling of logging and mining firms to get the jump on one another. At least twice, airplanes have landed unannounced on the reservation airstrip loaded with "presents." In each case, the presents were initial signals in cross-cultural diplomacy by firms who planned to negotiate for "rights" to prospect or log in a given part of the reservation. The goods arrived unbidden, and later the firms disappeared from the scene without setting up operations. The opposite, of course, has occurred more frequently. Timber has been removed from the reservation without the expected planeloads of goods as compensation. Xikrin have noticed that some firms exceed others in the quantity of goods they offer. Competition between firms is interpreted in terms of the qualities of firm owners, preference being given to those who are more generous.

If we focus on the flow of goods entering the Xikrin village from the outside today, neither gift nor commodity exchange nor barter aptly characterizes the cross-cultural transactions through which Xikrin receive manufactured goods from the current crop of logging and mining extractivists. The Xikrin certainly receive Western commodities, but the resources taken from their reservation are not transacted as commodities by the Xikrin. Economic structures are insufficient to provide channels of exchange, and the political structures that organize the flow of goods are predicated on new forms of chiefly power.

EXTRACTIVIST-XIKRIN TRANSACTIONS

If the Xikrin do not sell commodities, what determines the value of the goods they receive from the outside? Along with this question we should also ask about the social mechanisms that maintain the stability of this value. To answer this question we note that the goods received from extractivist firms resemble nothing so much as repeated "peace offerings" that might be proffered to a potentially hostile party in return for safe passage. Passage without disruption is precisely what loggers and miners seek in return for the use of Xikrin resources. From their perspective, contacts with Xikrin should produce a decision, enforceable on the community as a whole, to abstain from confrontation. Hence the need for chiefs who can conduct negotiations and act as native conduits to enforce a code of conduct on the entire group. That is, as long as chiefs can rein in "dissidents" who would take advantage of the proximity of logging work-parties to provision themselves with desired goods, firms conclude that there is benefit in dealing with chiefs.

The difference between dealing with a centralized and an "acephalous" polity, of course, is often critical for cross-cultural trade. Goody (1978, 536), citing an African example, points out that traders in northern Ghana had to make different types of payments within different types of polities. "They stood the chance of being raided in the acephalous areas and were often forced to pay tolls or other dues in the centralized states."[1] In evaluating the value of the toll and whether to pay it, traders had to weigh both their potential gain and the power of the chief. In the Xikrin case, the dialectic is quite complicated since extractivists and Xikrin commoners each evaluate chiefly power from a different vantage point, both of which must be taken into account in the calculations of the chief himself.

Firms must gauge the level of control and cooperation that a chief may command from his followers, while followers gauge not only the quantity of goods channeled to the chief but his ability and disposition to fulfill their individual expectations. A good example of the complexities in this regard are the actions that Jaguar took to force Surubim to return the pistol stolen from the logging camp. In so doing, Jaguar risked further alienating Surubim but was able to propose a raid on a mining camp so that Surubim and others like him could acquire manufactured goods without chiefly mediation (see page 165). Other examples of Jaguar acting to restrain villagers in the interest of longer-term relations with extractivists are not hard to find. In a very real sense, such incidents are part of the process whereby chiefs and extractivists arrive at a mutual valuation of payments to the Xikrin since such payments are only very loosely pegged to the value of the natural commodities extracted.

The following incident illustrates how Xikrin collective power lies in the Xikrin ability to add production costs not directly related to the extraction process itself. The value of goods directed toward chiefs is determined through the exercise of this power. In a clever coup, my friend Cleared Path succeeded in absconding from the logging camp with three canoe motors, hauling them up a small creek to the Bakajá River and then back to the village itself. Advised of the incident by the head of the logging crew, Jaguar pressured Cleared Path to return the motors. If the loggers could not convince Jaguar that his cooperation in stemming theft would eventually result in the village receiving more than the value of three canoe motors, he would be hard-pressed to offer any assurances to Cleared Path that it would be better for all concerned to return the motors ("Geesh, they were like new," lamented Cleared Path on recalling the incident). From the vantage point of the company, what they will extend by way of goods becomes a quantity somewhere between the value of the motors *to the Xikrin* and the potential value of the natural commodity *to the extractivists.* These latter strongly protested the theft of motors, because production would be disrupted if they were subject to wildcat raids by individual Xikrin rather than because the motors exceeded the value of the mahogany or the price the firm was willing to pay.

Xikrin raiding potential, based in the final analysis on their ability to act collectively, which includes, of course, the ability to collectively refrain from action, imposes a baseline value for the maintenance of peace. The quantity of value this assumes within Xikrin society, however, cannot be pegged to a set cash price but to *specific commodities that satisfy the redistribution necessary to maintain loyalty to a chief.* The absolute price is unimportant compared to the evaluation of items according to the Xikrin system of values. However, from the perspective of a Xikrin commoner, *the evaluation of goods is not formed relative to the values taken by extractivists from the reserve but within the framework of the obligations of chiefly reciprocity incurred as a result of their participation in publicly sponsored activities.* The cultural process by which Xikrin arrive at a level of remuneration in trade goods is of a different order than that of extractivist firms. Only the extractivist firm is in a position to gauge the value of one commodity (what is taken from the reservation) for another (what is shipped to the Xikrin village). Xikrin commoners judge the value of trade goods in relation to the obligations incurred as a result of participating in joint activities without reference to the market value of natural resources.

Xikrin chiefs have perhaps the most complicated optic of all. Their position is ultimately based on Xikrin social forms, but social approval rests on their furnishing goods to their followers that they must procure from extractivist firms. Having no independent source of commodities outside extractivist firms and no social base outside traditional social organization, the power they wield, in some sense, is not their own. It rests on the particular linkages between social forms regnant within the village and within the regional economy. The kinds of coordinating roles the chief will be obliged to assume differs according to the outsider with whom he is associated. Miners, loggers, the FUNAI, even other Kayapó village leaders, all impose different sorts of pressures and constraints.

The notion of linkages can be thought to have a physical meaning as well. The opening of a road, for example, or the depletion of a gold site, the pollution of a traditional fishing venue can all have dramatic effects on the movement of people and hence the exercise of influence and control.

From the chief's point of view, a straightforward donation of the canoe motors by the company would not be particularly helpful or desired. While Cleared Path would have been ecstatic over having his own canoe motor, this would have generated jealousy, divisiveness, and dissidence, undermining the basis for further collective action under chiefly auspices. What the chief requested instead of the motors were a number of different items that could serve to symbolize the ongoing relationship of reciprocity between himself and his followers. As might be expected given the prominent role of food in ceremonial and interhousehold exchange, foodstuffs comprise a large proportion of these goods.

Is there a sense that transactions between extractivists and Xikrin chiefs can be considered barter? Humphrey and Hugh-Jones (1992, 8ff.) point out that during barter the transacting parties are "on their own" if they decide one object can be swapped for another. The momentary mutual estimation of worth is all that matters. Unlike exchange systems involving commodities, there is no overall criteria through which a system of equivalencies can be calculated: "Goods are often unlike and incomparable." The authors also contend that a perfect balance is obtained at the completion of a transaction. Appadurai's (1986, 9) definition of barter distinguishes it from exchange by labeling it an act that is accomplished with the "maximum feasible reduction of social, cultural, political, or personal transaction costs." Although Humphrey and Hugh-Jones point out that barter rarely comes out of the blue, as it occurs in predictable social contexts, swapping one item for another and going one's separate ways unencumbered with further social obligations makes barter a paradigmatic form of transaction between strangers operating outside a common set of assumptions.

It should be clear that by these definitions, barter does *not* describe the basis for transactions between Xikrin and extractivists because at no time are objects exchanged for one another or are mutual estimations of worth arrived at by parties to the trade. Never is any consensual decision reached regarding the equivalent worth of X number of boxes of crackers, flashlight batteries, and cheap cognac, and Y cubic meters of mahogany. Moreover, as we have seen, transactions between extractivists and Indians are bipolar only if we fixate on the contrasting identities of Indians and non-Indians. In reality, such transactions are neither bipolar nor simultaneous estimations of values because at least three parties—extractivists, chiefs, and commoners—are always involved. In addition, as the previous discussion of the contrast between systems of production and value made clear, Xikrin chiefs are not engaged in transacting resources that they "own" in any individual or collective sense. Neither gold nor mahogany was ever owned nor did the Xikrin ever recognize a loose sort of nontransmissible usufruct right, as they do for stands of Brazil-nut trees. Moreover, the threat of collective Xikrin violence is always balanced against the potential for violence of thugs hired by extractivists. The balance of force and counterforce as well as the firm's ability to withdraw and seek natural products elsewhere are principal ingredients in the delicately balanced array of forces that bring extractivists into contact with Xikrin society. As might be expected, the crystallization of proper conditions for the movement of trade goods can also be rapidly reversed with potential costs and benefits for both sides. This concatenation of nonequivalencies underlines the confusing complexity involved in transactions between Xikrin and extractivists. Such transactions do not fall into any neat categories comprehensible in terms of the articulation of modes of production, barter, or exchange, or even of any simple Xikrin dependency on steel tools for survival.

The primary significance of these considerations is that transactions, such as those in which mahogany is exchanged for Coca Cola and crackers, that look senseless when seen as examples of barter *are* senseless as barter; they are never the result of mutual estimations of relative worth. Only from the perspective of the extractive firm can this be the case. From the Xikrin point of view, we are already dealing with multiple, contested perspectives that conjoin the calculations for the maintenance of collective social forms and the need for a channel by which essential manufactured items can be obtained.

Conservationists and supporters of Indian communities who are concerned mainly with getting Indians "a fair deal" for their commodities necessarily think in terms of the direct exchange of one commodity for another. The issue for them is how to force an equitable rate of exchange so that native communities receive fair value for their resources and will not have to sell these off so quickly. This could allow for more careful harvesting practices and time for the natural habitat to regenerate. If harvesting naturally regenerating resources were carefully managed, in theory, such an activity could be sustainable, that is, continued indefinitely with no overall degradation of the environment or loss of income. Unfortunately, because of the factors we have adduced above, the Xikrin are not involved in a "swap of commodities." In order to understand the indigenous perspective in this case, it is necessary to come to grips with the manner in which chiefs use commodities to exercise power within their communities. We must come to grips with the logic of indigenous power, both bottom up and top down, within the particular set of extraordinary circumstances that characterizes the extractive hollow frontier during the late 1980s and 1990s. Let us turn, then, to some concrete examples of the way control of trade goods both heightens chiefly power and is the object of chiefly control.

CHIEFLY CONTROL

The chiefs' lot among the Xikrin is far from an aristocratic life cocooned and shielded from the "masses." The masses, one must remember, are not only kinsfolk, lovers, nieces, and nephews but people who have known them all their lives and have a more or less complete understanding of their strengths and frailties.

On a typical morning, Jaguar could be roused from slumber by his wife's classificatory mother's husband brusquely announcing, "I'm going fishing today, and I need tiny fishhooks for bait as well as hooks to catch Pescada." At this, the chief might motion to his son to retrieve the requested supplies from a storage space, only to confront the wife of a poorer family fast approaching, clutching a small red basin. "Give me manioc flour, we've nothing to eat at our house," she says. While the bravado of her words are belied by her tentative manner, Jaguar would likely nod to his wife to retrieve a gunnysack full of farinha from under a wooden bench and fill the woman's basin. And so it goes; numerous mornings I have seen a bleary-eyed chief field a number of demands for goods before he has yet to raise his head from the foam rubber mattress!

A witness to this scene might think that the disparity in possessions was not then a sign of entrenched inequality but merely one phase in a cycle of acquisition and redistribution. By honoring requests, the chief may claim to act only as a repository of goods for the benefit of the entire community. Anthropological studies can be cited to support the view that leaders, including Kayapó chiefs, of relatively egalitarian communities may even be poorer than others (e.g., Werner 1980). This is presumably because chiefs constantly need to reassert their generosity as part of their claim to leadership. Such a view does not accurately describe the recent power acquired by Xikrin chiefs within the hollow frontier.

As we have seen, chiefs do not receive accolades for their generosity. What generosity they do display seems more akin to the kind of fending off of accusations of stinginess (cf. Peterson 1993, on demand sharing) and the blatant handing out of favors to cement political loyalties. Many requests made to the head chief go unfulfilled, and people, especially relatives of one sort or another, complain how sad they become when they request items *kaigo,* or "fruitlessly," from their foremost relative in the village. Chiefs, for their part, claim they *have* to be firm, for after all, not only do people misrepresent their real needs (men always claim to be without ammunition, for example), but soon they would have nothing left if every request was honored. In fact, during my last stay in the village, Jaguar gave me this precise counsel himself, warning me to dole out my trade goods only slowly in carefully measured quantities.

The demands of kinship and solidarity from Xikrin villagers forces us to confront the question of the struggle to diminish material inequality currently being waged within the village. It is important to establish whether or not control of access to goods translates into political influence. From the chief's perspectives, goods are sought less for their intrinsic advantages (being awakened daily with demands for goods is hardly an advantage!) than for other reasons. The pressures of the office are great. He may eat a bit better and do less physical work, but he is always on stage. In his role as leader, distribution of goods comes to occupy an increasingly important part of his everyday existence. An obsession with goods is reflected in his relations with his own kin and other villagers, and this obsession tends to fill up his life.

MATERIAL INEQUALITY AND CHIEFLY STRATEGY

The survey revealed that the ability to stockpile significant quantities of goods belonged exclusively to chiefs. Additionally, the types of goods stockpiled reflected the chief's role as an organizer of collective activities. As the survey results show, only chiefs had stores of extra food. The underchief Krô'i had three thirty-kilogram sacks of salt that would be used if he was successful in organizing his followers to catch and salt fish for sale in Altamira or the gold-prospecting site of Ilha da Fazenda near the mouth of the Bakajá. In the corner of his bedroom rested a hulking motor taken during the raid on the mining camp. While men from poorer families, such as Surubim and Female Land Turtle, were grabbing what they could of household items, firearms, or even a chicken or two, Krô'i was clearly thinking in terms of larger collective projects. Only a chief would have the resources to keep the motor maintained and filled with gasoline and lubricants. Moreover, only a chief could sponsor the sort of collective activities that would make the possession of a motor worthwhile. Although the motor was not operational, if it could be fixed, it would prove a valuable asset.

Although he was a recognized underchief and was successful in maintaining followers through periodic redistribution, Krô'i was still subordinate to the principal chief. We can contrast Krô'i's hopes for employment of the motor with those of a commoner to better understand the distance between chiefs and commoners. During the same raid in which Krô'i managed to transport his motor back to the reservation in an small aircraft, one commoner, "Roberto," triumphantly pounced on an abandoned chainsaw as his booty from the raid. Not having the luxury of return air transport, which was restricted to chiefs and favored followers, he slung the device over his shoulder and began the three-day trek back to the village. The load was heavy, he complained, and nobody offered to help him during the trip. Nonetheless, he persevered, spurred on by visions of trees almost felling themselves in his garden plot and astronomical success in the gathering of wild honey. On his return, he explained, he managed to use the chainsaw a single time in his own garden plot before it ran out of fuel. Since no chief was willing to diminish his own stock of fuel, Roberto was forced to discontinue use of the chainsaw. It now sits, unused, dusty, rusted, and nonoperational in his house. Even if he could get fuel, it is doubtful that he could run it. In a society in which kinship looms large, one might imagine that the assiduous demands of relatives could be a principal block to acquiring and keeping valuable productive resources of one's own. Such is not the case, especially when we recall that only a minuscule number of manufactured items are exchanged between households. Rather, for a number of concrete reasons, as we shall see, the productive advantages that lie solely with chiefs are not easily usurped.

Collective activities in gardening and hunting are not merely the result of chiefly sponsorship aimed at increasing individual productivity through the use of Western items. Collective activities also represent the exercise of chiefly power. Chiefs not only act to "collectivize," they act to disempower and block the use of similar productive technology by commoners in the village. In storing his motor, Krô'i was well aware that it would either be used with the agreement of Jaguar, who could help get it repaired and supplied with fuel, or against the wishes of Jaguar, in which case Krô'i would have to arrange his own outside supplier independent of Jaguar.

Krô'i is making an attempt to appeal to the younger Xikrin, and he directs most (but not all) of the bachelors and younger married men. Plenty of audiocassettes of backland Brazilian music are an indispensable asset for the young chief. He opens up his house as a pseudo-nightclub in the evening. The fifty or so music tapes are blasted through large speakers and attract young people to his house where they can socialize and create a spirited attitude that will carry over to his work parties and other projects.

Krô'i, who is playing his cards to perhaps one day assume the principal chieftaincy has carefully stored twenty toothbrushes awaiting distribution to loyal followers. On a recent trip to Tucumã, he purchased ten sleeveless overall jackets, like those de rigeur for Hell's Angels and other motorcycle gangs. Where gang colors would be displayed on the back is the insignia of the National Indian Foundation, a feather headdress, around which is inscribed, "Federal Security Bakajá Village." The jackets were distributed to select followers of Krô'i and were obviously imitations of those worn in other Kayapó reservations where Indians have formed a native "police force," to patrol reservation boundaries and village social functions as well (Verswijver 1992, 244–46). Although no such organization exists at Bakajá, the jackets give their owners a jaunty contemporary feeling of being in step with their more prosperous and sophisticated bethren in other villages. Not coincidentally, this fits in well with the image that Krô'i projects as a savvy world-experienced leader who can help bring the village up to speed in its dealings with the outside world.

Nonetheless, sponsoring pseudo-Brazilian "socials" or buying a handful of fashionable jackets is hardly enough to enable oneself to be recognized as a legitimate chief. Chiefs are held responsible for supplying their followers with goods.

This responsibility can be seen from the purchases made by another aspiring sub-chief, Bep Pruin. On one trip to Altamira he purchased two boxes each of .16 and .20 gauge shotgun shells, and boxes of .38 and .22 bullets. He himself hunts with a .38 carbine and most of the ammunition was purchased for the sole purpose of redistribution. Double-checking my survey records, I find that the ammunition gauges fit the gauges of weapons he has bought for men he would like to recruit as followers. In other words, supplying ammunition for guns he has previously purchased is part of a continuing campaign to ensure the loyalty of these men by upholding his end of reciprocal transactions.

Although the generosity and honesty of Bep Pruin are acknowledged, and his purchase of firearms for commoners is particularly popular, his organizational skills are limited. While he buys things for followers, he has difficulty mobilizing them to plant gardens or go hunting. His skills in accounting and dealing with foreigners are on a par with his organizational skills. While he wields some influence as a chief, he is referred to derisively as the *palmito benadjwỳrỳ*, or "palm-heart chief." This alludes to his role in ostensibly overseeing contacts between mahogany loggers and the village, and it also points out his ineffectiveness. With devastating irony Xikrin liken him to the spindly comestible palm-heart, the palmito, rather than "export" wood. While both species live in the forests, only mahogany is called "wood" *(pĩ)* and has lasting weight in the affairs of the village. This well illustrates some of the ambivalence Xikrin commoners feel about their chiefs.

Chiefs are quite sensitive to public opinion in the village, which agitates incessantly for justification of material privilege of any kind. Chiefs have reacted by encouraging commoners in their role as followers to formulate specific requests for trade goods. They may then use their privileged access to food and imported goods to initiate what they hope will be a continuing relationship involving political loyalty and participation in sponsored work parties. Or commoners may take the lead and direct requests to a known aspirant of chiefly standing, offering their potential receptivity to chief-sponsored initiatives in the future. In short, both chiefs and commoners work to fashion new social channels through which commoners might have access to goods but they do so in a way that enhances the de facto authority of the chief.

THE SPIRALING EMBRACE: CHIEFS AND RETAINERS

A number of individuals from poorer households work directly for Jaguar as personal retainers. They prepare food for his household or for work groups under his sponsorship. They fetch firewood, run errands, and perform multiple chores. In return they are fed by the chief's household and receive special clothing and even sleep some nights under the chief's roof. During the course of the survey, the finery of these personal retainers sharply contrasted with that of others in their families. When Jaguar returns from a trip to the city he often brings special tokens to these retainers. This arrangement serves as an escape hatch for some individuals and affords them a chance to break out from the confines of work with age-mates and their domestic group. "Thick Skin," for example, is an exceptionally intelligent and sensitive lad of fourteen who takes to wearing flowers in his hair and is more attuned to listening to the radio and unsettling others with his humorous social commentary than with the rigors of the hunt. "Big Eye" is a single mother who seems to have no disposition to marry, while "Howler Monkey" was captured long ago from the neighboring Parakanã tribe and was given as a spouse to Jaguar's aged father who recently died. All seem happy with their role as assistant to the chief, and the extra labor helps Jaguar expand his domestic activities and act as a frequent host to those seeking food.

By recruiting retainers, chiefs acquire a good deal of responsibility for their welfare. The effect is to provide an alternative to the supports of the existing system of kinship ties. The three retainers labor little within their own households and do not receive much in the way of food, clothing, and tools from their coresident families. Their households of origin feel relieved from much of the responsibility for their material well-being, which has been turned over to Jaguar. Chiefs adopt an ethos of kinship when dealing with retainers, as they do with their followers. By invoking familiar kinship values, chiefly assumption of support for their retainers can be justified as an example of ideal social behavior rather than as an amassing of power at the expense of domestic loyalties.

In a similar vein, chiefs are in a position to offer their generosity to entire families of nonrelatives, using the ethos of kinship to increase their constituency of supporters. During the spring of 1995, an entire poor family took refuge under Jaguar's roof. A compartment was made in the room of Jaguar's daughter and son-in-law where they could hang their hammocks. Beatings repeatedly administered by a maternal aunt living next door had precipitated the flight from their household. In a way reminiscent of Jaguar's personal retainers, this family is clearly marginalized. They had never been able to get help from village kin to plaster their hut walls with mud, and their house remained the only structure exposed in this way. The woman has long been tagged as antisocial: She often flies into a rage and strikes her children; she rarely decorates them with body paint as an attentive mother should; and some years earlier she did not even plant her own garden. I have seen her several times scavenging alone in the gardens of distant relatives, a sharp contrast to the spirited sociality of the merry groups of women who garden regularly together. Her husband is an outsider who was born long ago in the village of Gorotire and found his way to the Bakajá settlement at the end of the 1970s along with the remnants of the Kararaô band of survivors.

Jaguar treats this family with some reserve and makes a point not to be overly generous with them. At some point they will gather their few possessions and move again, but for the time being Jaguar's actions have helped dampened tensions among the neighboring houses. When a new village is constructed they plan to erect a house next door to Jaguar's and presumably enter into the society of cooperating females that links Jaguar's residence with its neighbors.

NON-KAYAPÓ RETAINERS

In the last decade numerous Kayapó villages have recruited non-Indian Brazilian employees to serve their chiefs. In some cases, these employees may serve specialized technical functions such as those of pilots or drivers. However, in many cases, employees have worked as laborers, tending the gardens, houses, and even, in the case of the Kikretūm village, the cattle herds of the chief. If there is any doubt about how Kayapó chiefs, such as Jaguar, who do not know how to read or write and whose knowledge of Brazilian society is scanty, are able to acquire Brazilian workmen, the answer lies in the tremendous poverty and marginalization of much of Brazil's population. Landless peasants flock to Brazil's Amazon region to escape the misery rampant in other rural regions. Such was the case of the "Oldtimer," who Jaguar plucked off the streets of Tucumã after he had worked for years as a personal servant to the Kayapó chief Pombo in the Kikretūm settlement. He later worked at the Xikrin reservation of Cateté and claims to have worked with Indians since he was young and living in his native state of Maranhão. Oldtimer sought employment from Jaguar because he lacked identification and working papers. Without such documents it was impossible for him to legally find work anywhere. Although he claimed to be working for the monthly Brazilian minimum wage, while on the reservation he had never actually been paid.

His most important function was to provide agricultural labor. Through Oldtimer's effort, Jaguar was able to create the largest surplus of locally grown food on the reservation, as attested by the sacks of manioc flour stockpiled in his house. Perhaps Oldtimer produced a greater proportion of his own food locally than did any of the Xikrin. His clothes were filthy tatters. He was given time off from garden, repair, and construction work in order to hunt and fish. Occasionally, when Jaguar returned from one of his forays to the city, Oldtimer would be given a bit of raw sugarcane alcohol. He built his own house single-handedly and did much carpentry work in the rebuilding of Jaguar's own house and storage area after these had been inadvertently destroyed by fire. At times he would be called on to operate Jaguar's chainsaw, when his followers were clearing a garden. While an industrious worker, his knowledge of motors was limited. To make up this deficit, Jaguar began casting about to add to his "foreign" workforce.

An ideal solution seemed to be found in the person of a scintillatingly intelligent young black man who worked as a laborer for a logging company based in Tucumã. Whereas, Oldtimer had fled poverty in the northeast, "Big Black" had sought out the Amazonian frontier by traveling away from the cattle country of the central state of Goiás where his brothers and father were employed as farmhands. He was "loaned" to Jaguar by the logging firm, and came to live in the Bakajá village. He was very popular and often worked alongside Jaguar's workers, and his energy, vitality, and good humor were highly valued. Noting his linguistic facility, curiosity, and openmindedness, Xikrin began sharing their insights into their culture and their opinions with him. Big Black rapidly became a popular fixture in collective work parties in which he operated canoe and chainsaw motors. After approximately six months, however, he left to resume work at the logging camp. In the interval, Jaguar was promised another laborer who would also help with cooking.

Superficially, the presence of Oldtimer and Big Black did not change many aspects of village life. Nonetheless, in many ways their presence helped to bolster Jaguar's power. When they worked, they answered directly to Jaguar. Normally, a Xikrin work party engages in give-and-take and collectively reaches a consensual decision regarding the right amount of work to do, taking into account the difficulty of the job at hand and the participants' frame of mind and energy level. While sponsored by others, collective work is very much an affair deriving from group consensus rather than a leader's ability to command. Having his own personal workers also exacerbated the material inequality between Jaguar and everyone else. Finally, the presence of these outsiders was seen as a token of chiefly influence with extractivists and other foreigners. That their own chief could attract and retain Brazilians to work for him helped prove the influence Jaguar enjoyed with powerful outsiders. Given the precariousness of their situation, non-Kayapó laborers for the chief held no moral claims to his assistance and so were only a negligible drain on his resources.

In addition to the workers in the village, the Xikrin cultivated the idea that they employed two men who looked after their interests in Tucumã with the logging companies. These men, one of whom was married to a Kuruaya Indian woman, had worked with timber companies on other Kayapó reservations. They were supposed to oversee needed purchases and maintain communication between the logging firm and the Xikrin. In return, they were to receive a small percentage of logging profits. In reality, during the 1994–95 period, when these men were "employed" by the Xikrin, they were simultaneously working for the loggers as their "Indian agents." One of these men boasted to me that he had been overseeing timber operations on Kayapó reservations since 1986 and had never yet been kicked out of a reservation. Upon their arrival in the village, Jaguar and the other chiefs would make a big show of closeting themselves with their logging representatives so as to debrief them of the latest events.

So far we have examined how Jaguar used his position to attract native village retainers, who worked with him in preference to their own household groups, and outsiders, who worked as field and domestic labor, ostensibly in return for pay. There is a third class of people who in some sense are intermediate between these other two, namely persons of indigenous origin who fluently speak both Xikrin and Portuguese. One such man is a longtime Bakajá resident, having come from his native Gavião village in the mid-1970s. He already boasts several grandchildren in the village and, although only still a strapping mid-forty-year-old, is considered part of the older men's age grade by virtue of his grandchildren. At age fourteen he was sent by his chief to mission school in the city of Belém. He attended for several years and learned how to read and write, and he gained some knowledge of the strange ways of white society. Marco's position among the Xikrin is hardly unique, since many Gê-speaking groups have outsiders who have been incorporated into the village, learned the language, and acquired a whole set of kin relations. What *does* differentiate Marco is that his knowledge of the outside world makes him invaluable as a translator, traveling companion for Jaguar, and, in past times, an emissary to mining camps. He has used this position to acquire privileges—the cement floor of his house and a stereo system, for example. Nonetheless, these privileges are gained at the cost of subservience to Jaguar.

Marco complains that he is on call to lend all kinds of assistance to Jaguar but has no freedom. In fact, Jaguar has threatened that if he ever leaves the village without his permission, he will not be allowed back to take up residence with his wife, children, and grandchildren. Marco's lot is not always comfortable, since commoners have dubbed him, in imitation of Brazilian organizations, a "secretary" of the chief. Marco is thus neither fish nor fowl. He does not enjoy the confidence of commoners, or even of other chiefs, who say that he is very stingy with his knowledge of Brazilian ways. They protest that he has never taught anyone to read or write, although he is fully literate himself. Also, he can never assume full rank as a chief. This limitation is not a result of his foreign birth but of the low regard in which he is held by many of the commoners as well as the determination of Jaguar to maintain him as an aide-de-camp.

The "Little Backwoodsman" falls roughly into the same category as Marco. He is a mestizo, borne of a non-Indian mother and a Kayapó father. He speaks Kayapó fluently and has lived on a number of different Kayapó reservations. Many Xikrin commoners say that he was expelled from these because he raised the ire of chiefs who had suspicions of his contriving to sell reservation resources to extractivists for his own benefit. Such rumors would never have reached me if they had not been repeated by Xikrin commoners at Bakajá, indicating that his integration into the village was still viewed with suspicion. Gossip has it that he has stashed away a considerable sum in some unknown location and is seeking to add to this at the expense of the village. Other villagers, however, seemed to accept him as an adopted relative, and Little Backwoodsman is careful to favor his adopted relatives with presents. He married a Xikrin teenager while she lived with her family at Trincheira and accompanied her family upon their return migration to the Bakajá village. He had quickly become a favorite of Jaguar, who not only adopted him as a name-receiver (in distinction to Marco, whom he classified as "brother-in-law"), but lavished him with gifts, such as a stereo, a canoe motor, and firearms, far beyond anything ever received by Jaguar's other real or adopted kin relations.

Little Backwoodsman had tastes quite different from other villagers. A table in his house prominently displayed shampoos, conditioners, and soaps in an assortment that called to mind a suburban bathroom rather than a straw-thatched jungle hut. He had strung his house with tiny Christmas lights, wore prescription glasses when ill, and boasted a mammoth stereo system. Two suitcases full of new clothes also attested to his relative opulence. The survey revealed that he did stockpile some food items and he used the promise of distribution of goods to raise a work party of men to help him clear an area for his garden in 1995.

Little Backwoodsman was skilled in mediating encounters between loggers and miners. I myself heard him negotiate the amount chiefs would receive in spending money during a weekend trip to the town of Tucumã. He had many opportunities to enrich himself at the expense of both sides of these cross-cultural transactions, as evidenced by a chainsaw he had received from one of the logging firms. As a cross-cultural mediator, he seemed to revel in his role as teacher and, when fancy struck him, would spontaneously launch into his interpretations of the cultural basis of Xikrin behavior and beliefs. For whatever reason, he regarded the FUNAI as an adversary and succeeded in calling the honesty of local FUNAI employees into question so that they were ordered off the reservation by Jaguar.

Both Marco and Little Backwoodsman, along with all of the underchiefs—and unlike Jaguar—engaged in a full range of subsistence activities. Although Little Backwoodsman supplemented his narrow range of kin relations by offering payment in exchange for garden help, he had to hunt and fish regularly to keep his family supplied with protein. Having his own canoe motor and chainsaw, however, made his chores easier and he did not labor together with other men in collective gardening work or other chores, besides hunting.

Marco, on the other hand, relied on the work of his extended household, including sons and sons-in-laws, and was a habitué of collective gardening work. Being illiterate and knowing little about Brazilian society, Jaguar depended greatly on the assistance of his "secretaries." By favoring one over the other and keeping them in a state of competition with one another he received a full range of opinion and prevented them from pooling forces to strike deals to their own advantage. Jaguar kept both men closely tied to him by acting as concerned patrician and stern disciplinarian, alternating offers of prestigious imported items and party junkets into town with threats of expulsion from the reservation. In addition, their distance from commoners, by virtue of their material acquisitions and relatively few kinship ties, and the fact that they were not held highly in the opinion of most commoners, meant that they were in a poor position to attempt to usurp Jaguar's status as the primary chief.

In sum, over the past several years Jaguar has steadily acquired a retinue of poor Xikrin, Brazilian peons, and translators who enhance his ability to act as a redistributive intermediary between extractivist firms and male and female collective organizations. The translators, in particular, compensate for Jaguar's limited experience outside the village and his rudimentary command of Portuguese. Others assist him in procuring and preparing food for the work parties under his sponsorship and, additionally, allow him to extend spontaneous hospitality to kin and followers on a daily basis. His retainers are also essential in keeping him informed of events in the outside world that are pertinent to his dealings with extractivists. Retainers are called on to serve as culture brokers, but always in a subservient role that does not threaten Jaguar's own position. It is worth underlining that first and foremost, he is able to recruit these helpers through generosity with trade goods rather than through mechanisms of coercion. Furthermore, the particular characteristics of extractivist firms, with their access to marginalized Brazilian labor, their lack of interest in possession of land, and their wealth, favor the development of chiefly retinues. A key factor, as well, is the extractivists' ability to use their ties with merchants, pilots, and the like so as to avoid the use of cash in their transactions with Xikrin who are straitjacketed into relationships with extractivists through the coercive use of credit, while simultaneously excluded from a cash economy that would allow them to make other decisions regarding suppliers of trade goods, hired labor, and markets for the products of extractivism. When extractivism is illegal, as it was after the moratorium placed on mahogany exports in July 1996, extractivists succeed in making chiefs co-conspirators against government regulation and intervention in the often destructive activities of the industry.[2]

The chief's ability to garner goods for himself has made an appreciable difference in the overall configuration of village social relations. The trend, at present, is for material inequality to become more pronounced because Jaguar "reinvests" his goods in relations that will help him amass more goods and reinforce his role as the primary redistributor of manufactured goods in the village. Personal retinues who owe their primary loyalty to Jaguar independently of their participation in men's clubs, age grades, or domestic groups constitute a new dimension of social organization and a significant factor in village politics. Personal retainers have an interest in the maintenance of a redistributional role of a particular person rather than a particular office. The result may well be an increase of the personal authority of chiefs as they become less constrained by the traditional expectations associated with age grade and men's club leadership.

Jaguar's considerable personal acumen aids him in his assessment of personal character and helps him weigh the consequences of the almost Machiavellean maneuvers he has used to enhance his influence and prevent any significant challenges to his authority. Nonetheless, as we will see in Chapter 10, there are many reactions to inequality evident among commoners. Some of the complexities involved in acquiring retainers can be glimpsed through the misadventures of one of Jaguar's rivals for the chieftaincy.

Observing Jaguar's success, Bep Pruin also sought to recruit an outside ally who would assist him as a culture broker. Unfortunately, not blessed with Jaguar's superior judgment, he ended up badly compromised. Bep Pruin was receptive to Little Backwoodsman's half-brother's marriage to a seventeen-year-old girl from his household, the daughter of his wife's widowed sister. He discovered only afterward that the stranger under his roof was a fugitive from Brazilian justice, who was thus nullified as an asset in any cross-cultural negotiations in Brazilian towns, being subject to immediate arrest. Nevertheless, he slipped into nearby towns on occasion, and he contracted a venereal disease that he passed to his new wife. Thus the health of Bep Pruin's classificatory daughter and grandchildren was put at risk. Moreover, Bep Pruin's new household member has a badly deformed hand, which makes him less than ideal as a gardener or a hunter.

In short, rather than obtain a capable dependent who could assist him in dealings with extractivists and in this manner help him consolidate a following within the village, Bep Pruin acquired a host of problems and concerns that will make it more difficult for him to be an effective chief.

One possible misconception regarding the chiefly exercise of power is of significance at this point. It may seem that chiefs are primarily motivated by personal ambition to obtain trade goods and influence and in the process raise themselves above their fellows. Conversations with chiefs belie this notion. All chiefs express ambivalence about the office, and almost all, except for Jaguar, have threatened to step down at one time or another, particularly in the face of what they see as a lack of appreciation expressed by followers. Actually, the option of renouncing the office is seen as an alternative to being thrown out *(bōm kumē)* if one is unsuccessful at obtaining trade goods or if one "divides them poorly" *(mỹja angàrà punu)* among followers. Chiefs experience shame *(piaàm)* when they are not able to meet the expectations of followers they have known their entire lives. They also know that sometimes the needs of their own kinsfolk will be slighted in order to pass goods along to political allies. Moreover, chiefs have constantly to deal with outsiders *(kubēn)*, as part of their office, even if they find doing so tiring or distasteful. Finally, we have already seen that chiefs field constant demands for goods and that the task of remaining generous *(o djuwa mêj)* at all times can be tiring.

In large part the strain felt by chiefs is a reflection of the fact that they still participate in the same moral economy proper to the kinship realm. They share the same obligations toward kin and other villagers as any other Xikrin, yet in contrast with the average villager, they have responsibilities for acquiring trade goods and are beholden to a large number of followers and their families. In their dealings with outsiders, chiefs are constantly pushed to assume a greater influence over the behavior and loyalty of their followers. Both the FUNAI and extractivists prefer "strong" leaders for obvious reasons, since they facilitate administration and control.

While the amount of influence a chief can exercise within the village remains limited, similar limitations do not exist within Brazilian society, where gross inequalities on the basis of wealth are accepted and even glorified. In other Kayapó villages, some leaders, on acquiring cash from extractivists, have set themselves up in houses in the frontier towns of Redenção or Tucumã, where they enjoy cars, airplanes, servants, and the lifestyle of wealthy Brazilian regionals. These chiefs have begun to spend increasing amounts of time away from their villages, stressing their role as *representatives* of their villages within larger Brazilian society (Turner 1995, 106). The opportunities afforded them as representatives within a foreign society allow them to enjoy the privileges of wealth to a degree not possible in a Kayapó community in which the moral imperatives of kinship continue to reign unchallenged. In short, many privileges of the chieftainship, if they are to exist as a compensation for withstanding the pressures of the office, must be exercised outside of the village in nearby Brazilian towns.

Nonetheless, Xikrin chiefs do not rise to chiefly status or remain there on the basis of personal ambition alone. Xikrin society demands coordination and leadership, not only to procure trade goods but to coordinate and organize public activities both ritual and secular. Most but not all chiefs begin their careers as young gourd-rattle leaders *(ngôkonbàri)*. As young unmarried men, they were encouraged to assume leadership of their age cohort and, through persuasion and personal example, to animate others to work well at whatever task was indicated. Upon marriage, gourd-rattle leaders give up their office, but may be "drafted" later into a leadership role. While they must be popular enough with a number of people to assemble a group of workers *(meanhõapêj)*, chiefs must be designated by senior chiefs. Elder chiefs have an interest in choosing hard-working, popular junior chiefs who are not likely to openly oppose their authority.

There is always pressure on young men to become leaders, and this pressure is not easily dismissed since elders exercise almost total influence over how one fits in and is accepted within a small enclosed community. On the other hand, popular leaders are encouraged to become chiefs because it is thought that they will be successful in obtaining trade goods and honorable in their redistribution. It is not easy to ignore public opinion within the confines of a village. Commoners feel they have a stake in a functioning chieftaincy and press for those among them with leadership qualities to become chiefs, for without them they run the risk of receiving no trade goods. Chiefs risk censure and experience shame by not living up to the expectations of their followers, but capable men who evade the role of chief also risk popular disapproval. Once a man enters into the game of chieftainship, he has to play to win, that is, to function effectively in this capacity. However, even success is ambivalent, since it incites spontaneous resentment against a glaring material inequality for which there is no cultural precedent or justification. Despite the association between material gain and chiefly position, a stockpile of goods alone would never make a man a chief.

THE MAINTENANCE OF MEDIATING POWER

As in other communities assailed by hostile outside forces that seek access to resources under the control of community members, the maintenance of community boundaries is an important defensive strategy (Wolf 1957). The creation of a closed corporate social structure erects a defense against destruction of the community and ensures a particular role for the chief. The fashioning of a corporate identity does not mean the absence of movement in and out of the community, as Jaguar's buildup of a retinue illustrates. Instead the boundaries around Xikrin society alert us to the fact that control over the movement of people and goods across these boundaries comprises part of the exercise of power within Xikrin society. We must briefly consider how chiefs act to preserve the village and the reservation as a corporate enclave. This entails repelling outsiders but also controlling the movement of insiders.

In the first place, chiefs lead men of the village to preserve whenever possible the integrity of reservation boundaries. The threat of expulsion by painted warriors is a powerful deterrent against landless peasants seeking to occupy land. It seems to be less of a deterrent to large ranchers and others who have commonly employed private guns against Indians and peasants. Xikrin chiefs have sought to negotiate with the Liberato and Silva ranching consortium that threatens incursions into the eastern portion of their reservation. However, behind these negotiations lies the threat of collective force.

If the collective action of Xikrin warriors succeeds in keeping people out of the reservation, the difficulties of transportation help to keep Xikrin villagers within the reservation. Overland routes not only require weeks of foot travel through the forest, but reservations are now bordered by potentially hostile populations—squatters, *agrovilas,* and cattle ranchers—whose presence tends to inhibit seepage of Indians out of the reservation. We have seen how chiefs control most of the outboard motors and fuel supplies needed for long-distance river travel. Difficulties in reaching the nearest town are considerable, due to the isolation of the village, and require either numerous days of motorized water travel or expensive air transportation. The latter is also scarce and plane passengers are screened by chiefs. Of course, collusion between miners, loggers, the FUNAI who own the planes, and chiefs are necessary to preserve this screening authority. Apparently, however, in other Kayapó villages that own airplanes outright, chiefs exercise the right to determine who uses them. Movement in and out of the villages is therefore not free to all.

Although difficult access certainly helps to preserve the productivity of hunting and fishing, to some extent, isolation is not regarded favorably by most young commoners. For them, the ability to get to towns represents a "productive" activity since they may encounter opportunities to acquire desired trade goods. Paradoxically, as shown by the survey results, the misfortune of family illness is a principal means through which commoners get access to trade goods in nearby towns, as they accompany their close kin for medical treatment. Although com-

Figure 8. Adult men engage in target practice on the village plaza in 1994, as bachelors keep busy rolling green papayas. (Photo by author)

moners are generally confined to a squalid room at the FUNAI-run Indian House, they may succeed in trading some crafts items or otherwise contrive to obtain some desired good.

Approximately a dozen men have worked at one time or another for various logging or mining firms. As previously discussed, on only several occasions did men leave to work on their own initiative. Usually men agree to work outside the reservation only with the permission of a chief, or at his suggestion. In return for their work they receive a small compensation, but most of the income from gold or timber reverts to the chief. Thus, after spending from June to August 1995 at a logging camp within the reservation, three young men from Bakajá claimed they were owed one hundred Brazilian reais (approximately U.S. $100) that they would receive in the form of merchandise ordered from Tucumã by the logging company. It is a stretch to say that these encounters open up widespread opportunities for work away from the village. They do serve to spread hearsay about the outside, including the world of Brazilians and other indigenous communities. In a sense commoners have much more knowledge about the world beyond the village than ever before, but not more access.

Figure 9. Jaguar's followers prepare a makeshift silo in 1985 to store Brazil nuts for eventual shipping to Attamira. (Photo by author)

This explains the enthusiasm of ordinary Xikrin for the construction of a road linking their village with neighboring towns and agrovilas. They reason that movements of people and goods would be more feasible and affordable in trucks or cars than it is presently by air. The trickle of goods that presently are accessible mainly to chiefs might be increased and raise the living standard of everyone. They are also aware that other Kayapó villages have been rebuilt using building supplies such as sawmill lumber, cement, and roofing material, which could only be realistically transported in sufficient quantities for everyone to benefit through ground transport. Sentiment in favor of a road does not reflect a desire to merge with Brazilian society but to expand commoner access to manufactured goods by making a chiefly monopoly more difficult to maintain. As the notion of corporate community implies, by controlling movements in and out of the community, chiefs also strengthen themselves politically—especially when community sentiment for enforced corporateness remains high.

9 IN THE MAELSTROM OF EXTRACTIVISM

Both the extractive industries and the collective anxiety of commoners contribute new complexity to the chiefly role of coordinator of collective activities. Succession to chiefly office has become a conflict-ridden and uncertain process. Powerful logging and mining interests act, where possible, to pit indigenous peoples against the FUNAI and the government. Furthermore, in the current circumstances, Xikrin realize that they must attempt to set limits on their contacts with wider Brazilian society as the settlements encroach on reservation territory. While struggling to rebuff invaders, they also seek certain kinds of connections—above all a road—between their village and neighboring Brazilian settlements.

In short, although the frontier remains physically distant and normally unseen, it has left its imprint. The latest wave of extractivism within reservation boundaries represents a new stage that in some qualitative sense must result in a break with the past, if only because there are no more exits: Whatever solutions reached must be within the context of a reservation encircled by "development" that includes groups of social actors each with distinct interests.

At the time of my first field stay in 1984, logging was practically unknown, and certainly mahogany was not anything like the "green gold" it was to become only a short time later. The 1981 questionnaire of the Ecumenical Center for Documentation and Information (CEDI), widely circulated in indigenous areas, does not even mention "logging" among the activities that might undermine the viability of reservations. Not until the mid-1980s does logging take its place along with colonization schemes, cattle ranching, mining, road building, and the construction of hydroelectric dams as a real threat to indigenous lands. The expansion of the timber industry vividly shows the mammoth power of the extractive industries in the Amazon. During the ascension phase, their influence is so extensive as to draw other regional actors into their orbit, either willingly or unwillingly. Their power to undermine the basis of preexisting forms of social organization is only matched by the rapidity with which they undermine their own basis for existence by overharvesting the natural resources on which they depend. The greater the hold they command and the more rapid their expansion, the more rapid their evanescence. Through no choice of their own, the Bakajá Xikrin were drawn into the vortex of the timber rush at a crucial moment in their recent history. Rather than detail an exhaustive laundry list of each of the relevant firms and contacts, this chapter focuses on key events that throw light on the dilemmas forced on the Xikrin by the ubiquitous pressures of extractivism.

The manner in which the Xikrin confronted the invasion of loggers onto their reservation owed a good deal to the previous arrangements struck with gold prospectors operating along reservation borders northeast of the village during the 1980s. Gold prospecting has a long history in the area of the Xingu/Bakajá, it had begun at least by the end of the last century (Umbuzeiro n.d.). However, in the 1980s prospecting activities in the area of the Bakajá reservation expanded greatly with the discovery of placer gold deposits along the Manezão stream. Several Xikrin had made their way to the *garimpo do Joel* at the headwaters of the Bakajá around 1979 where they learned the rudiments of mining work. By 1985 some of these same men had spent time at the Manezão site. Beginning in 1986, under the impetus of a FUNAI employee posted to the Bakajá village, the Xikrin began to receive payments from miners, sporadically at first and later on a regular basis. Between 1987 and 1989, the nongovernmental organization CEDI (1991, 325) reports that the Xikrin entered into a succession of agreements with miners, as mine ownership changed hands rapidly. At one point, after a new owner failed to continue payments, Xikrin invaded the mining encampment, and shortly afterward, agreed-on payments resumed.

Begining in 1985, the village also began to receive some aid from the Vale do Rio Doce Company (CVRD), which was engaged in the colossal ore export project in the Carajás range to the south of the reservation. This aid was not extensive and did not change village life to any extent. Vidal (1985) indicates that CVRD targeted U.S. $1,000 per month for the Xikrin, including projected needs for food, air travel, ammunition, gasoline, and machine repairs. She notes that the administration in Altamira was using this money to pay FUNAI debts and suggested withholding part for future use. Although the Xikrin village seemed to get a small portion of the budgeted funds, CRVD financial assistance helped to establish a new vocabulary for engagement with the outside world.

In the reports of FUNAI officials and anthropologists consulting with the CVRD, the "development project" was born, and *projeto* quickly made its way into the Xikrin vocabulary. Although there was never any creative elaboration of any real "projects," the language of development was eagerly seized on by all parties as a term around which multiparty agreements could be conducted. By way of example, we can see how the hyperdevelopmentalist spirit of the times is reflected in an accord signed by Xikrin leaders and gold prospectors in which development rhetoric is loosely wedded to payments in return for "harmonious" relations.

Among both gold prospectors and Xikrin, there is no doubt that the term *development* served as a screen for the more readily intelligible and enforceable terms of "no payoffs, no peace." Agreements with miners and loggers are often of dubious legality, and the actual process of "courtship" and haggling between Indians and extractivists rarely occurs in the presence of third parties. However, there does exist a limited number of instances in which agreements or contracts were actually drawn up and these give a fascinating glimpse into such transactions— from the point of view of the extractivists, of course, since the documents are ponderously written in legal-sounding Portuguese. For example, consideration II of the agreement between prospector representative Raimundo Nonato Alves and the Xikrin (Anonymous 1990), which purports to pave the way for realizing "projects of community development," reads "that the [Xikrin] community has aspirations of well-being and social development," and consideration III continues, "that the community and miners intend during the period of the development of the works in the area of Projeto Cajazeiras [gold mine] to create and maintain relations of fraternal, pacific and respectful coexistence, collaboration and mutual support." Cutting through the jargon the agreement's bottom line consists of monthly payments of two hundred grams of gold (or 6.43 ounces worth approximately U.S. $2,500 at official 1990 rates, less at local unofficial rates) to the Xikrin, along with one flight a month between the Xikrin village and the outside world as well as a promise on the part of the miners to observe the reservation boundaries. In return the Xikrin agree to not press for possession of the disputed gold mining area on their reservation's edge or to disrupt mining activities. According to stipulations, FUNAI was to be present at any meeting between Xikrin and prospectors.

These conditions appear to have been more or less standard terms agreed to between chiefs and miners since late 1986 when Xikrin were to receive Cr 20,000 per month (approximately U.S. $1,426 at November 1986 rates) from mine operator Nelson Wilson Bahr (Parise et al. 1986). CEDI (1991, 325) reports that in December 1989, the Xikrin were receiving a monthly payment of appoximately U.S. $472 (U.S. $209 at black market exchange rates) from the wildcat miners who had taken over the area.

Shortly after the signing of the 1990 agreement, tensions flared between rival miners, and the mining leaders who had been signatories were either killed or run off. Violence and the decrease of gold yields caused near anarchy along Manezão, which signaled by 1992 the breakdown of the agreement between the Xikrin and the miners (Vidal 1992a). In their agreements with mahogany loggers, the Xikrin sought to reinstitute the same sort of stable monthly payments they had received from miners. They also continued to use the language of development by portraying such payments as support for chiefly sponsored projetos.

Despite protestations that they were concerned primarily with the integrity of reservation boundaries and thus opposed illegal logging, FUNAI policy also pushed the Xikrin into the arms of loggers. To maximize its ability to administer to the needs of the different Indian peoples under its authority, the FUNAI since the mid-1980s has instituted a de facto system of triage. Resources are channeled to people in some indigenous areas while others, such as the Xikrin, thought to be more acculturated and more susceptible to the influence of outsiders, are left to find their own way by entering into agreements with local extractive entrepreneurs. Only monies from programs sponsored by outside businesses and administered on a regional level, such as the Body Shop or the Companhia Vale do Rio Doce, continued to be directed toward the Xikrin. The CVRD money has also been spent on projects that are not perceived by the community as of immediate significance, such as the erection of a new dispensary in 1995. While the dispensary and the Body Shop showers were being built with donated cash, the Xikrin were expressing an urgent need for a teacher so that basic reading and mathematics could be learned.

When FUNAI has been lax in providing for the needs of the community under their charge, loggers and gold miners have been quick to step into the breach, as noted in Chapter 6. In a written plea for funds from the CVRD, the head of the Bakajá Indian Post admitted that "The FUNAI has done little or nothing for this group since 1985" (Ventura 1991). Without competition from the FUNAI, loggers (and miners and others) had only to supply the basic medical care and capital goods needed for subsistence production in order to command access to the natural resources located on the Indian reserve. That is, the rise of logging activity was not the only reason for the increased Indian involvement in logging. What made their pressure irresistible was the concurrent decline in political and economic weight of FUNAI. Without the ability to protect the integrity of reservations under its administration and the financial means to ensure even the health and requirements of basic subsistence, the FUNAI came to occupy a very curious place in the local political economy, acting essentially as a broker between powerful interests in government agencies and the private sector. According the the Xikrin, the FUNAI head in Altamira often flew in to preside over monthly payments of the gold miners to the Indians.

Xikrin acceptance of logging may also be attributed to their understanding of the experience of other Kayapó villages in the earlier phase of the mahogany boom as it moved northward from southern Pará. The mid-1980s was the beginning of a period of prosperity for the Kayapó community of Kikretūm, and this prosperity was to have tremendous influence on the future course of the Xikrin settlements to the north. During the mid-1970s, in the wake of the founding of the town of Tucumã as a privately planned community (Moran 1990), sawmills sprang up in the region. By the mid-1980s, Tucumã's proximity to both Kikretūm and the Xikrin reserve at Cateté made it a common meeting place for members of the two Indian communities. With the rise of the timber industry and nearby gold prospecting, and the influx caused by large-scale government-sponsored development in the Carajás range, Tucumã became a burgeoning frontier settlement. While contemporary Bakajá Xikrin became familiar with the town only in the late 1980s, it was already a part of their traditional orbit. Late in the nineteenth century, the site of the present-day town was a Xikrin settlement called Roiti djam (Tucum grove) after the same Tucum palm that gave the contemporary town its name (see Chapter 2). By the mid-1980s Kikretūm leader Pombo was profiting from both mahogany and gold. T-shirts imprinted "Souvenir from Garimpo Rio Branco, Colonel Pombo, Manager" were a common sight on Tucumã's dusty, unpaved streets.

The road construction boom in the Amazon undertaken by the federal government in the 1970s and early 1980s made the commercialization of previously inaccessible timber a profitable possibility (Schmink and Wood 1992). As mahogany stands were exhausted in the south of Pará, the center of activity moved to the axis formed by a state highway, PA 279 between the towns of São Félix do Xingu and Xinguara (Verissimo et al. 1995). This road, along which Tucumã was constructed, lies between the vast unified Kayapó reserve to the south and the Cateté reservation to the north. Some 120 kilometers above PA 279 lies the southern borders of the large combined indigenous reserves of Apyterewa, Koatinemo, Ipixuna, and Bakajá-Trincheira. Logging companies have been responsible for constructing roads that branch off from government-built PA 279 and illegally penetrate indigenous reservations. Verissimo and coauthors (1995) estimate that by the time of their field research in 1992 approximately three thousand kilometers of such roads have been built by loggers. Along these roads colonist families and even larger groups of ranchers were able to spread

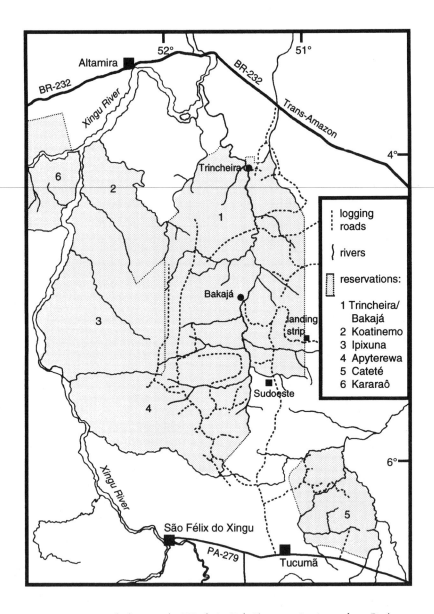

Map 3. Logging roads threaten the Trincheira-Bakajá reservation in southern Pará. (Ann Peters, based on CEDI 1993, Verissimo, et al., 1995, and author's interviews)

out in search of available land. Of the settlers interviewed by Verissimo, most had come from the central west or northeastern region of Brazil and none were from the Amazon itself.

Once an area has been logged out, subsequent colonization and use of land for pasturage and agriculture is as much a threat to the future ecological viability of the region as logging itself, which, while destructive of particular species, is quite transitory. Snook (1993) points out that the process of eliminating the mahogany tree population is rapid because of the large machinery currently available for road building. While loggers worked for over four hundred years before extracting the available mahogany from a band sixty kilometers wide in the Yucatan pennisula in Mexico, the current pace of road construction in Pará can accomplish a comparable harvest in a matter of months. The greatest danger to both the ecosystem and the Xikrin lies in the road-building capabilities provided by new industrial technology.

One of the innovations developed by Kayapó communities to the south of PA 279 are sentry posts located along the reserve borders to prevent illegal incursions. In contrast, the combined demarcated reservation lands lying above PA 279 between the Xingu and Bakajá Rivers, where sentry posts have not built, may be entered with impunity. As it stands now, the demarcation of borders, without adequate safeguards, serves mainly as a legal justification for Indian groups that want to attempt to frighten off, fight, or otherwise remove illegal squatters. The presence of a demarcated reserve can serve as a legal shield in the face of any subsequent retaliation.

The companies that extract timber move from one Indian reserve to another, searching for new sources of mahogany as old ones become depleted. For this reason, promises offered by loggers to improve living conditions among the Xikrin were very effective; the Bakajá Xikrin believed they had a chance to adopt some of the advantages enjoyed by the larger Kayapó villages at Cateté and Kikretūm that had more experience dealing with Brazilian society and longer periods of contact. During the time that Kikretūm Kayapó village was enjoying its period of prosperity, for example, loggers had used equipment and workers to plant a huge garden and open a cattle pasture for use by the Indians. Additionally, they constructed roads and bridges to haul wood from the reserve. Bakajá Xikrin also point out that the wattle-and-daub huts of the Cateté Xikrin have been entirely replaced by concrete and cinder block constructions with aid supplied by CVRD and logging interests.

While the decline of gold payments, FUNAI omissions, and the experiences of other Kayapó with the mahogany trade made conditions ripe for the timber companies, Xikrin still may have rejected even temporary occupation of their reservation. Instead, they were presented with a fait accompli after logging companies secretly invaded Xikrin territory. Late in 1988 loggers who had invaded the northern part of the reservation were halted by residents of the Trincheira village. From that point on, the reservation was subject to unrelenting pressure from logging interests.

In June 1989, noting a steady flow of air traffic in a distant part of the reservation, men of the Bakajá village were sent to reconnoiter the area. They discovered areas of cleared forest, logs stacked on the ground, and workers busily entering the reserve from an area in which a gold mine had previously been established. Xikrin confronted workers on the site and blockaded the recently constructed dirt road into the reserve. The appearance of a group of young Indians adorned for war, faces painted and arms at ready, sent a truckload of workers fleeing from the site. Realizing that the destruction was the work of someone of influence, the Xikrin set out to discover the organization behind the invasion. Shortly thereafter, a delegation from the village, consisting of Xikrin chiefs and their translators, paid a call to the offices of Perachi Exporting Limited in Tucumã. The head of the company, Idacir Perachi, offered an immediate payoff, but, shortly thereafter, personally flew to the Xikrin village in order to negotiate the removal of the timber that had already been felled, as the removal continued to be blocked by the Xikrin. The resulting agreement foresaw the removal of approximately 1,500 cubic meters of mahogany before the onset of the rainy season. The price was set by the company in terms of BTNs, or Bonus do Tesouro Nacional, a mechanism developed by the Brazilian Central Bank to peg exchange rates to the U.S. dollar. Trees with a circumference of less than 180 centimeters were to be sold at one half the price of the established rate of 4.6465 BTN/cubic meters (Anonymous 1989).

The money to be paid after the measurement and shipment of each lot of 200 cubic meters was to be deposited in the Banco do Brasil agency in Altamira where it was to be used for the "maintenance of aid, health, quality of life improvements, water and waste infrastructure and the equipping of the Bakajá Indian Post and its members, according to the orientation and leadership of the signatories to this contract, in common agreement" (Anonymous 1989).

Under the terms of the contract, the company was forbidden to fell any new trees or to bring timber workers to the Bakajá settlement (ibid.). As drawn up by the company, the contract makes the grudging admission that the sale of the timber already on the ground is being negotiated "since it has already been seized by the Xikrin." The predatory attitude of the logging companies is evident in their treatment of exportable hardwoods as a "free" resource; if the Xikrin had not taken any action, the timber would simply have been removed without payment.

For several months, until the start of the rainy season, the Xikrin reaped the benefits of the agreement—goods were delivered by small airplane on a regular basis. The following year, Perachi did not seek to extend the contract, presumably because the small quantity of remaining timber rendered irrelevant the clause that opened the door to negotiate new terms for the upcoming season.

Instead, Perachi moved on to new and lucrative areas. Not coincidentally some of these happened to be in other Indian reserves neighboring Bakajá, such as Apyterewa, Ipixuna, and Koatinemo (CEDI 1993, 24–25). While the Xikrin had received some indemnity for the Perachi invasion of the eastern border of the reserve, the familiar air traffic and echoes of heavy machinery were soon heard in the southern and western parts of the reserve. Once again, Perachi had "inadvertently" invaded Xikrin lands and once again was forced to withdraw. This did not mean, however, that Perachi folded up shop. In subsequent years, filled with the sense of entitlement typical of the local elite, he continued the covert removal of mahogany from various Indian reserves in the area. Shortly thereafter he even entered into an agreement with the Cateté Xikrin to extract mahogany from the Cateté reserve some two hundred kilometers southeast of Bakajá (CEDI 1993, 13).

Mahogany does not grow in pure stands but is interspersed with other forest trees. The usual logging company procedure in lands that are uncharted is to send scouts through the area to locate harvestable trees. Each scout labels the tree with his own distinctive mark and is paid between two and three dollars for each "find." Once a tree is located, scouts take care to leave a noticable trail *(picada)* so that the company workers can find it again. Although termed a *trail,* the fast-moving scouts do the minimum possible to mark its presence, which is only indicated by an occasional sapling felled by machete or a twig broken off at waist level. If too many seasons pass after scouting, it is necessary to reidentify trees and mark new trails.

With some idea of the number and size of trees in a particular area, loggers can move to the next phase, which consists of building an "esplanade." This is the grandiose name given to the main road along which trucks and supplies will run. The idea is to construct this road in such a way as to minimize the length of connecting feeder roads to individual trees. Individual trees are dragged or skidded along such feeder roads whence they can be stockpiled, measured, and shipped out of the area. Large industrial machinery is used to make the road, and the booming whine of tractors and bulldozers as they strain against their heavy loads resounds over miles of forest. In a place without phones, automobiles, or the sounds of machinery, the rise and fall of working motors is alternately threatening and oddly hypnotic. Because it is seasonal, work is frantic. The intense activity of the dry season is offset by complete idleness during the wet season, when any felled timber lies until the next season.

This process of road construction cannot go unnoticed, particularly by air. Moreover, logging operations involve setting up an encampment, often with its own dirt runway for small planes, and in a landscape without machinery, industrial-size motors resound for miles. Why then does illegal logging continue? Part of the reason lies in the technicalities required to convict an offender, part lies in the domination of the elites within the extractive economies of the Amazonian frontier, and part, in some cases, lies in the connivance of Indian peoples. A complete answer would take us far from the subject of this book, but in broad outline such a question tells us much about the world within which the Xikrin must manuever to assure their subsistence.

The power of the wealthy in a land where everyone—including it must be said, local government agencies—is impoverished, is hard to overestimate. They retain what amounts to a practical monopoly on means of communication and transportation in the area. Through their political influence elites ensure that local government agencies that could exercise a restraining influence are kept underfunded and essentially irrelevant. In the fall of 1995, for example, faced with a steady stream of intransigent invaders in open defiance of clearly demarcated reserve borders, Xikrin impounded a truck, some chainsaws, and some other equipment. As might be expected, this created quite a bit of tension, and there were threats of reprisals on both sides. The response of the Brazilian Indian Agency, responsible for the integrity of reserve borders, was to send a team, composed of an advisor to the Ministry of Justice, two FUNAI officials, and a single federal police agent to collect information on the incident. With no resources budgeted for transportation, unable to rent an airplane or even a car to view the locale from which colonists had been surging into the Xikrin reserve, the investigation team was dependent on local officials for transportation, lodging, and access! All of these officials, the team noted in their subsequent report, were actively agitating against the demarcation of Indian lands (Cruvinel 1995). Thus local elite control of access and communication make the very reporting of legal violations and the establishment of basic facts largely dependent on their cooperation.

According to a FUNAI official in Altamira, neither the FUNAI nor the federal police have the authority to arrest illegal loggers and impound their equipment. This authority rests with the Brazilian Institute for the Environment and Renewable Natural Resources (IBAMA), which exercises duties roughly belonging to the National Park Service, Forestry Service, and the Environmental Protection Agency in the United States. To compound matters, arrests must be made in flagrante delicto and the FUNAI, IBAMA, and federal police must coordinate their actions when the illegal logging occurs on Indian land. Once the equipment is impounded, the owner is permitted to retrieve it by paying a sum *(fiança)*, guaranteeing his appearance in court. Since the powerful are never convicted, heavy equipment is simply removed to another area, where it is immediately put to work opening more roads and felling more trees. In one case, after his apprehension for illegally logging in the Apyterewa Reserve, one logger had the arrogance to suggest that he should bill FUNAI for the improvements—the roads and clearings—he had made while in the area (Marques, personal communication)!

In the small towns of southern Pará, illegal loggers take their place among the elite owners of mining companies and large cattle ranchers. They frequent the town solemnities and social clubs. Their public cordiality is matched by the ruthless control they exercise over their workforce and their willingness to hire gunslingers to fend off threats to their domain, be they landless peasant squatters, rubber tappers, Brazil nut gatherers, or Indians. For many, their operations in the Amazon represent only part of their total financial holdings (Verissimo et al. 1995). Much of the timber trade is directed by men with experience in the southern part of Brazil who were lured by the new export regulations and financial incentives offered during the 1980s by the Brazilian government (Browder 1987).

After Perachi ceased to provide more goods, the Xikrin saw the writing on the wall. The clarity with which they assessed their options was not due to any sophisticated understanding of business procedure or government policies but was based on their experience of the boom-bust economy of the region—with which they were intimately familiar. It was clear that the area around their reserve was being targeted for mahogany extraction by numerous companies. The entrance of loggers coincided with a decline and eventual halt to payments from the gold mine at Manezão. To make matters more complicated, Xikrin were aware of the efforts of prominent indigenous rights activists to establish a greatly amplified reservation that would include the splinter settlement of Trincheira and the Bakajá village. Xikrin were fearful that logging would rob their future reservation area of much of its value even before it had been demarcated. The Xikrin were forced to choose between two evils: risk the loss of a needed source of income or collude on the sale of timber and risk compromising the integrity of reservation borders even before their demarcation. This second option also promised to alienate the FUNAI and indigenist rights activists, as well.

The diplomacy involved was daunting because the FUNAI and loggers were in direct conflict in many areas and the Indian Agency would be less likely to support the Xikrin with needed personnel and funds to demarcate the reservation if the Xikrin were collaborating with loggers. In addition, there was the serious problem of land invasion following the opening of the road. Once timber was extracted, logging companies had no further interest in the land. When not serving as infrastructure for a large cattle farm, logging roads often provide means of access for landless peasants to occupy hitherto inaccessible areas. As of this moment, the most serious threat to the Xikrin may not be loggers but the infiltration of landless peasants over the southern border of the reservation along timber roads.

Although the experience with Perachi was short-lived, it gave the Xikrin a taste of the power of loggers and the goods they could provide and, given the events surrounding the reservation, made their future involvement with loggers almost inevitable. The Xikrin decided that they could either wait for their lands to be invaded and risk the theft of more timber or they could approach loggers themselves in the hope of striking a deal that would provide them with benefits not forthcoming from other sources. We must remember that by the time of this decision, the FUNAI had gone for several years without supplying the Xikrin with needed manufactured goods.

Pressure continued to build during 1990 as the eastern border of the reserve was penetrated by a road originating at a neighboring ranch, Old West (Velho Oeste). Old West was a property owned by a man nicknamed Mikuin, who operated as part of an outfit called Liberato e Silva, which in turn was part of a consortium of companies with real estate and cattle interests in the area. A former gold prospector on Indian lands, Mikuin operated a dirt airstrip constructed on the eastern edge of the reserve or actually within reservation borders, depending on the source of one's information. Cruvinel (1995), a FUNAI anthropologist who visited the airstrip, believes that it lies within the boundaries of the Bakajá-Trincheira reservation.

The "Old West" appellation, after the shoot-'em-up image of the North American frontier, served quite well to characterize the regional climate. Old West served as a jumping-off point for gold prospectors, colonists, and adventurers. Lying along the border of the reserve, the airstrip is often rife with rumors about imminent attack by the Xikrin. This works to the benefit of the owners, who pose as friends of the Xikrin in order to terrorize smallholders and squatters. The belief that they can set the "Indians" on opponents within the area acts to deter potential land invasions.

Following the incursions made from the Old West, the logger Angelin Ório, whose base of operations is Tucumã, presented a new threat. Without Xikrin permission he began logging within the proposed reserve and even within the previously demarcated areas close by the Xikrin village. Although new to the Bakajá Xikrin, Angelin was no stranger to Indian reservations or to the Kayapó. He had been extracting mahogany from the Kikretũm Kayapó area since 1983.

Agreements between his company, Industria e Comércio de Lâminas Nossa Senhora da Aparecida Ltda, and Colonel Pombo of Kikretũm were initially authorized by the FUNAI (CEDI 1993, 23; Ventura and Marques 1993, 6). Angelin's firm continued to remove timber from Kikretũm until 1991, around the time he was contacted by the Xikrin.

After consultation among the villagers, chiefs Jaguar, Bep Keiti, and two translators sought out Angelin in his home in order to ask for payment. The idea from the beginning was not to stop logging but to get a fair share for the resources being stolen. With the appearance of the Xikrin at his home, Angelin wined and dined them and together they agreed on a price of U.S. $40 per cubic meter of mahogany. While no longer getting the timber for free, Angelin calculated that the price per cubic meter was still attractive.

For their part, the Xikrin imposed limits within the reservation beyond which no logging was to be undertaken. In this way the village was to be saved from direct exposure to logging employees, and game resources would be conserved over large areas. Xikrin have observed that the noise from the large machinery causes all animals within earshot to flee. In addition to these promises, Angelin also made a commitment to build a road to a traditional fording place along the Bakajá near the Xikrin village. Furthermore (and this was the most attractive aspect for the Xikrin), he agreed to build an entire new village out of modern building materials—cement, cinder blocks, and aluminum roofing. Originally, the offer was only to construct houses for the chiefs. This triggered hostility and resentment toward the chiefs and the logging firm on the part of Xikrin commoners, and it appeared that violence aimed at the loggers and possibly the chiefs was a real possibility. In the end, commoners preferred to have no cinder block houses built than allow chiefs to enjoy this exclusive luxury.

After two years of work within the boundaries of the proposed reserve extension, Angelin withdrew, alleging that pressure from the federal police and the IBAMA environmental authorities made it too risky to continue, particularly in light of the small number of harvestable trees that remained. Needless to say the long-hoped-for modern village was never constructed. The Xikrin remain unconvinced regarding his claim of a timber shortage and believe he simply wanted to avoid the extra expense of building a road directly to the village. Becoming disenchanted with Angelin, some Xikrin stole a few items from his encampment, an action they called "payback stealing" *(amipãjn oawakin)*.

In 1994, after Angelin had retired from the field, the Xikrin still hoped for the construction of a road between their village and nearby Brazilian towns. The logger who stepped forward to make new promises along these lines went by the nickname Panther. Along with his brother, Gemivan, he had been active in wildcat logging in the area for years. While apparently not as well financed as more-established firms such as Perachi and Angelin, he had more highly developed negotiating skills with indigenous communities. For several years he had contracted with the young Xikrin leaders on the Cateté reserve. Without a doubt, his experience in working with indigenous communities gave him advantages over rivals. He was adept at working with the middle men *(gatos)* who actually transported sawed trunks from the reserve to the sawmills in Tucumã. Timber from the Xikrin reserves was channeled to the sawmill owned by Osmar Ferreira, who had direct experience striking deals with Indian leaders, in contravention to existing legislation making logging on Indian reservations illegal.

ROAD CONFRONTATION

Panther entered the field with promises of new houses for all Xikrin. The materials for this large construction project were to be transported along the road he had opened up from Tucumã directly to the Bakajá village. For Xikrin commoners, the roadway held out the possibility for greater equality among Xikrin. Not only would it be possible for everyone to enjoy the (dubious) benefits of cinderblock construction, but a roadway would help break the monopoly on travel and access to trade goods enjoyed by the chief, as detailed in previous chapters. Additionally, Xikrin were learning just how expensive air transportation costs could be and hoped that a road would allow them access to greater quantities of goods. A tactical consideration also argued in favor of road construction between the Xikrin village and the outside world. The Xikrin were aware of the incursions of loggers and landless peasants in the southern portion of the reserve along roads that penetrated the reservation from the direction of Tucumã. This created a situation in which loggers and peasants enjoyed unimpeded access to the reservation with motor transit while the Xikrin were forced to reach these areas on foot, putting them at a severe disadvantage. A roadway extending from the border to the village would allow Xikrin to use the road system to rush warriors to the scene of any confrontation.

Xikrin commoners' hopes were dashed when the FUNAI chose the moment of the inauguration of Panther's road into the village to mobilize a raid on illegal logging activity (cf. Marques et al. 1994, for FUNAI version of events). Two planeloads of federal police and IBAMA officials descended on the village. They impounded the heavy equipment used in building the road and they rounded up Panther. It appeared as though the long years of FUNAI hedging in the face of illegal logging had come to an end. The coordinator of the FUNAI office had gotten funds to overfly the region twelve times in 1992 and four times in 1993 (Marques, personal communication) but did not arrest anybody. Now, however, FUNAI sought to reestablish control over the reservation by expelling Panther and halting illegal timber removal.

Between FUNAI's promise of support in the future when they would find buyers to purchase the timber already on the ground and the concrete accomplishment of Panther's road construction, the Xikrin had ample reason to side with the logger and reject FUNAI's intervention. They surmised that given the FUNAI's record of inaction, even if such promises were made in good faith, a likely scenario would be a painfully long interval between current promises and future action, during which time what timber did remain on the ground would most likely be stolen. They would be left without their modern village, their road would fall into total disrepair, and having accomplished a highly publicized action, FUNAI would, once again, retreat into inactivity. Sentiment against the FUNAI was heightened because the Indian agency intervention seemed to be sabotaging commoners' efforts to achieve greater parity with the chiefs in trade goods. Rightly or wrongly, Panther seemed to represent a chance for every commoner household to reap the benefits of the timber boom, while the FUNAI appeared to be supporting a status quo in which chiefs were necessary as intermediaries and favored as privileged recipients of trade goods. In a brave act of confrontation with the federal police contingent, Xikrin commoners prevented the detention of Panther and sent the FUNAI and federal police planes on their way. Jaguar remained largely on the side during the confrontation.

GARIMPO RAID

Earlier in 1994 Jaguar had not remained so passive during militant confrontation with outsiders. As mentioned previously he had taken the lead in organizing a raid on the Manezão mining operation with the aim of consolidating an alliance with the new owner and also coopting commoner discontent. The owner of the mining company Valley of the Swallows (Vale das Andorinhas) found himself in the uncomfortable position of having invested money in mining rights to an area where he was unable to assume de facto control of operations. Tough, independent wildcat prospectors refused to give up their lucrative prospecting on the mere technicality of paper ownership. A mop-up or police operation was called for, and the Xikrin served as willing participants. They were genuinely angry because previous financial arrangements depended on stable mine ownership. The shooting death of the previous owner and the reigning anarchy among independent operators had served the Xikrin poorly. They found themselves with an unruly mob of prospectors poised to overrun their reserve in search of gold and, on top of this, were no longer recipients of any kind of financial consideration from the mining company.

After promises of renewed financial support from Vale das Andorinhas, the Xikrin acted. They performed the requisite ceremony, gathered herbal medicines from the forest to assure success, and adorned themselves with war paint. Fierce anger burned in their bellies as they set out for the mine locale. It was hardly a fight. When an advance group of four Xikrin had barely appeared over the hill, prospectors took to their heels, abandoning their possessions and running for their lives. Several got good beatings, but Xikrin were content to give most a good scare and score as much booty as possible. Several prostitutes plying their trade in the mining camp were taken prisoner and made to serve as cooks for the next several days, as the Xikrin carefully combed the site for useful items. Helped by a Vale das Andorinhas company plane, Xikrin shuttled back and forth on the twenty-minute flight between the mining camp and the Bakajá village transporting chickens, clothing, and even Krô'i's motor (discussed in Chapter 8), among other items.

NEW ADMINISTRATIVE REQUIREMENTS

In their confrontations with the prospectors and the federal police, Xikrin proved themselves able military adversaries. However, it would be mistaken to see belligerance or a propensity for violence as stemming solely from the nature of Xikrin culture. Although men are trained to be courageous and skilled with weaponry, such incidents occur because of the structure of the regional political economy in which the Xikrin seek to advance their own agenda by allying with one side against another. Unlike other Xikrin and Kayapó peoples who have young people with some Western education, Bakajá residents do not as yet seek to establish direct administration over resources such as gold, timber, or other extractive products. They realize that they lack the basic familiarity with Brazilian ways that would allow them to profit from sole control. When Xikrin fight today, they do so with an eye for gaining allies. The potential for mobilization seems greatest when Xikrin commoners feel they are fighting for outcomes that will result in a more equal distribution of benefits. The only maneuver that can shift, even if slightly, the large advantages of logging and mining firms over the Indians is the possibility of pitting potential competitors against one another and, in the process, raising the costs they will pay for access to resources.

The use of military tactics and the need for allies serves to reenforce chiefly influence because the chief becomes an indispensible coordinator on such occasions. The complexity and delicacy of his position is heightened by the shifting sets of alliances and opposing groups within which the Xikrin seek to operate. The coordination of movements within the reserve creates administrative tasks that were nonexistent in the past. An example should help the reader see the enormity of the job.

As previously mentioned, during the fall of 1994 the FUNAI announced that it would begin demarcating the enlarged Xikrin reservation that was originally decreed in 1992. The original area, demarcated in 1979, amounted to 192,167 hectares, while the newly proposed boundaries would encompass 1,655,000 hectares. The enlarged area would not only include the Trincheira village, where the Xikrin were first settled by the SPI, but also resources, such as fishing spots and Brazil nut groves, the frequent use of which took Xikrin beyond their official reservation boundaries. The new area abutted reserves of the Araweté, Assuriní, and Parakanã peoples, thus eliminating a corridor between them. Such a corridor would have made all their lands more susceptible to invasion. By 1992 the logger Perachi had already established an airstrip in the corridor (Vidal 1992b) and the new reservation boundaries were challenged on the ground and in court by logging and ranching interests such as Alquirino Bannach (Anonymous 1994). On 15 January 1993 a federal judge in a suit brought by the Brazilian NGO, Nucleus for Indigenous Rights, ruled that loggers Perachi, Maginco, and Impar had ten days to withdraw employees and equipment from reservation lands. FUNAI and IBAMA were judged negligent in their protection of reservation territories.

For the Xikrin, the immediate concern was whether or not a particularly rich gold deposit along the Manezão creek would fall within the new reserve boundaries. A group of young men were dispatched to accompany the surveying team so that goldminers would not surreptitiously use their influence to determine the line laid out by surveyors. While this was going on there were continuing invasions into the southeastern portion of the reserve by squatters organized and led by a group called MATER (Movimento dos Agricultores Sem Terra do Pará, a movement of landless peasants). Decisions had to be made about whether it was feasible to meet this threat through direct confrontation or to try and get the FUNAI to take action against the invaders. However, if the FUNAI *did* take any kind of action against the invasion, administrators would necessarily become aware of the Xikrin-sanctioned logging activities within the reserve. Administrative reaction might jeopardize the support of the FUNAI for the completion of reservation demarcations. Meanwhile negotiations were continuing with Panther in the wake of the confiscation of his equipment as to what kinds of services he

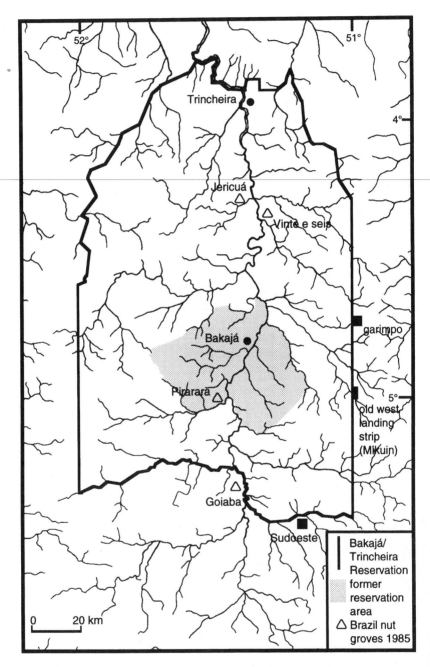

Map 4. Trincheira-Bakajá Reservation. (Ann Peters, based on FUNAI maps of Trincheira/Bakwajá Indigenous Area, 8 June 1990 and 14 November 1989)

would provide the Bakajá community in exchange for the timber already harvested. Failure to counter the squatter invasion and loss of FUNAI support would call into question the viability of the demarcation process. Meanwhile the negotiations with Panther took place against the backdrop of a large debt that had accumulated in the name of several chiefs among the merchants of Tucumã, threatening to make the purchase of needed items impossible. Along with external threats and diplomatic negotiations, ordinary organizational matters, such as the coordination of garden planting, also cried out for the chief's attention.

The movement of different people to distant parts of a reservation with a perimeter measuring 710 kilometers meant that personal visits to all the trouble spots were out of the question. The chief was required to receive what intelligence was available from whatever source as it came into the village. Warriors on foot, radio messages, logging company representatives transported into the village by air, and any other information source all required someone in the village to make sense of it all and respond as necessary. On top of it all, it meant rolling out of bed in the morning to the incessant clamorings for goods from the chiefly stores.

Such duties are not in the job description of any tribal leader. There exists no respite from the pressures unleashed by whirlwind extractivism, and chiefs are forced to make daily decisions about events and processes whose logic and impetus originates in national and regional capitals and markets throughout the world. As we saw, the current chief had assumed a leadership role based on his ability to coordinate the activities of work parties, his intelligence in absorbing traditional knowledge and stories, his talent for keeping people enthralled for hours at a stretch as he orated, pontificated, and dramatized in public speeches before the village. His knowledge of the outside world was recent, his Portuguese poor, and his judgments often seemed unreliable. He was a man of action—a performer and a fighter—rather than an administrator or a cross-cultural mediator.

The chief felt the pressures of his new duties keenly. At times he tended to drown all in excesses of alcohol and he often talked about passing on his office. But to whom? Engineering a transfer of office when there was no obvious capable successor but several competing pretenders was itself a daunting task. Conducting such a transition appeared to be as difficult and risky to the village as any other responsibilities, and so he remained a leader fully aware of the delicate transition period through which his people were passing.

One of the tragedies of the current situation in the Bakajá village is the difficulty in grooming a chiefly successor through traditional means, including instruction in important ceremonial chants. Such training requires a close association over a period of time during which the chants can be memorized. The new administrative position of the chief, and his accumulation of trade goods, has had the effect of distancing him from his fellows. While the outward difference in material circumstances between chiefs and commoners is not glaring by Western standards, the chief no longer lives like the rest of the villagers. His contact with his fellows is no longer one between coequals but one in which unequal obligations of allegiance and generosity tend to create formality and distance. A kind of estrangement results between the chief and potential successors as well as between the chief and the population at large, and, while the chief continues to be liked by most in the village, those he has approached have refused to accept his tutelage.

If the array of outside information that the chief must analyze and respond to is daunting, commoners also remain closely attuned to outside contacts. The arrival of manufactured goods deserves special emphasis since this process determines much about the quality of everyday life. Xikrin are well used to the chaos of redistribution and, by way of analogy, liken it to the confusion that reigned when all arrived simultaneously to gather kernels from the great corn tree of myth. They also point out that the distribution of meat commonly led to fights in the past. While distinctions are made between grades of people organized with respect to gender and age, within these categories there is no hierarchical ordering of persons along a commonly recognized scale. As a result Xikrin feel strongly that all are entitled to equal treatment; one often hears requests for items or shares of food or goods justified by reference to what others have already received. Shares are not tidily set aside for each recipient, and in the case of redistribution of manufactured goods, the portion each person receives depends on the chief's calculation and on a person being present. Those not present often receive nothing.

It is easy to imagine the surge of anxiety that arises among commoners with the arrival of a plane loaded with merchandise. Under the watchful eyes of all present, items are taken to the chief's compound where they are immediately redistributed. Since flights are often delayed, sometimes by many days, this creates a serious dilemma for those who plan activities away from the village. An all-day fishing or hunting trip or even an excursion to a distant garden plot may mean not receiving some desired good. The result is that reliance on manufactured goods has consequences that go beyond their use and derive from their manner of distribution. Those who have their own stock of desired items or who make plans to do without rice or cooking oil or a new shirt are in control of their work schedule. Those who cannot or will not are forced to stay close to the village in case of the arrival of an expected flight. This is yet another determinant of the rhythm of village production that tends to force people to cleave to the chief's collective production organization. People get fed up waiting for prom-

Figure 10. Chiefs arrive with merchandise as a logging company employee waits in the foreground to hitch a ride back to town in 1994. (Photo by author)

ised supplies and take off on their own to go fishing, hunting, or gardening for the day, however, not everyone feels they can afford to do this. Small wonder the Xikrin praised those outsiders who were punctual with regard to flight times and brought precisely the goods agreed on. Thus the mine owner Nonato was renowned for keeping his word, while the FUNAI was criticized as a particularly egregious offender. Any ethnographic description of village life cannot afford to ignore the irritation, the feeling of treading water and doing nothing while waiting for a promised shipment of goods into the village. Far from being a time of joyous abundance, arrivals are inevitably anticlimactic disappointments that engender further bitterness at dependency on the white man's goods.

The arrival of planes represents not only a show of chiefly power but also provides individual Xikrin with the opportunity to circumvent chiefly monopolies on goods. Xikrin men try to strike individual deals with pilots, offering to trade items such as feather headdresses or skins for goods to be delivered on a return trip. Women may try to barter bead necklaces they have made. Occasionally anger at the privilege represented by an uneven distribution of goods boils over— directed not at chiefs but at their dependents, the translators and outsiders who receive extra goods. Thus Little Backwoodsman or his brother (who married into Bep Pruin's household, see Chapter 8) must be quite careful that the unloading of the plane is not the occasion to divest them of their own goods. In one instance the brother was making his way back to his house carrying a plastic bag filled with bread that he had purchased in Tucumã. In the crush to unload, the bag was jostled, the plastic ripped, and in an instant snatched from its owner as men, women, and children grabbed their fill and happily left the scene munching on the stolen loaves. Such open redistribution "from below" may be unusual, but it shows some of the resentment underlying the current concentration of chiefly power. While not openly challenging the right of chiefs to control redistribution, such acts reveal dissatisfaction with how redistribution is carried out in practice and puts the chief on notice that he must be more equitable or risk losing influence.

As their reservation lands and resources are assaulted from without, isolation from the outside world is no longer an option for the Xikrin. The maelstrom of extractivism forces the Xikrin to foster alliances with or against groups of competing miners, loggers, and FUNAI officials in order to gain access to needed goods and defend their lands and resources, often at the expense of providing allies with access to the same. Chiefs organize the collective expression of Xikrin force, which is key to the formation of alliances, much as it must have been during the rubber boom. However, the instability resulting from economic expansion and contraction of extractivist industries is heightened by the uncertainty of temporary and shifting alliances. Furthermore extravillage alliances are not neutral with respect to divergent interests between chiefs and commoners and men and women within the village. Panther's promise of a road was pleasing to Xikrin commoners on the one hand but his close association with younger chiefs at Cateté was threatening to the older Bakajá chief because he felt the latter may have championed a contender to his own leadership within the Bakajá village. Jaguar may well have preferred to deal with the known quantity of the FUNAI but felt forced to accede to popular sentiment in favor of Panther while attempting to bolster his relationship with the Vale das Andorinhas mine owner and commoners through his raid on the gold prospectors. Reliance on the whims of the outside world forces shifting alliances, even as it pits villagers against one another.

In some important ways the current process of redistribution undermines the villagers' abilities to make autonomous decisions regarding their own subsistence activities and impels greater reliance on chiefs. The attention that must be paid to outside events and the tempo of goods shipments affects the entire flow of village life, which particularly during the dry season is always breathlessly poised to capture distant signals and thus seems never fully absorbed in the activity at hand. Before leaving the field in August 1995 I accompanied men on a forest trek undertaken with the objective of getting meat for a naming ceremony.

Discussion about the timing of future goods shipments formed a frantic undertone to the whole expedition and eventually overrode all other factors in the decision to head back to the village. Such timing, of course, is not solely the concern of commoners. To the burden of making decisions about foreign and little-understood external institutions and actors, the Xikrin chief, increasingly estranged from his fellows, must make delicate judgments regarding the consequences of redistributive and organizational decisions on the Xikrin body politic.

10 | THE POLITICS OF WORK

A major contention of this book has been that Xikrin subsistence activities represent an arena of contestation and ambivalence that is caused by their operation within the extractive frontier and the reservation system. In other words, one effect of frontier living is a politicization of everyday life. Decisions about how production is to be organized carry previously unknown distributional consequences; this makes the carrying on of "tradition" a problematic affair. Controversies center around the legitimate control different groups and networks—kin networks, households, men's and women's clubs, chief-led political factions, and age grades—exercise over local production and the redistribution of imports. People invest themselves in social institutions not only with a view to meeting requirements of livelihood or of defense against invaders but with a view toward halting and containing the trends toward inequality that have been unleashed within Xikrin society. It is precisely the resistance to such trends, be they the unequal distribution of trade goods, productive advantages in subsistence due to introduced technology, or unequal advantages in dealing with outsiders because of facility with Portuguese or limited literacy, that creates the politicization of daily life. Xikrin resistance to these developments is based on a sense of how the world should be, which is in turn shaped by internalized, remembered, and shared experiences. The present chapter attempts to come to grips with current controversies and conflicts in the village by contextualizing them within Xikrin history and currently circulating ideas regarding alternative ways of organizing production.

Previous anthropological accounts of Gê peoples differ regarding the relationship between conflict and symbolism and social forms. Maybury-Lewis (1967) asserts that factionalism is independent of dual organization, while Da Matta

(1982) believes that factional strife may be diminished through dualist artifices. In the latter case, no opposition is ever allowed to fester as a source of conflict because means always exist to cross-cut the initial opposition with a second so that standing groups of people may never be permanently polarized with respect to one another. Neither author attempts to sociologically characterize the origin of conflict. Conflict simply erupts because of jealousies, passions, and idiosyncratic disagreements seemingly rooted in personal differences. Social mechanisms either function to dampen such conflict or fail to address it, depending on the author cited. Turner's position regarding the origin of conflict is close to that of both Da Matta and Maybury-Lewis, since he assumes that conflict will erupt in the absence of positive reciprocity or mechanisms to bring people together. Thus, the "basic reason for the instability of the Kayapó moiety system is implicit in the negative nature of the relationships modeled by the moieties. These relations . . . take the form of negative separation and inhibition" (Turner 1979, 209).

Bamberger, for her part, attributes the social root of conflict to the diffuse Kayapó system of political authority. The ease with which a section of the village may split off and recreate society entirely anew, while in the process leaving conflict behind, has resulted in a Kayapó history that "reveals a population in the throes of an endless mitosis." Bamberger points to a lack of developed mechanisms whereby collective input can be generated to work out problems. People do not believe individual leaders or public institutions will seek to meet the needs of an ongoing constituency. She asserts that the

absence of loyalty to figures of authority seems to be symptomatic of a general Kayapó problem, one that is also manifest in the ease with which marital ties are dissolved and new marriages established. This flexibility and fluidity in the matter of changing both spouses and political affiliations must be viewed in conjunction with the lack of any real opportunity to effect a structural change in the nature of institutions, which are so firmly fixed by custom that personnel changes would scarcely affect them. (Bamberger 1979, 141, 144)

In this view, Kayapó allegiances are fluid precisely because structure is so rigid. Conflict may be attributed to purely internal structural causes. Bamberger does prove prescient in describing how the appearance of chiefs appointed by outsiders is a significant event in the development of a new Kayapó voice that can agitate in the defense of indigenous struggles for land and the well-being of communities.

My analysis of the Xikrin world within the hollow frontier builds on previous ethnographic understanding of indigenous social forms but sees these as responsive to larger systems of power. There is an urgent need to reexamine descriptions of social organization with a view to locating the development of internal contradictions in the course of longstanding interactions within a frontier context. In this chapter some examples of the politics of subsistence help to illustrate that while binary oppositions are relevant, such oppositions alone do not explain conflict nor are they irrelevant to conflict. Social forms generated within a pervasive logic of binary oppositions determine both the mode of articulation with outsiders such as extractivist firms and the government, on the one hand, as well as the resistance to the creeping inequalities that are part of the dynamic organizing the flow of goods from the outside. By way of example, we can see how such symbolic oppositions as the association of males with the public sphere and females with the domestic sphere have become an axis of struggle regarding the organization of production and control over subsistence.

WOMEN'S OPPOSITION TO CHIEFLY GARDENS

As it is customary for garden work to be undertaken collectively by members of a men's club, the followers of one chief agreed to slash a large plot in exchange for trade items such as machetes, whetstones, shotgun cartridges, and food. This involved clearing dense liana-cluttered vegetation with machetes, after which larger trees were felled with axes. At the end of each workday, collective meals for the participants were prepared using food stores provided by the FUNAI. Work proceeded steadily on an almost daily basis for about one month in the summer of 1984. Fifteen able-bodied men comprising one of the men's clubs worked together for thirty days clearing the forest. After this, the cut vegetation was allowed to dry in preparation for burning. Planting, which was to begin at the onset of the rainy season, did not, however, go smoothly.

Women who were to furnish both the labor for planting and the manioc cuttings from their own gardens were decidely unenthusiastic about the men's "collective" garden. In domestic plots, men and women often plant together. In the collective plots, women were asked by the chief to supply manioc clippings from their own gardens as planting material; they were then expected to plant these in the plot cleared by the men. Female public activity was to mirror that of the men since women's clubs are formed by the spouses of men in a given men's club under the leadership of the chief's wife. In their capacity as men's club counterpart, women were called on to complete the garden work begun by their men in the chief-sponsored garden. However, in order to perform their tasks, women had to take material from their own gardens, which they strongly resisted.

The women's response was not complete refusal but halfhearted compliance.

They did plant some manioc and once or twice they weeded the areas where manioc had been planted. However, a large part of the area cleared by the men was left untouched, and the partially planted garden lay completely untended for seventeen months. Thus female noncooperation resulted in a garden neither planted nor tended in proper fashion. The fairly small amount of manioc eventually harvested was appropriated by the chief for redistribution to followers engaged in the Brazil nut harvest (see Chapter 5).

Most Xikrin men and women held that it was perfectly correct for the chief to distribute trade goods in sponsoring the cultivation of a large garden. The timing of the distribution of goods had been coordinated with the local FUNAI official stationed at the post who provided food and trade goods for the purpose of expanding horticultural effort. Xikrin commoners saw chiefly sponsorship of a collective plot as necessary if they were to have access to the tools and goods they desired from the FUNAI. Some sort of intermediary was necessary to coax the FUNAI to supply goods to the Bakajá village. For his part, the FUNAI official saw his role as that of "encouraging production." An increase in food production was projected to result in greater security and well-being for the community as a whole. Hopefully, good "work habits" would be cultivated as well. Should these take hold, the FUNAI employee voiced the hope that the Xikrin would be able to sell produce at the farmers market in Altamira. Thus, "encouraging production" served both the short-term goal of demonstrating his administrative effort to higher-ups and the longer-term goal of stimulating regular Xikrin production for markets, which would presumably make them self-supporting and less of a drain on FUNAI resources.

After they had received food and tools, commoners expected the chief to divide up the large garden area into smaller plots that would be managed and harvested by married couples. In this form, the "collective" garden would have served as a complement to domestic plots. Women had expected to plant their manioc clippings in areas that were to be reserved for their own eventual use. When the chief refused to make such a division, female participation was grudging. Females planted at the urging of their husbands, who had already received trade goods and food. Incidently, while the FUNAI provided food for male workers during clearing, no food was offered during planting operations.

In the end, both men and women resisted the chief's appropriation of their labor and the women's garden resources for use at his own discretion. All would have been quite willing to work manufacturing manioc flour for their own use but were reluctant to furnish the chief with such a resource at their own expense. Far from seeing the collective garden as a way of stabilizing their own food supply, as the FUNAI naively envisioned, Xikrin commoners saw it as a way for the chief to gain influence over their actions. Not only did they feel that the chief had overstepped his legitimate authority by determining how they were to use their labor, such activities also seemed to furnish the chief with a potential means of coercion, namely the large stores of manioc flour that commoners had produced themselves. "Why should the chief have so much manioc flour anyway," they grumbled. Most of all, however, people publicly worried about the time they were spending away from their own plots, over which they had total control. They saw work on the "public" garden as a potentially threatening trade-off. If people were not able to produce sufficient subsistence on their own plots because of the time they spent in chief-sponsored work, they would be dependent on chiefly largesse. They would have to request the manioc flour they had made themselves. It was not that chiefly generosity would not be forthcoming, only that the acceptance of food under such circumstances would place commoners in the chief's debt. They would therefore be compelled to reciprocate, not with a return gift of food but through further participation in activities under chiefly sponsorship. Xikrin were not worried in this case about being dependent on outside goods such as machetes but on indebting themselves to their own chief. When he was a producer of imported manufactures, chiefly generosity was celebrated. It was resisted when he offered handouts of food people could produce domestically.

In this case, the organization of Xikrin life and space into opposed public and domestic spheres did not organize a timeless and stable set of oppositions, nor was it irrelevant to the renegotiation of power within the village under the impact of the frontier and reservation system. Chiefs use their ability to mobilize men as a means of inducing outsiders to turn over goods to them. The ability of cooperating groups of female kin and their male spouses and relatives to maintain control of their agricultural production represents an attempt to impose a limit on chiefly power and maintain subsistence autonomy within the domestic sphere.

However, from another point of view, given the trends described in Chapter 5, both horticulture and group hunting and fishing provide the rationale for the consistent cooperation of stable groups, which requires chiefly coordination in much the way that the trading of wild products between age groups did formerly (see Chapter 3). Chiefs must mobilize their followers on a consistent basis in order to receive goods from the outside. However, the ability of the chief to parlay his control over manufactured goods into control over the timing and distribution of horticultural production was resisted by women because it would have radically changed their status. Women's labor contribution and control over reproductive plant stock such as manioc clippings would have been subordinated to the political uses the chief made of manioc flour redistribution. This would have signified a shift in the relationship between the public and domestic domains as well as in the relationships between men and women. Women seemed to be reacting to the possibility that they might become more subordinate to their husbands in particular and to men in general. The labor, resources, and cooperation of women would no longer have been mobilized at their own discretion within the contexts of domestic pursuits organized by related women but at the behest of the chief and their husbands acting in concert to provide the chief with the means to sponsor further collective activities.

Women did not resist the introduction of manufactured goods into the village. In fact, they were vocal in their desire for such goods (cf. Murphy and Murphy 1985). They were unwilling, however, to allow their families' well-being to be dependent on a system of redistributive patronage. Thus the relations between center and periphery, public and domestic, male and female, and chief and commoner defined in terms of binary oppositions common to the Gê become redefined within changing Xikrin relations to the power centers of the frontier. In the aftermath, women mostly got what they wanted: The garden yielded little, and despite the month of clearing by men, it took only two days of collective labor to harvest and prepare manioc flour for the chief. This turned out not to threaten female influence and resources nor did it detract from the time men and women spent together on their domestic plots. In addition, both women and men were fairly satisfied with the tools men received for their work during the initial clearing operation. Only the chief suffered a drop in credibility, both among his followers and their mates and among the FUNAI who had supplied him with goods to "encourage agricultural production."

The basic issues illustrated by this episode have continued to be controversial, of course, and remain ongoing. During the summer following the incident just described, the same chief announced that his followers should cooperate with one another in clearing one another's *domestic* plots. Instead of working for weeks with close in-laws and relatives as had previously been the case, men of a given men's club were to assemble and clear each other's plots over the course of a single day. This was possible because of the greater number of labor hours men's groups could provide compared to that of groups of kin, which were invariably smaller. The plot of each participant was to be allotted a single day of the group's effort after which such plots would be cared for jointly by domestic groups composed of wives, husbands, and others. In order to explain what amounted to a different division of labor from that of preceding years, the chief explained that such collective effort would make individual men less susceptible to fatigue and hence less vulnerable to illness. Thus his organizational improvisation took the standard form of most Xikrin calls to observe tradition in which people are exhorted to act correctly in order to preserve the health and well-being of members of the community.

Having been unsuccessful in absorbing the women as auxiliaries to the men's horticultural production in the public sphere, through the new work arrangement the chief attempted to extend collective men's club solidarity to the domestic sphere. Whether he sought in this manner to allay female fears and opposition or to lay the basis for a subsequent attempt to corral female labor is open to question. Men did in fact all work on each other's domestic plots that year. In subsequent years they have relied for the most part on kin for the chore of garden clearing. However, the whole tenor of the importance of collective gardens changed following 1986 when the FUNAI halted shipments of goods to the village that had been earmarked to encourage horticultural production.

Since that time men continue to work jointly to clear chief-sponsored garden areas but much of the work complementary to male public labor has been assumed by Brazilian laborers rather than women. In 1994 Oldtimer (see Chapter 8), working the chief's garden, claimed to have harvested about 330 kilograms of rice and had planted enough to harvest 1,000 kilograms, if all went well. Although rice is a recent introduction to the Xikrin, Oldtimer also planted bitter and sweet manioc along with corn. Women are called on less frequently for planting and harvesting in chief-sponsored plots.

In sum, the use of non-Xikrin labor has made the process of collective gardening much less contentious because both men and women work less and do not have to give up jealously guarded time in their domestic plots. However, a new development in the continuing struggle between the legitimate control of public and domestic resources and labor occurred in 1995. At this point some of the underchiefs and translators opted to use timber company–supplied peons to clear their domestic plots. In doing so they avoided calling on kin and in-laws for labor help, which would have required them to reciprocate in like manner when called on. By this means the underchiefs avoided incurring debts toward kin and in-laws, confident that their individual households could be at least partially self-sufficient. By seeking to broaden their base of support from chiefs to encompass his close allies and collaborators, timber companies sought to shore up their support within the village. Thus, over time, the use of non-Xikrin labor by chiefs to appease commoner concerns about the autonomy of domestic production leads to further developments that call into question the current structure of domestic production, which relies on reciprocal help within bilateral networks of kin. When non-Kayapó labor is used in domestic plots it threatens to erode the reliance of domestic production on female-centered kin networks and may allow other Xikrin in addition to chiefs to accumulate surpluses of food or goods without the leveling obligations of reciprocity to check individual accumulation. Causal factors are complex, and such developments owe their occurrence both to extractive industry intervention and a distinctive Xikrin worldview built on a series of binary contrasts. It is the combination of these factors that resulted in the particular way contradictory processes unfolded within the village.

BRAZIL NUTS AND FEMALE LABOR

If women initiated protests against what they saw as a threatening extension of public chiefly influence over conditions of production in the domestic sphere, they also contested the terms under which male public associations organized extractivist activities. In this case, the women aimed their fire at the Brazil nut harvest, which, like large chiefly gardens, is an occasion for redistribution of manufactured goods. Brazil nuts are often collected jointly by men and women. However, men do the public work of hauling Brazil nuts to the common storage area, and I discovered that men are not responsible for the entire harvest only by calculating the number of boxes of Brazil nuts for which individual men took credit against the number of days worked. Sometimes the totals claimed by a man are greater than humanly possible. In reality, public organization subsumed female contributions to that of the spouse or male kin. The wife or daughter's portions were lumped together with the man's portions because women had, of course, no voice in what was defined as a public male activity. As a corollary women had no control over the leader's redistribution of collectively delivered goods to men's club associates. But, then again, male followers also felt that they had distressingly little influence on these occasions.

As described in Chapter 5, redistribution of trade items after the harvest follows a mixed criterion. On the one hand, for each box of Brazil nuts they collect, men retain a single nut as a way of keeping a count of their individual contribution; on the other hand, since the goods are delivered directly to the chief, who then apportions them on the basis of personal allegiance and other considerations not linked to productivity, the accounting system serves less as a way of establishing the value of a man's labor contribution than as a hedge against what may be considered an abuse of redistributive power by the chief. As a last resort, a man will take his Brazil nut tokens to the FUNAI representative with a request that the latter dip into his own stores in order to redress the wrong suffered. Although the insistence on maintaining a record of individual work implicitly challenges the redistributional authority of the chief, open contestation of this authority was only initiated by several unmarried women who began collecting Brazil nuts. The women used a similar accounting device and demanded compensation directly from the FUNAI official at the post.

The women who engaged in this action felt that the current organization was not serving them well. They suffered what might be called a double dependency: They depended on trade goods such as machetes to produce their livelihood and they depended on men to furnish these since the chief apportions goods only to his male followers. This placed discretion for handing out goods squarely in the hands of male kin and marriage partners. Women chafe under this arrangement whereby their ability to produce is determined by male relatives and affines and the product of their labor is treated as if it were work performed by their husbands or fathers. While a woman may receive some trade goods from the men in her life, the prerogative rests with the male. Male monopoly over trade goods in complicity with the Indian Agency for the first time gives males some control over female labor since women are forced to work as "silent" partners whose work is subordinated to that of men.

In attempting to counteract new controls over their lives, women appeal to the FUNAI representative at the post to distribute goods directly to individual workers, male and female, rather than turn them over to the chief for redistribution. In doing so they seek to undermine the ability of the chief to redistribute goods on the basis of political expediency to their husbands and fathers. Once again, we see that the opposition between center and periphery described as fundamental for the Gê-speaking peoples' village life (Maybury-Lewis 1979) is liable for refiguring and rerepresenting. As new powers of control over previously nonexistent goods have been appropriated by chiefs, neither chiefly control over trade goods nor male control over female labor can be regarded as an extension of traditional customs. Rather than openly challenging the authority of chiefs, which tends to undermine the position of male authority generally, men react by "tweaking" the system. They seek as individuals to establish direct ties with the FUNAI personnel or other outsiders. This can take the form of offering presents of meat to the on-site employees or taking them fishing. Women, on the other hand, react by seeking to reposition the legitimate powers that may be retained by the male public sphere and its chiefs by challenging the right of chiefs to redistributive authority.

If we accept that Xikrin are indeed contesting the terms in which social relations are cast, this raises the issue of whether divergent points of view and interests are in fact rooted in social organization or are merely idiosyncratic expressions of personal perspectives. In the former case, men and women take a certain stance on the issue of collective gardens because they formulate issues according to generalized dispositions of males or females within Xikrin society. In the latter case, conflict is unavoidable but is rooted in differences in personality or a general human propensity toward conflict rather than in structural factors. The first hypothesis forces us to look for evidence that different social positions actually do influence people to take different stances on issues, to see things differently, or to describe things in terms of different language. The second hypothesis would have us place little emphasis on conflict since it would appear to be unrelated to specific social relations that organize Xikrin life. There does appear to be evidence that despite the close quarters and intimate association of all villagers compared to people in, say, North American suburbs, Xikrin do not view their world in terms of an undifferentiated community interest. Cooperation within social institutions therefore involves people acting together while not necessarily sharing the same underlying set of assumptions regarding the aims of their activity. The following personal experience of a man who began life as a commoner and eventually became a chief sheds further light on the kind of differentiation of interest and perception that exists within the Xikrin community.

A CHIEF'S TALE

"It's only recently that we've had *benadjwỳrỳ,* known as *chefia,*" explained one man from the last generation born before official contact. His use of the Portuguese "chieftaincy" to explicate a thought formulated in Kayapó was significant. The mixing of languages appears itself to represent the impossibility of understanding the function or office of chief in exclusively insider or outsider terms. "The benadjwỳrỳ only appeared with pacification," he continued. "Only recently with chiefs that work with whites do we have an explosion in the number of young chiefs. In the past there were no rich or poor Indians." Xikrin hold chiefs responsible for the unwanted inequality they see in their midst. They distinguish between the benadjwỳrỳ, the chiefs of today, and the *ngôkonbàri,* the chiefs of yesteryear, in a way that surely does some violence to history since benadjwỳrỳ were surely present before contact as well. However, there is truth to this contrast as well, since present-day chiefs *are* different from their precontact predecessors.

Today all chiefs are considered "foreigner chiefs" *(kubēnnhôbenadjwỳrỳ).* This has a number of related connotations. A large part of chiefly responsibility, as we have seen, lies in dealing with outsiders, and hence recognition by outsiders is essential in order to exercise chiefly office. The Xikrin version of a typical encounter of outsiders approaching their village begins with the common request to meet the *cacique,* as indigenous leaders are referred to throughout the region. When the outsider is taken to the chief, he is said to throw his arms around his shoulder in the comradely style of the Brazilian *abraço,* or hug, and cry out, "Amigo." The recounting of this social satire sets listeners to snickering, but nonetheless is revealing for its insights into Brazilian attitudes toward Xikrin leadership and society. If the Xikrin are to interact successfully with Brazilians, they are forced to take foreign ideas into account. Hence, many current standards of chiefly conduct mimic practices borrowed from Brazilian authorities, which tend to differentiate the status of chiefs and commoners more fully than Xikrin find comfortable. On the occasion of outsider visits, the chief will sit in a chair, for example, while his followers sit on the ground. This artifice is discarded when outsiders leave. It is thought, however, that chiefs must act in accordance with foreign standards of leadership.

Nonetheless, despite their designation as "white men chiefs," they are not considered pawns of the FUNAI or other outsiders. Instead they owe their continued exercise of authority to the support they enjoy from followers within a particular community. Validation of chiefly legitimacy relies on cultural capital generated both inside and outside the village. It is entirely possible to fail as a chief by not getting sufficient goods to redistribute (see Chapter 7).

In describing the duties of a chief, the commoner point of view differs from the chiefly point of view. As befits a "hybrid" institution, analogies are drawn from both inside and outside Xikrin society. Such analogies are attempts to understand and rhetorically portray the highly improvisational role of the chief. These understandings, then, attempt to define and circumscribe the power of chiefly authority, but in different ways. The rhetorical nature of the discussion of chiefs is starkly obvious in the following interview with a young chief who is compelled to switch viewpoints midstream as he first recounts his motivations as a commoner and then switches, later in the interview, to the viewpoint of a chief.

In recounting his career and how he became a chief, a man with whom I had extensive conversations over several months related how he had initially worked for other chiefs. Duck even referred to himself during this time of his life as a peon, or *peão*—the regional Brazilian term for a manual laborer. In this capacity he collected Brazil nuts and helped clear and prepare the plot for the chief's garden. However, he was frustrated because he received nothing for his efforts in the way of trade goods. Every boat that returned from delivering its load of Brazil nuts brought someone else a shotgun or other goods, but never anything for him.

Duck finally decided to approach the other village chief, Mauré, who at the time led a rival faction opposing Jaguar, about working with his followers. By way of explanation he diplomatically stated that in his present group there were many people and not enough "stuff" to go around. Mauré agreed to take him on, and he went to work with great energy. He collected Brazil nuts, he slashed a large garden for the chief, and then a second garden. He began to receive things: a pair of shorts, a T-shirt, rubber thongs for footwear, and even a new shotgun. According to him, he collected eleven boxes of Brazil nuts (the number must have stuck in his mind) in return for the .20 gauge shotgun. He liked his weapon a lot and was very happy.

In this account there is no doubt as to Duck's criteria for choosing one chief over the other. As a follower he had received food and other favors from both chiefs. However, he expected access to significant durable and semidurable goods, including a shotgun. Beyond receipt of certain trade goods, opting for one chief over another had several consequences. Duck was forced to formally change his men's club affiliation, for example. Even his choice of domicile became a factor, and he did eventually leave the village for approximately five years when Mauré's followers split off from the main village to found the settlement at Trincheira. As an unmarried man and an orphan, his choices were less complicated than those of many others since he did not have to coordinate his options with those of any close relatives.

In his early twenties, Duck was approached by elder chiefs to become a "new" chief himself. There were several reasons why he was uniquely qualified. His father had been a chief, and, after being orphaned, he had been raised in the house of a respected elder from whom he had mastered much oral tradition. His command of Portuguese was superior and his knowledge of the outside world was greater than most village men, since he had worked outside the reservation on different logging projects. In the course of this work, he had visited other Kayapó villages as well and had even married in the Cateté village. Thus he fulfilled the formal criteria of chiefly descent, had displayed the necessary intelligence and learning of traditional and outsider knowledge, and fit well into the political projects of the preexisting array of chiefs. They saw him as a popular younger leader who would be able to energize bachelors and younger married men in collective activity.

Despite his knowledge of Brazilian society Duck remained illiterate and innumerate. However this lack of formal education in the Brazilian school system was actually a mark in his favor since the Bakajá chiefs were fully aware of the challenge that an educated chief would pose to their own authority. Bakajá chiefs had observed from afar the rise of a new group of younger chiefs at Gorotire and other Kayapó villages who, educated in Brazilian schools, used their literacy to amass tremendous influence and wealth as cross-cultural mediators (Turner 1995). Crafty Bakajá leaders had no intention of allowing the same challenge to their authority and therefore refused to send youngsters to study in Altamira, insisting that any education of young people in Portuguese and mathematics take place within the village. If lack of literacy made him a good prospect as a younger leader subordinated to the older leaders, so to did his lack of an immediate family aside from a single brother. His relative isolation in the village made him dependent on elder chiefs for a base of support.

Duck was hesitant at first and older chiefs spent months recruiting him. Finally, one of the elder chiefs took him to Altamira where he was put up in a hotel and, after a few days of persuasion, sold him on the idea of becoming a chief. Duck's fear of the social shame and stigma that would result if he failed as a chief was at the root of his reluctance. He also was unenthusiastic about the social hardships chiefs undergo by having to face unrelenting demands for food and goods by other villagers on a daily basis. In addition to the enormous social pressures within the village, chiefs also frequently deal with outsiders, and he was concerned that this would be tiring and even distasteful. Brazilian society was strange and uncomfortable, for the most part, and Brazilian food often literally made him sick. However it is precisely because chiefs are in theory, answerable to their followers that they are forced into contact with outsiders. *O djuwa mêj*, or fair/ample giving refers to generous behavior that is expected equally from chiefs and from kinship relations. Chiefs must show largesse toward their followers (*meanhõapêj*—literally, "his work people") and can only do so effectively through their contacts with outsiders. If dissatisfied, followers can reject chiefs or desert them. The stigma of suffering the public humiliation of failing as a chief is onerous, since in the aftermath, one is faced with continued village life at close quarters among those whom one had aspired to lead.

Upon his return, having overcome his initial reservations, Duck began a period of apprenticeship of several months under the elder chief Jaguar. Another underchief offered Duck one of his daughters in marriage. Although this meant she would have to abandon her current husband, the girl accepted. At the same time, in agreeing to this new marriage, Duck definitively gave up any notion of returning to the wife he had left at the Xikrin Cateté reservation. Thus he was touted as a new chief only after he was firmly tied to older chiefs through very close social ties. He did, however, insist on building his own house rather than residing with his father-in-law. His new house featured a large, open common room with slats, rather than the mud walls of private homes. This marks the chief's house as a public gathering space within the village. The transformation from commoner to chief was effected only through the reconfiguration of close social relationships and the space occupied in the village. While many people may be referred to as chiefs (see Chapter 7), it is the ability to resituate oneself politically so as to make factional alliances with both kin and nonkin that distinguishes effective chiefs from those who may merely claim the title benadjwỳrỳ. A politically effective chief must have something to offer to nonkinsfolk who, in accepting to become his "work people," expect generosity in return. A chief should have food at his house, where followers can come and eat their fill. A chief should also give away various types of goods, including trade goods *(àrodja)*. A similar analogy underlies relations between kin and between a chief and his followers. Persons recognized as kin should be treated with unrestrained generosity while nonkin are never favored with the same treatment. In a similar vein followers of a chief expect to be treated like kin. When requests are directed to the chief, he should be forthcoming (i.e., *aprã*—"to supply a need," whether this be food or any other items such as shotgun shells). Like a good kinsman, a chief should never ask for anything as payment in return. This would give his gesture the appearance of interested behavior motivated by a desire for a payback. Unrestricted generosity, on the other hand, demonstrates that the chief likes his "followers" or, as these are often referred to currently, "the community" (Fisher 1998). "Shame" or feelings of restraint, in theory, govern the conduct of both chiefs and commoners. Followers would feel "shame" in approaching any chief other than the one they work for to request a trade item. Chiefs feel shame if they are not able to satisfy the desires of their followers or if they are accused of being stingy.

In explaining his current practice as chief, Duck rhetorically frames his dealings in terms of the morality of kinship; he does not acknowledge that he "pays" people to work for him and adamantly holds that everything he provides to followers is given freely and without calculation. However, commoners are quite open in discussing the relative generosity of their chiefs—"he pays well" *(pãjn raj)* or "he pays poorly" *(pãjn ïxtiri)* are commonly heard. While such comments are exchanged among commoners within the Xikrin village, I have also heard similar commentary among Kayapó from different villages during visits to the FUNAI Indian House in Altamira or Belém.

SOCIAL ORGANIZATION AND THE STRUGGLE FOR THE FUTURE

Commoner and chiefly representation of the role of the chief diverge in crucial particulars. Forged in the crucible of extractivist and bureaucratic intervention, Xikrin leadership is understood in terms of the conflicting systems of meaning drawn from different areas of experience. As a young man discussing his future aspirations, Duck talked about his expectations as a "peon" in terms used by commoners. He openly stressed the type of payment he desired in return for his loyalty and effort, and compared the generosity of different chiefs. The axis of description changes, however, when describing his current duties as chief. In this context he speaks in terms of obligations overtly similar to those between kin and angrily rejects the idea that chiefs engage in payments of any kind to maintain their leadership. Nonetheless, analogies used by Duck and others in the village to characterize the relationship between chiefs and commoners draw upon the language of extractive firms and the FUNAI bureaucracy. "He's an employee" *(empregado)* or "he pays well" are commonly sprinkled throughout village speech. At the same time the values that frame the relationship between a chief and his "work people" continue to be drawn from the domain of kinship. Chiefs should be generous *(o djuwa mêj)* and, as Duck claimed, "followers are relatives" *(meanhõapêj ombikwa)*. It is as if two different vocabularies are used to describe relationships that escape definition as either wholly indigenous or wholly Brazilian. Even more to the point, the *content* of the chief's role and the standards by which generosity or other behaviors are judged necessarily changes as a result of struggles within Xikrin society and the changing policies and practices of the FUNAI and extractivists.

Any description of the chief's role as a mediator between the Xikrin and wider Brazilian society cannot rely on statements and definitions but must contextualize the part played by chiefs in the contradictory processes that tie Xikrin to extractivism even as they seek to develop areas of stable relationships independent of the boom-bust cycles and the supply of manufactured goods. Observations on social organization are essential to understanding how Xikrin are coping with the wider world and with the rise of disturbing inequalities within their own village. As Sider suggests, "the fundamental language of this confrontational and incorporative dialog is not found in words, or even in symbols. It is rooted, rather, in the domain of social organization, in which words and symbols are contextualized in a struggle to harness emergent differentiation or, from below, to develop and redevelop autonomy" (Sider 1987, 22).

Duck's tale reminds us that the difficulties of balancing obligations between kin and nonkin work people may be personally painful for the chief as well. At least one prominent man has withdrawn from chiefly office, refusing to play an uncomfortable game in which he felt followers and relatives competed for his favor. Jaguar's relative isolation and bouts of depression and drinking (Chapter 9) are similar reminders of the difficulties of leadership, which stem from the administrative complexities and also from the basic ambiguity of the institutional role.

NEW ORGANIZATIONAL INITIATIVES

Xikrin social institutions such as the chieftaincy are not chartered by a cultural script unanimously subscribed to by all villagers. Instead, they are often best seen as contending attempts to tilt the scales in favor of some people to the relative detriment of others. With this in mind, organizational forms characteristic of past periods may be touted as superior to the present-day emphasis on men's clubs under chiefly sponsorship. Between my period of fieldwork in the mid-1980s and the mid-1990s there was a revival of the food exchanges between age grades known as *aben kadjy mỹja o ba* (described in Chapter 3). Xikrin elders hold that persuasive oral harangues and enthusiasm for dance and work originating with gourd-rattle leaders were instrumental in initiating and coordinating such exchanges, in effect, collectivizing production according to age grades. Currently, such exchanges take on a different cast. In advocating such exchanges, old men carp in the men's house about their hunger and desire to eat well and the importance of providing food for women, children, nephews, and nieces. While such speeches were surely made in similar fashion during precontact times, given the current reliance on chiefly sponsored collective hunting and manioc flour produced by individual households, such advocacy of age-grade exchanges is a not-so-veiled criticism of the current configuration of social arrangements.

In fact, in the aben kadjy mỹja o ba exchanges of today, the most prominent chiefs are invariably absent. In the commentary surrounding these collective feasts, one hears reference to the impoverishment of the village and its lack of goods. Vegetable fish poison is used on these occasions; no metal hooks, nylon lines, or outboard motors received from the outside world in the person of chiefs or their emissaries are required. Fishing technique relies on the collective effort of dam building, plant collecting, and capturing the oxygen-deprived fish as they wildly try to escape. Similarly, the food contributions of the age grades remaining near the village are comprised of either corn, bananas, or sweet manioc. None of these require the extended preparation time of manioc flour, and, more important, they do not rely on the "modern technology" of flour making—the metal griddle, the mechanical grinder, and fuel. The collective food exchange recalls precontact times in both its organization and its selection of foodstuffs.

Chiefs are not absent by accident from the aben kadjy mỹja o ba. By turning their backs on all the necessary goods that chiefs supply, commoners on such occasions are making a statement. It is as if such occasions are compensations for the failings of the current mode of leadership and food production to provide what people really want.

Besides furnishing abundant food, these gatherings are occasions for developing a collective consciousness about the past. Out of the current population of nearly three hundred people, there are perhaps twenty-four who were actually alive when the aben kadjy mỳja o ba system provided the bulk of subsistence. While no one advocates discarding steel tools or canoes, such revival of tradition is less about a return to the past than about confronting the present inequalities and the system of authority in the village. The success of such organizational initiatives in instilling a sense of history can be gauged by the fact that any number of young people in the village could authoritatively pontificate on the way gourd-rattle leaders acted in contrast to the current crop of benadjwỳrỳ. Historical citations of this sort do not emerge from a unified authoritative version of the Xikrin past but from different perspectives within society—between those better and worse off, between women and men, and chiefs and commoners. Such citations provide a basis for organizational initiatives that, while remaining within the repetoire of tradition, take on an oppositional character.

UNSPOKEN DIFFERENCES

In fact, Xikrin are quick to take advantage of new opportunities, even those that appear unlikely at first glance. While logging roads may provide a channel onto the reservation for unwanted invaders, they also attract land tortoises drawn to the warmth of the open roadbed. Very quickly the logging road to the Bakajá village has also become a favorite collecting spot for single, divorced, and widowed women, and even one or two whose husbands show little taste for hunting. Frequently in the early mornings, as the Bakajá River emerged from layers of mist, I would watch small groups of women silently paddle across to the road. They would spend the day along the road and its immediate perimeter looking for tortoises. Normally women in the foraging group did not belong to the same household or female-centered network of kin. In their makeup, these parties resembled male hunting parties rather than garden groups of related women. While individual women go out foraging, other women in the household can engage in garden work, cooking, and child care. In many ways the male/female division of labor between the husband who hunts and the wife who remains in the village is mimicked by this new organization of female foraging. The practice seems to be a response to a complex social situation that includes, among other factors, a dramatic increase in single mothers and a rise in the self-sufficiency of younger men who, able to acquire trade goods directly through their chiefs, are less dependent on parents or in-laws.

Figure 11. Adult man with headdress, 1984. (Photo by author)

Females foraging on the road will not replace males as primary providers of meat nor will this practice be a panacea for any of the problems confronting the Xikrin. For the time being, at least, it seems not to have generated any controversy. Such cases warn us against oversanctifying native pronouncements about the social place of males and females and suggest that we pay careful attention to what people are actually doing. Direct observation, including interviews with the actors, allows us to see how Xikrin society is differentiated in more ways than we could ever know by recording descriptions of cultural expectations regarding age, gender, or ceremonial status. Activity is never an automatic response to a preexisting cultural script.

In many ways female foraging for land tortoises is perfectly compatible with the new trends toward the collectivization of hunting trips by men and the self-sufficiency of manioc flour production by households. It serves a useful purpose for those households well served by the current dominant trends. After all, only a minority of women forage for tortoises. We need to see such differentiation of roles and initiatives as part of a complex interplay of contradictory social trends rather than as something given by a cultural charter for masculinity or femininity. As with the ambiguities inherent in the contemporary role of chief previously discussed, continued differentiation within the community entails a reconceptualization of meanings associated with gender, age, and other social distinctions without implying any eventual agreement among the entire population.

Indigenous life within the extractive frontier is lived in complex relations with the wider world and is not easily characterized as either "traditional" or "changed." Depending on one's viewpoint and what one chooses to emphasize, either term might easily apply. What can be definitively stated, however, is that subsistence is organized today as much for political purposes as for sustenance. By way of illustration, we have seen that Xikrin gardens worked jointly by related female kin do not merely produce food, but that through them, women seek to maintain the domestic group's power to determine the expenditure of its homegrown labor in the face of possible demands from the chief. Under the impact of relations with the wider world, Xikrin society has become differentiated in ways previously unknown. The accumulation of material inequalities affecting a person's access to the requirements of livelihood are part of this process. Different organizational combinations examined in the course of this chapter and of the book have been employed by Xikrin in an effort to change the terms of access even as they appeal to specific traditions. In order understand this process I have stressed that people do not blindly accept roles assigned to them in a division of labor. Rather, people seek to define their place in the process of subsistence production by defining their relationships with others according to a familiar cultural idiom. Under current conditions, people produce food and define their relations with others within the context of processes that extend beyond the village and are contained within it. That food production, distribution, and consumption should stimulate the advocacy of conflicting traditions and innovations seems in large part due to the uncertainties and inequalities introduced as part of the frontier situation and internalized within Xikrin society.

11 CONCLUSION

I returned to work with the Xikrin in 1994 fully aware of media denunciations of Kayapó avarice and corruption. The media described the "sale" of natural commodities and relied on general notions of universal human greed to make sense of Kayapó actions. Now that Kayapó had access to cash, so the accounts went, they wanted to acquire and consume like all the rest of us, and the myth of their ecological stewardship was nothing but a delusion of environmental and indigenous advocacy groups. Kayapó culture, social relationships, the history of the frontier, and FUNAI policy swings were not part of "the story." It is fair to say that very few other indigenous peoples have been so widely associated with the movement to preserve the Amazon forest. Regardless of the unique circumstances, the Kayapó case has relevance for conservationists, policy makers, and social scientists confronting the divergent interests and competing alternatives within tropical forest areas.

This work has been my attempt to address what I saw as the relevant issues. Why, I wondered, did it seem that Xikrin would sell their grandchildren's environmental birthright just at the moment when reservations were finally being demarcated and boundaries guaranteed for generations to come? My analysis has focused on the Bakajá Xikrin and should not be construed as explaining the trajectory of other Kayapó villages. Most of these other communities show important differences, such as a class of young leaders educated outside of the community and a longer history of contact. FUNAI financial support of the Bakajá community over the past thirteen years appears to be at lower levels than that of other villages, and lack of alternatives has certainly played a significant role in throwing the Xikrin into the arms of extractivists. In all cases, however, indigenous subsistence and social needs have been shaped by years of frontier contact, and developments within communities are essential elements for understanding the escalating involvement with extravillage protagonists.

The documented events on the reservation, however, do not relieve state authorities from their obligation to enforce laws governing protected reservation territories, even if this must be done against the resistance of local elites. Governments can and should ensure reservations adequate for indigenous peoples' use of traditional natural resources. Sedentary village life within the confines of reservations also requires tools and infrastructure. But reservations and indigenous communities have always been components in more extensive networks of social relations and material flows. In a world teeming with desperate, landless peasants seeking a place to homestead, wealthy ranchers looking for cheap pasture (or tax breaks), and extractivists seeking quick profits, the competition for resources among these groups spills over onto unpoliced reservation lands. Within the Amazon, the government itself has had to compete with others for control over land, communication, and transportation, often at a disadvantage.

Indigenous peoples do not have a choice: If Xikrin were to choose to deal only with official government agencies, they would be unable to survive in their current environment. The past helps us understand much about the current form of Xikrin social life, but it is also a guide to the future. Barring an almost unimaginable expansion of resources and authority for the FUNAI and Brazilian environmental agencies, there is little question that Xikrin will continue to be part of a fairly unregulated frontier political economy. Within Amazonia, the informal economy continues to expand, sometimes at the expense of the formal economy (Cleary 1994). We can expect, and the Xikrin do realistically expect, that their profound dependence on imported goods will neither end nor be satisfied within smoothly oiled official channels. Reasonably, they expect the disarticulated Amazonian boom-bust economy to continue as in the past. Relations between loggers and miners and the Xikrin are not a result of corruption of leaders, a decay in tradition, unconcern with the natural resource conservation, cross-cultural misunderstandings, or even a rejection of Indian agency oversight. No scheme to entice the Xikrin to stop logging or ban miners from the reservation and its environs can afford to ignore past experiences and current hardships, or the character of the regional system within which reservations are set.

The policy embraced by most NGOs and conservationists—that of encouraging involvement in markets on the basis of fair prices and sustainable practices—remains problematic according to the results of the present study. In his article "Indian Development in Amazonia: Risks and Strategies," Marcus Colchester (1989, 249) considers indigenous Amazonians' widespread involvement with the market: "In searching for viable means of production of goods to exchange for modern industrial products, we can note three different strategies that Indians have been able to develop. They can either sell themselves, sell the surpluses of their traditional economy, or they can adopt new economic tactics to produce non-traditional products." While this seems on the surface like a reasonable generalization, the present work shows that notions of barter, surplus, and sale only loosely describe the transfer of goods mediated through indigenous social forms. If outsiders are to accord any weight to indigenous social practice and organization, they must recognize that the mere fact that natural resources leave the reservation and trade goods and food enter does not imply the existence of markets, money equivalencies, or even barter.

In the Amazon, politics overwhelmingly determines what may be marketed as a commodity and the social forms through which goods are transferred. The very existence of wildcat prospecting and reservation logging relies on the relative power of government regulation, police, service agencies, and local elites. The situation is complicated by the massive population movement of Brazil's poor, who are unable to eke out a stable livelihood in their communities of origin. Within the reservation, the exercise of chiefly power and resistance to chiefly monopoly access, rather than the demand for specific goods, stokes the movement of natural and manufactured commodities in and out of the reservation. The demand for hardwood and precious metal exports, especially to Europe, North America, and Japan, lies as an offstage incentive. But this demand may only find its supply if an influx of foreign currency can lever loggers and miners into a position where they may outcompete contending parties who would use resources for other ends. Within this context, to rely on markets implies reliance on the top dogs in ongoing power struggles, whose preeminent position—if past boom-bust cycles are any indication—is sure to be temporary.

The indigenous forms that develop do not conform to the inexorable logic of either the market or tradition but are actively created through the transformational techniques and organizational arrangements valued by Indians themselves. Subsistence and organization are never imposed from without in any mechanical sense; as indigenous creations, they have their own dynamic tendencies and contradictions that must be analyzed. Xikrin have adopted technologies that favor certain crops over others, that fits in well with both pursuit of extractive products such as Brazil nuts and the decreased access to various plant and animal resources as a result of their attachment to the FUNAI post. The Xikrin may still be thought of as indigenous ecologists whose hunting, gathering, horticulture, and fishing remain not only a mainstay of their lives but a rich repository of knowledge and tradition. However, their ecology is not merely an adaptation to a natural environment but to a social environment as well.

The frontier is not only an external constraint but a part of Xikrin life that has been internalized in the form of awareness of certain recurrent patterns, outside actors, and tensions within the community itself (cf. Roseberry 1989). If we see the current work organization and disposition of natural resources as a result of this process, we can better understand Xikrin ecology as responsive to tradition and changes in a "landscape" that is both natural and social. Xikrin resource use stems from more than their residence within a certain environment. They are dependent on this environment for their livelihood, but they are equally dependent on inflows of Western goods for the maintenance of subsistence and social organization.

Xikrin are forced to collectively shoulder their isolation from access to goods under conditions that make such goods increasingly necessary. Indigenous social organization derives at least part of its efficacy and ability to transform itself from contending networks of power outside the reservation. Bakajá villagers do not suffer from ever-increasing market encroachment but from radical swings, as the extractivist economy of a particular locale expands or evaporates along with FUNAI funds. The social forms of age grades and men's clubs have been successful in projecting Xikrin collective power. For example, the introduction of projects—of the sustainable or unsustainable variety—to garner trade goods takes place under the auspices of chiefly sponsorship and thus is an extension of age grade and men's club organization. Attempts by individuals to work for cash are discouraged overtly by chiefs and commoner peer pressure and implicitly by cultural values of exchange that make it quite difficult to trade manufactured goods between village residences in return for food and other necessities.

The frequent village splits among Kayapó peoples are often related to different orientations toward links with the outside world. The desire for cash and opportunities to sell Brazil nuts, salted fish, and garden products to extractivist workers around the Xingu River helped precipitate the exit of the Trincheira faction to form their own village. While some try to improve their access to goods through splits within villages, unequal distribution of manufactured goods will remain the rule. Barring exceptional circumstances, individuals or households who wish to acquire a new firearm or metal pot will look to goods channeled in by a chief rather than to kinsfolk or friends from more lavishly stocked households. Moreover, both men and women are "locked in" to a rhythm of work that alternates between chief-sponsored activities and those within extended households. Within dependent social formations, a chief's ability to set parameters on the tempo and organization of work is more crucial in maintaining influence than his ability to control any surplus produced by villagers. Differences in wealth and material possessions are expressed through the accumulation of trade goods rather than through items produced and consumed within the community.

As chiefs seek to fulfill their obligations to followers, they acquire a retinue that can only be maintained through further consolidation of the chief's position as a redistributor of goods originating outside the reservation. Those among this retinue with the cultural competence to do so will attempt to establish their own networks of kinship relations using their access to the outside world, which remains their principal asset. Many within the Xikrin community will resist the unequal spread of strategically important subsistence tools and food items. Collective acts such as food exchanges between age grades, "boycotts" of garden labor, and "liberation" of private airlifted goods show a desire to forge alternatives to the status quo. On the other hand, private acts of theft are fairly common and only the poorest families do not have houses with locked doors to guard their possessions. The chief has storerooms and a padlocked fenced area to guard his possessions.

Although each Kayapó community is autonomous, events in other villages become reference points for ongoing discussions and disputes. Massive injections of goods and services, such as the support delivered from the Vale Rio Doce Company to the Cateté Xikrin, provide ammunition for critics of the Bakajá chief, who suggest that the absence of such support is a stark commentary on his effectiveness as a leader. The present study shows that ties between male commoners and chiefs are essential to ensure adequate domestic production. Unmarried men and sometimes entire nuclear families are tempted to place themselves within the orbit of effective leaders who supply them generously with desired goods. There has been an outflux of Bakajá villagers to Cateté and to Trincheira over the past decade. In the three years before 1995, there had been some reverse flow as the influence of kin and the relatively less-degraded environment around the Bakajá village began to exert a counterpull.

Once the initial influx of manufactured goods makes household and even nuclear-family subsistence autonomy possible, these relatively autonomous groups may circulate between Kayapó villages. There are always nominal kinship ties used to justify such moves, or men may find new marriage partners. Using census data collected in 1984, I discovered that immigrants to the Bakajá village and offspring born since their arrival constituted 29 percent of the total population. Thus, despite their corporate character, Kayapó communities are sites of greater population flow than would seem apparent. The processes discussed in the present work promise to increase the movement of people between villages as the mediating ability of chiefs to attract goods to the village waxes and wanes.

Every large-scale process, such as development or deforestation, has its hidden local side that consists of local developments and local perspectives. What is distinct about this local history is not captured in the contrast between external and internal because there is no way of excluding the foreign; there are only many alternative ways to come to terms with its presence. For the Xikrin, the politicization of daily life is a testament to the internalization of the external. As a consequence, from Xikrin perspectives, any outside intervention must be accepted or rejected in terms of ongoing political formulations. Every remedy envisioned by well-intentioned NGOs, anthropologists, or others to help stem pillaging of gold and timber must, by definition, challenge networks of established power. These are almost inevitably linked to the aims and organization of at least some village residents and will not be unanimously embraced by all.

In financial terms, Xikrin reliance on imports remains minuscule. Even if loggers and miners delivered on their promises, at no time do any of the agreements uncovered during the course of this research amount to more than several thousand dollars per month. These sums were never delivered in money but in merchandise, and air transport ate up a great proportion of the total. The small sums of money and merchandise are in sharp contrast to the enormous reservation area of 1,655,000 square hectares that risks being depredated. Although the outstanding debts owed in Tucumã exceeds U.S. $44,000, my own estimate of annual expenditures, based on what Xikrin claim they would like to purchase and the quantity of goods that actually arrive in the village, are between U.S. $30,000 and U.S. $40,000. The standing forest within the reservation itself has a value—in conserving undegraded land, biodiversity, and climatic stability—that would easily justify an outright donation far in excess of the sum currently spent for trade goods and community infrastructure each year in return for the exclusion of logging and prospecting (even if the salaries of FUNAI personnel and the cost of transport were added). Given the current level of dependence, the contracting of experts to evaluate the feasibility of sustainable production practices can easily cost more than is funneled through chiefs by extractivists. In fact, such projects become a new form for funneling material redistributed within indigenous communities.

The small scale of contemporary Amazon indigenous societies should not lead one to conclude that these societies are simple. Rather, they possess a dynamic and contradictions all their own. Too often it seems to me that schemes to involve indigenous people as sustainable producers or environmental stewards either treat them as an interest group or one cohort operating by consensus. On the basis of shared culture or even what anthropologists have taken to be a shared environmental adaptation, people are assumed to share unitary interests. A cultural order is assumed to be a product of shared understandings rather than an ongoing social process whose dynamic lies beyond the control of any would-be decision maker, whether elected or not. No less than our own familiar surroundings, the social world of indigenous peoples is composed of institutions that are culturally ordered *and* the cumulative products of individual decisions and strategies. Through their leaders, different Kayapó communities have accepted or rejected loggers' overtures, and such disparate choices are equally within the Kayapó cultural repertoire. When conceptualizing indigenous peoples' quest for a land base, human rights, and security, we must somehow conceptualize the issues in terms of societies that are both linked to and autonomous from a larger social order rather than as pure expressions of a culture logic.

Any social order consists of social divisions, tensions, contradictions, and differences of opinion. Politics, or the struggle of different interests, plays itself out differently within diverse cultural orders, and political leaders, such as Kayapó chiefs, must be seen as representatives of these interests, rather than as representatives of a "culture" or a "social order." To act otherwise is to insist that indigenous peoples learn the rules of a certain kind of politics, associated with an international order of nation-states—giving up parts of their own indigenous practice in the process. We are implicitly demanding of indigenous leaders that they be included at the table only when they have learned the ideological sleight of hand whereby political leaders come to present themselves as representatives of a "society" or a "culture."

Based on consideration of the Bakajá Xikrin case, for example, we might conclude that the Xikrin need to become literate and savvy in numerical calculations in order to deal with miners and loggers and receive a fair price for their resources. However, a move to educate the young may serve to disempower the old or uneducated, as has occurred in other Kayapó communities. Jaguar's refusal to let any children go to school in Altamira and his insistence that lessons be conducted in the village are far from irrational, for Xikrin rationality, like any other, must include considerations of power. Attempts to make redistributions less contentious by introducing a piecework system in which each worker is compensated in proportion to what he or she produces similarly raises problems of institutions and authority and, as such, is supported by some and opposed by others. When I was leaving the reservation, men were discussing the possibility of giving chiefs only half of the proceeds from the timber concessions and keeping half for the rest of the "community" of adult men. Such a solution obviously raises further problems and, given the precedent of collective female responses, would likely have unintended consequences beyond decreasing stores of chiefly trade goods.

In short, one of the most telling pieces of evidence in favor of the efficacy of local institutions, cultural values, and indigenous agency is the impossibility of ever proposing any neutral remedies to problems such as development or environmental degradation. Not only are these problems inserted into different chains of causality within indigenous communities, but there is never a case where "our" politics (even when disguised as purely humanitarian relief) do not meet "their" politics, often with unforeseeable consequences. This is not to argue against political engagement, for indigenous peoples' continued survival entails constant vigilance against the logic of states and the market economy, which views autonomy in any form with distrust, or worse.

Instead we must begin with the simple proposition that connections must be acknowledged. The large-scale processes that both link and isolate indigenous peoples from wider surroundings are refracted through institutions created by indigenous peoples for themselves, but not by themselves. Support for indigenous rights must be framed so as not to foreclose on any of the (often unstable) alternatives forged within dependent and hybrid political economies of the reservation system. In the end, the socially induced pressures and constraints of indigenous organization are a critical part of the environmental future of the far-from-inconsequential 11.74 percent of Brazil's mammoth territory designated as indigenous lands (Ricardo and Santilli 1997, 31).

NOTES

CHAPTER 2. THE RISE OF RUBBER AND RELIGION

1. This in itself is highly unusual given today's patterns. Kayapó women rarely venture from the settlement by themselves. However, as will be seen, during peacetime, and given the right opportunity, women will take to the forests for their own gain.
2. It appears, in fact, that São Félix was founded shortly after a road was opened connecting the Xingu and Araguaia Rivers (Audrin 1963, 95).
3. Known as Angmêkapran in the myths of Gorotire Kayapó and Apinagé, and Auké among other Timbira Gê peoples.
4. For a similar description of rubber extraction, see Gallais 1942, 228.
5. The situation in central Brazil differed from that in the western Amazon where systematic violence and enslavement was practiced against indigenous people in order to compel them to harvest rubber (e.g., Casement 1997).
6. The Colégio Isabel was founded in 1871 in Leopoldina along the Araguaia River by Couto de Magalhães who was the president (head administrator) of the state of Goiás. He asserted that all tribes of the Araguaia region were represented at the school's founding: "Immediately there entered twenty children of both sexes from the Shavante, Gorotires, Kayapós, Karajás, Tapirapé, and three from the extinct tribe of the Guajajara" (1977, 25 [my translation]). While it seems clear that both Gorotire and Irã'ãmrajre Kayapó were part of the entering class, there is no evidence that Xikrin were among them.
7. This may be the same village Vidal (1977, 27) refers to as Motikre.
8. Presumably the Gorotire Kumrẽn, which included the Irã'ãmrajre before they split.

CHAPTER 3. RENOUNCING THE FRONTIER

1. mỳkam na ga nô punu? (interrogative/pres. stative/two pers. sing./eye/bad).
2. Probably more Xikrin were killed, but it is doubtful that a Xikrin informant would have memorized many names beyond those of his or her own kin—that is, the names recounted to him by his or her own kin. The exception is when one is an eyewitness to events, in which case a person will attempt an account of all the actors involved.

3. Thus the Sanumá process of village naming in which villages are almost "invariably names of persons either living or dead" is quite different from that of the Kayapó, who have no lineages and no "official" version of history. For the Sanumá, "names are instrumental in the process by which certain agnatic groups obtain political hegemony in the village of residence" (Ramos 1995, 67).
4. The Pacajá River itself was named for this tree, *Bàtprà-mã -ỳr* (tree spp.-go-toward).
5. This is probably the historical origin of the two Parakanã groups known today.

CHAPTER 4. THE BEGINNINGS OF REDISTRIBUTION

1. The notion of "commoner" should not be understood as a literal translation of the Xikrin language but as a term that is used to emphasize the difference between chiefs and nonchiefs. The latter are referred to as *mekàtàp*. The etymology of this term is complex since the literal meaning "those with raw (i.e., unprocessed) skin," is a reference to people who have not received certain ritual prerogatives. These prerogatives received by non-*mekàtàp* may only be acquired in ritual contexts in which many persons act on behalf of the honored recipients. Thus, metaphorically, commoners are thought to act on behalf of chiefs (rather than the other way around), while chiefs supply the provisions that make ritual performance possible. No Xikrin feels himself or herself to be "common" or less worthy than any village mates. *Mekàtàp* can also refer to anybody leftover or left out.
2. This raises an intriguing explanation for the form of Xerente villages. The Xerente, close relatives of the Xavante, construct their villages in a semicircle. Given their history of splits, such a form may have been a way of labeling themselves as conciliatory rather than belligerent with regard to factional disputes.

CHAPTER 6. INCONSTANT GOODS

1. The Body Shop brochure "Trading with Communities in Need" (1995) lists the Kayapó as trading partners who supply the company with Brazil nut oil. However, the aid received by the Xikrin was disbursed by the Body Shop to the FUNAI in Altamira for aid to different groups under its administration. The Bakajá Xikrin do not supply any products directly to the Body Shop.
2. Xikrin would make the distinction between the "great chief" *(benadjwỳrỳ raj)* and "chiefs" *(benadjwỳrỳ)*.
3. The single exception is of a man who formerly lived at the nearby Xikrin settlement of Trincheira. He has a very small amount of money in a bank in Altamira left over from the time Trincheira sold salted fish.
4. I converted these sums from the exchange rates listed in the *Wall Street Journal* on the days of deposit.

CHAPTER 7. INFLATION, FOOD, AND THE NEW ECONOMY

1. Vidal (1977, 152) also remarked that a man called *capitão*, or chief, in fact, completely lacked any prestige.
2. See Halperin (1984, 263ff.) and Mingione (1991, 21ff.) for a discussion of the ambiguous distinction between reciprocity and redistribution in Polanyi's work. See also Wachtel (1977) for a discussion of the ideological use of this ambiguity by Inka rulers.

CHAPTER 8. THE SPREAD OF CHIEFLY POWER

1. The charging of a toll for safe passage is not foreign to the Amazon. Ramos (1996, 126, 134) describes the decision by the Yekuana Indian, Lourenço, to charge gold prospectors a toll for the use of an airstrip in the vicinity of his village.

2. The 21 July 1997 *New York Times* reports that 80 percent of Brazil's timber harvest is taken illegally.

REFERENCES

Albert, Bruce. 1988. "La Fumée du métal: Histoire et représentations du contact chez les Yanomami (Brésil)." *L'Homme* 28 (2–3): 87–119.

Anonymous. 1994. FUNAI Oficio (unnumbered) /CCJ/CJ/94. Brasília, 24 January 1994. ms. 14 pp. Copy in author's files. (Directed to Minister Humberto Gomes de Barros with information about the lawsuit of Alquirino Bannach to halt the demarcation of the Trincheira-Bakajá Reservation.)

———. 1990. "Termos de Compromisso N° 001/90 que entre si Celebram a Comunidade Indígena do PIN Bakajá e os Garimpeiros que Trabalham no Garimpo do Manezão Objetivando a Realização de Projetos de Desenvolvimento Comunitário." ms. 4 pp. Copy in author's files.

———. 1989. Contrato que entre si fazem a comunidade indígena Kayapó/Xikrin do Posto Indígena Bacajá do Município de Senador José Porfirio e a Exportadora Perachi Ltda—CGC 04.708.210/0006–51, Situada À ROD. PA 279, KM 157 em Tucumã—Pa. (August 23) 3 pp. Copy in author's files.

———. n.d. (Payroll, supplies, and census at Posto Francisco Meireles. 1960?) Microfilm. Sociedade de Proteção aos Índios. Inspetoria Regional 2, Film 374, Frame 1633, Setor de Documentação, Museu do Índio, Rio de Janeiro.

Appadurai, Arjun. 1986. "Introduction: Commodities and the Politics of Value." In Arjun Appadurai, ed. *The Social Life of Things: Commodities in Cultural Perspective.* New York: Cambridge University Press, 3–63.

Audrin, José M. 1963. *Os Sertanejos que eu Conheci.* Rio de Janeiro: Livraria José Olympio.

———. 1947. *Entre Sertanejos e Índios do Norte: O Bispo-Missionário Dom Domingos Carrérot,* O.P. Rio de Janeiro: Edições Púgil Limitada.

Balée, William. 1989. "The Culture of Amazonian Forests." In Darrell Posey and William Baleé, eds. *Resource Management in Amazonia: Indigenous and Folk Strategies.* New York Botanical Garden. Advances in Economic Botany 7:1–21.

Bamberger, Joan. 1979. "Exit and Voice in Central Brazil: The Politics of Flight in Kayapó Society." In David Maybury-Lewis, ed. *Dialectical Societies: The Gê and Bororo of Central Brazil.* Cambridge, Mass.: Harvard University Press, 130–46.

Body Shop. 1995. "Trading with Communities in Need." Distributed by the Body Shop, Wake Forest, N.C. (brochure) Copy in author's files.

Bourdieu, Pierre. 1977. *Outline of a Theory of Practice.* Cambridge: Cambridge University Press. Translated by Richard Nice.

Brooks, Edwin, René Fuerst, John Hemming, and Francis Huxley. 1973. *Tribes of the Amazon Basin in Brazil 1972. Report for the Aborigines Protection Society.* London: Charles Knight.

Browder, John O. 1987. "Brazil's Export Promotion Policy (1980–84): Impacts on the Amazon's Industrial Wood Sector." *Journal of Developing Areas* 21:285–304.

Bunker, Stephen. 1985. *Underdeveloping the Amazon: Extraction, Unequal Exchange, and the Failure of the Modern State.* Urbana: University of Illinois Press.

Burkhalter, S. Brian, and Robert F. Murphy. 1989. "Tappers and Sappers: Rubber, Gold, and Money among the Mundurucú." *American Ethnologist* 16:100–16.

Burris, J. L. 1941. *My Diary among the Savage Kayapó Indians of the Amazon.* Richmond, Va.: The Dietz Press.

Caiuby Novaes, Sylvia. 1997. *The Play of Mirrors: The Representation of Self As Mirrored in the Other.* Austin: University of Texas Press. Translated from the Portuguese by Izabel Murat Burbridge.

Carneiro, Robert L. 1983. "The Cultivation of Manioc among the Kuikuru of the Upper Xingu." In Raymond Hames and William Vickers, eds. *Adaptive Responses of Native Amazonians.* New York: Academic Press, 65–111.

———. 1979. "Tree Felling with the Stone Ax: An Experiment Carried Out among the Yanomamö of Southern Venezuela." In Carol Kramer, ed. *Ethnoarchaeology: Implications of Ethnography for Archaeology.* New York: Columbia University Press, 21–58.

———. 1973. "Slash-and-Burn Cultivation among the Kuikuru and Its Implications for Cultural Development in the Amazon Basin." In Daniel Gross, ed. *Peoples and Cultures of South America.* Garden City, N.Y.: Doubleday / The Natural History Press, 98–123. Originally in *Antropológica,* Supplement No. 2. 1961. *The Evolution of Horticultural Systems in Native South America,* Johannes Wilbert, ed.

Carneiro da Cunha, Manuela. 1993. "Les Études Gé." *L'Homme* 33 (2–4): 77–93.

Caron, Pére. 1971. *Curé d'Indiens.* Paris: Union Générale d'Editions.

Casement, Roger. 1997. *The Amazon Journal of Roger Casement.* London: Anaconda Editions.

Castelnau, Francis de. 1949. *Expedição às Regiões Centrais da América do Sul.* Vol. 1. São Paulo: Editora Nacional. Original French edition, 1850–51.

CEDI (Centro Ecumênico de Documentação e Informação). 1993. *O "Ouro Verde" das Terras dos Indios.* São Paulo.

———. 1991. "Aconteceu Povos Indígenas no Brasil 87/90." São Paulo.

Cleary, David. 1994. "Problemas na interpretação da história moderna da Amazônia." In Maria A. D'Incao and Isolda M. da Silveira, orgs. *A Amazônia e a Crise da Modernização.* Belém: Museu Parense Emílio Goeldi, 159–65.

———. 1990. *Anatomy of the Amazon Gold Rush.* Iowa City: University of Iowa Press.

Colchester, Marcus. 1989. "Indian Development in Amazonia: Risks and Strategies." *The Ecologist* 19 (6): 249–54.

Cook, David Noble. 1998. *Born to Die: Disease and New World Conquest.* Cambridge: Cambridge University Press.

Cotrim Soares, Antonio. 1971. "Assunto-relatório apresentado pelo sertanista sobre contatos com os índios Asuriní." Ms. In files of Instituto Socioambiental, São Paulo.

Coudreau, Henri. 1897. *Voyage au Tocantins-Araguaya.* Paris: A. Lahure.

Crocker, William H. 1990. "The Canela (Eastern Timbira), I. An Ethnographic Introduction." *Smithsonian Contributions to Anthropology* No. 33.

Cruvinel, Noraldino Vieira. 1995. "Relatório da viagem à gleba Sudoeste: A ocupação de parte da P. I. Trincheira-Bacajá." Fundação Nacional do Índio, Brasília. (6 October 1995) Ms. 5 pp. Copy in author's files.

Curtin, Philip D. 1968. *The Rise and Fall of the Plantation Complex: Essays in Atlantic History.* Cambridge: University of Cambridge Press, 92–96.

Da Matta, Roberto. 1982. *A Divided World.* Cambridge, Mass.: Harvard University Press.

———. 1970. "Mito e antimito entre os Timbira." In Claude Lévi-Strauss, Roberto Cardoso de Oliveira, Julio Cezar Melatti, Roberto da Matta, and Roque de Barros Laraia. *Mito e Linguagem Social.* Rio de Janeiro: Tempo Brasileira, 77–106.

Davis, Shelton. 1977. *Victims of the Miracle.* Cambridge: Cambridge University Press.

Diniz, Edson Soares. 1963. "Convívio interétnico e aglutinação intergrupal: Uma visão da comunidade do Posto Indígena Gorotire." *Revista do Museu Paulista* 13:213–20.

Ehrenreich, Paul. 1948. "Contribuições para a etnologia do Brasil." *Revista do Museu Paulista* 2:17–135. Originally published 1891. Translated from the German by Egon Schaden.

Ellison, Katherine. 1993. "Amazon Tribe Takes Villain Role: Chiefs Cash In on Rain Forest." *Times-Picayune.* A1. September 23.

Evans, Peter. 1979. *Dependent Development: The Alliance of Multinational, State, and Local Capital in Brazil.* Princeton, N.J.: Princeton University Press.

Fearnside, Philip. 1997. "Comment: Protection of Mahogany: A Catalytic Species in the Destruction of Rain Forests in the American Tropics." *Environmental Conservation* 24 (4): 303–6.

Ferguson, R. Brian. 1995. *Yanomami Warfare.* Seattle: University of Washington Press.

Ferguson, R. Brian, and Neil Whitehead, eds. 1992. *War in the Tribal Zone: Expanding States and Indigenous Warfare.* Santa Fe: School of American Research Press.

Fernandes, Fernando Henrique. 1971. "Relatório de reconhecimento P. I. Bakajá." 30 setembro 1971. Microfilm Sociedade de Proteção aos Índios. Inspetoria Regional 2, Film 374, Frame 1636, Setor de Documentação, Museu do Índio, Rio de Janeiro.

Ferrari, I., et al. 1993. "Saúde, garimpo e mercúrio entre os Kayapó: Estudo exploratório." *Salusvita, Bauri* 12 (1): 113–26. Cited in Terence Turner. 1995. "An Indigenous People's Struggle for Socially Equitable and Ecologically Sustainable Production: The Kayapó Revolt against Extractivism." *Journal of Latin American Anthropology* 1 (1): 110.

Ferreira, Jorge, and Henri Ballot. 1953. "Os Chikrin." *O Cruzeiro* N° 39 (11 July), pp. 56–59, 40, 44.

Fisher, William. H. 1998. "The Teleology of Kinship and Village Formation: Community Ideal and Practice among the Northern Gê of Central Brazil." *South American Indian Studies* 5:52–59.

———. 1996. "Native Amazonians and the Making of the Amazon Wilderness: From Discourse of Riches and Sloth to Underdevelopment." In Melanie DuPuis and Peter

Vandergeest, eds. *Creating the Countryside: The Politics of Rural and Environmental Discourse.* Philadelphia: Temple University Press, 166–203.

———. 1994. "Megadevelopment, Environmentalism, and Resistance: The Institutional Context of Kayapó Indigenous Politics in Central Brazil." *Human Organization* 53 (3): 220–32.

———. forthcoming. "Social Age and Gender among the Xikrin-Kayapó." In Donald Tuzin and Thomas Gregor, eds. *Gender in Melanesia and Amazonia.* Berkeley: University of California Press.

Flowers, Nancy M., Daniel R. Gross, Madeline L. Ritter, and Dennis W. Werner. 1982. "Variation in Swidden Practices in Four Central Brazilian Societies." *Human Ecology* 10: 203–17.

Folha do Norte (Belém) 20 September 1958.

Fried, Morton. 1975. *The Notion of Tribe.* Menlo Park, Calif.: Cummings Publishers.

———. *The Evolution of Political Society.* New York: Random House.

Frikel, Protásio. 1963. "Notas sobre os Xikrin do Cateté." *Revista do Museu Paulista* 14:145–58.

Gallais, Estevão-Maria. 1942. *O Apóstolo do Araguaia: Frei Gil de Vilanova, Missionário Dominicano.* (São Paulo?): Prelazia de Conceição do Araguaia. Translated from the French by Frei Pedro Secondy e Soares de Azevedo. Originally published in 1906.

Gallois, Dominique. 1986. *Migração, Guerra e Comércio: Os Waiapí na Guiana.* São Paulo: Faculdade de Filosofia, Letras e Ciências Humanas/Universidade de São Paulo.

Giannini, Isabel V. 1996. "The Xikrin do Cateté Indigenous Area." In K. H. Redford and J. A. Mansour, eds. *Traditional Peoples and Biodiversity Conservation in Large Tropical Landscapes.* Arlington, Va.: The Nature Conservancy, 115–36.

Globo (Rio de Janeiro). 1 November 1957.

———. 30 October 1959.

———. 31 October 1959.

Gonçalves, Aguinaldo, et al. 1992. "Garimpos, mercúrio e contaminação ambiental." In N. C. Leal et al. *Saúde e Desenvolvimento: Processos e Consequências sobre as Condições de Vida.* Vol. 2. São Paulo: Hucitec—Abrasco. Cited in Terence Turner. 1995. "An Indigenous People's Struggle for Socially Equitable and Ecologically Sustainable Production: The Kayapo Revolt against Extractivism." *Journal of Latin American Anthropology* 1 (1): 110.

Goody, Jack. 1978. "Population and Polity in the Voltaic Region." In J. Friedman and M. J. Rowlands, eds. *The Evolution of Social Systems.* Pittsburgh: University of Pittsburgh Press, 534–45.

Graham, Laura R. 1995. *Performing Dreams: Discourses of Immortality among the Xavante of Central Brazil.* Austin: University of Texas Press.

Gross, Daniel, George Eiten, Nancy M. Flowers, Francisca M. Leoi, Madeline L. Ritter, and Dennis W. Werner. 1979. "Ecology and Acculturation among Native Peoples of Central Brazil." *Science* 206:1043–50.

Halperin, Rhoda H. 1984. "Polanyi, Marx, and the Institutional Paradigm in Economic Anthropology." *Research in Economic Anthropology* 6:245–72.

Hartmann, Günther. 1982. "Bei den Mekubenokré-Kayapo, Brasilien: Aus de tagebuchblättern Wilhelm Kissenberths." *Zeitschrift für Ethnologie* 107 (1):153–62.

Hecht, Susanna, and Alexander Cockburn. 1990. *The Fate of the Forest: Developers, Destroyers, and Defenders of the Amazon.* New York: HarperCollins.

Hemming, John. 1987. *Amazon Frontier: The Defeat of the Brazilian Indians.* Cambridge, Mass.: Harvard University Press.

———. 1978. *Red Gold: The Conquest of the Brazilian Indians.* London: Papermac.

Hipsley, E. H., and N. E. Kirk. 1955. "Studies of Dietary Intake and the Expenditure of Energy by New Guineans." South Pacific Commission Technical Paper No. 147. Mimeo. Cited in Norman, et al. 1984. *The Ecology of Tropical Food Crops.* Cambridge: Cambridge University Press.

Hugh-Jones, Stephen. 1992. "Yesterday's Luxuries, Tomorrow's Necessities: Business and Barter in Northwest Amazonia." In Humphrey and Hugh-Jones 1992, 42–74.

Humphrey, Caroline, and Stephen Hugh-Jones, eds. 1992. *Barter, Exchange, and Value: An Anthropological Approach.* New York: Cambridge University Press.

Ianni, Octavio, 1979. *A Luta pela Terra: História Social da Terra e da Luta pela Terra numa Área da Amazônia.* 2d ed. Petrópolis: Editor Vozes.

Jornal do Brasil. 1980. "Indios Txukarramães interditam a Rodovia Manaus-Brasília." 14 August 1980.

Jornal do Comércio. 1959. (Rio de Janeiro). 17 November 1959.

Kensinger, Kenneth. 1995. *How Real People Ought to Live: The Cashinahua of Eatern Peru.* Prospect Heights, Ill.: Waveland Press.

Lea, Vanessa. 1986. "Nomes e Nekrets Kayapó: Uma Concepção de Riqueza." Ph.D. diss., Universidade Federal do Rio de Janeiro.

Lévi-Strauss, Claude. 1969–81. *Introduction to a Science of Mythology.* Four volumes. New York: Harper & Row. Translated by John Weightman and Doreen Weightman.

Lukesch, Anton. 1976. *Bearded Indians of the Tropical Forest.* Graz, Austria: Akademische Druck-u. Verslagsanstalt.

Magalhães, Couto de. 1977. *Viagem ao Araguaya.* 2d ed. São Paulo: Companhia Editora Nacional.

———. 1975. *O Selvagem.* Belo Horizonte, Brazil: Livraria Itatiaia Editora. Originally published 1876.

Magalhães, Francisco José Pinto de. 1852. "Memoria sobre a descoberta e fundação da povoação de S. Pedro de Alcantara, apresentada ao governador da Capitania de Goyaz Fernando Delgado Freire de Castilho em 3 de janeiro de 1813." In Candido Mendes de Almeida, ed. *A Carolina ou a Definitiva Fixação de Limites entre as Províncias de Maranhão e Goyaz.* Rio de Janeiro: Typ. Episcopal de Agostinho de Freitas Guimaraes.

Marques, Benigno Pessoa, Walter Avelino da Silva, Nerci Caetano Venturi, Carlos Alberto Conde, R. Adelberto Queiroz, Carlos Alberto N. Araújo, and Inácio Medeiros de Andrade. 1994. "Relatório referente á fiscalização conjunta IBAMA/FUNAI/PF/SAE na Área Indígena Trincheira/Bakajá-período 17 september to 20 september 1994." Ms. 6 pp. Copy in author's file.

Matos, Raymundo José da Cunha. 1874. "Chorografia histórica da província de Goyaz." *Revista Trimestral do Instituto Histórico, Geográfico e Ethnográfico do Brasil,* Rio de Janeiro. Vol. 37, Part 1: 213–398; 1875. Vol. 38, Part 1, 5: 150. Originally written in 1824.

Maybury-Lewis, David, ed. 1979. *Dialectical Societies.* Cambridge: Harvard University Press.

———. 1968. *The Savage and the Innocent.* Boston: Beacon Press.

————. 1967. *Akwe-Shavante Society*. Oxford: Clarendon Press.

————. 1965. "Some Crucial Distinctions in Central Brazilian Ethnology." *Anthropos* 60:340–58.

Mingione, Enzo. 1991. *Fragmented Societies: A Sociology of Economic Life beyond the Market Paradigm*. Cambridge, Mass.: Basil Blackwell.

Ministério das Minas e Energia. Federal Government of Brazil. DNAEE/DCRH Estação Aldeia Bacaja, Município Senador José Porfírio, Estado PA, Subbacia 18, Entidade 01, Unidade 07, Código 00451000, Years 1984–86. Copy in author's files.

Moffett, Matt. 1994 (December 29) "Kayapó Indians Lose Their 'Green' Image: Former Heroes of Amazon Succumb to Lure of Profit," *Wall Street Journal* A6.

Moran, Emilio. 1990. "Private and Public Colonization Schemes in Amazonia." In David Goodman and Anthony Hall, eds. *The Future of Amazonia: Destruction or Sustainable Development?* London: Macmillan Press, 70–89.

Moreira Neto, Carlos de Araújo. 1960. "A cultura pastoral do Pau d'Arco." *Boletim do Museu Paraense Emilio Goeldi, N.S. Antropologia* (10): 12.

Murphy, Isabel. 1995. "Kayapó Kinship and Two-Way Radios." Paper presented at the meeting of the American Anthropological Association, Washington, D.C., November.

Murphy, Yolanda, and Robert F. Murphy. 1985. *Women of the Forest*. 2d ed. New York: Columbia University Press.

Nimuendajú, Kurt. 1952. "Os Gorotiré (relatório apresentado ao Serviço de Proteção aos Índios em 18 de abil de 1940)." *Revista do Museu Paulista* 6:427–53.

Norman, M. J. T., C. T. Pearson, and P. G. E. Searle. 1984. *The Ecology of Tropical Food Crops*. Cambridge: Cambridge University Press.

O'Connor, Geoffrey. 1998. *Amazon Journal: Dispatches from a Vanishing Frontier*. New York: Penguin Putnam.

Parise, Fiorello, Nerci Caetano Ventura, and Ocirema S. Días de Oliveira. 1986. "Relatório da comissão de sindicância instituida pela ordem de serviço N° 061/86/4ª SUER de 14.10.86." (FUNAI document). 4 pp. Copy in author's files.

Peters, John Fred. 1973. "The Effect of Western Material Goods upon the Social Structure of the Family among the Shirishana." Ph.D. diss., Western Michigan University.

Peterson, Nicolas. 1993. "Demand-Sharing Reciprocity and the Pressure for Generosity among Foragers." *American Anthropologist* 95 (4): 860–74.

Picchi, Debra. 1995. "Village Division in Lowland South America: The Case of the Bakairí Indians of Central Brazil." *Human Ecology* 23 (4): 477–98.

Pires, João Murça. 1978. "The Forest Ecosystems of the Brazilian Amazon: Description, Functioning, and Research Needs." In UNESCO, *Tropical Forest Ecosystems*. Paris: UNESCO-UNEP, 607–27.

Posey, Darrell. 1989. "From Warclubs to Words." *NACLA Report on the Americas* 23 (1): 13–18.

————. 1985. "Indigenous Management of Tropical Forest Ecosystems: The Case of the Kayapó Indians of the Brazilian Amazon." *Agroforestry Systems* 3:139–58.

————. 1979. "Ethnoentomology of the Gorotire Kayapó of Central Brazil." Ph.D. diss., University of Georgia.

Rabben, Linda. 1998. *Unnatural Selection: The Yanomami, the Kayapó, and the Onslaught of Civilization*. Seattle: University of Washington Press.

Ramos, Alcida. 1996. "A Profecia de um boato: Matando por ouro na área Yanomami." *Anuário Antropológica/95*, 121–50. (Rio de Janeiro).

———. 1995. *Sanumá Memories: Yanomami Ethnography in Times of Crisis.* Madison: University of Wisconsin Press.

Ricardo, Fany P., and Márcio Santilli, orgs. 1997. *Terras Indígenas no Brasil: Um Balanço da Era Jobim.* São Paulo: Instituto Socioambiental.

Riviere, Peter. 1984. *Individual and Society in Guiana. A Comparative Study of Amerindian Social Organization.* New York: Cambridge University Press.

Roseberry, William Clinton. 1989. "Americanization in the Americas." Chap. 4 in *Histories and Anthropologies.* New Brunswick: Rutgers University Press.

Ross, Eric B. 1978. "The Evolution of the Amazon Peasantry." *Journal of Latin American Studies* 10 (2): 193–218.

Rubinstein, Steve Lee. 1993. "Chain Marriage among the Shuar." *Latin American Anthropology Review* 5 (1): 3–9.

Russell-Woods, A. J. R. 1989. "Frontiers in Portuguese America: Reality, Myth, and Metaphor." 70 pp. mss. Copy in author's files.

Salisbury, Richard F. 1962. *From Stone to Steel: Economic Consequences of a Technological Change in New Guinea.* Victoria: Melbourne University Press, on behalf of the Australian National University.

Santos, Leinad A. O., and Lúcia M. M. de Andrade, orgs. 1988. *As Hidrelétricas do Xingu e os Povos Indígenas.* São Paulo: Comissão Pró-Índio de São Paulo.

Santos, Ricardo V., and Nancy M. Flowers, Carlos E. A. Coimbra, Jr., and Sílvia A. Gugelmin. 1997. "Tapirs, Tractors, and Tapes: The Changing Economy and Ecology of the Xavante Indians of Central Brazil." *Human Ecology* 25 (4): 545–66.

Schmink, Marianne, and Charles H. Wood. 1992. *Contested Frontiers in Amazonia.* New York: Columbia University Press.

Seeger, Anthony. 1981. *Nature and Society in Central Brazil: The Suyá Indians of Mato Grosso.* Cambridge, Mass.: Harvard University Press.

Segurado, Dr. Ruffino Theodoro. 1848. "Viagem de Goyaz ao Pará." *Revista Trimensal de História e Geographia* 10:178–212.

Sharpe, Lauriston. 1952. "Steel Axes for Stone-Age Australians." *Human Organization* 11:17–22.

Sider, Gerald. 1987. "When Parrots Learn to Talk and Why They Can't: Domination, Deception, and Self-Deception in Indian-White Relations." *Comparative Studies in Society and History* 29:3–23.

———. 1986. *Culture and Class in Anthropology and History: A Newfoundland Illustration.* New York: Cambridge University Press.

Smith, Gavin. 1989. *Livelihood and Resistance: Peasants and the Politics of Land in Peru.* Berkeley: University of California Press.

Smith, Nigel J. H. 1982. *Rainforest Corridors: The Trans-Amazon Colonization Scheme.* Berkeley: University of California Press.

———. 1980. "Anthrosols and Human Carrying Capacity in Amazonia." *Annals of the Association of American Geographers* 70 (4): 553–66.

Snook, Laura K. 1993. "Stand Dynamics of Mahogany *(Swietenia macrophylla King)* and Associated Species after Fire and Hurricane in the Tropical Forests of the Yucatan Peninsula, Mexico." Ph.D. diss., Yale University.

Soares, José Carlos de Macedo 1928. *A Borracha (Estudo Econômico e Estatístico).* 2d ed. Paris: L. Chauny et L. Quinsac.

Spalding, Karen. 1984. *Huarochirí: An Andean Society under Inca and Spanish Rule.* Stanford, Calif.: Stanford University Press.

Stern, Steve J. 1982. *Peru's Indian Peoples and the Challenge of Spanish Conquest: Huamanga to 1640.* Madison: University of Wisconsin Press.

Stout, Mickey, and Ruth Thomson. 1974. "Fonêmica Txukuhamei (Kayapó)." *Série Linguística* 3:153–76.

Turner, Joan B. 1967. "Environment and Cultural Classification: A Study of the Northern Kayapó." Ph.D. diss., Harvard University. (See Joan Bamberger.)

Turner, Terence. 1995. "An Indigenous People's Struggle for Socially Equitable and Ecologically Sustainable Production: The Kayapó Revolt against Extractivism." *Journal of Latin American Anthropology* 1 (1):98–121.

———. 1993. "The Role of Indigenous Peoples in the Environmental Crisis: The Example of the Kayapó of the Brazilian Amazon." *Perspectives in Biology and Medicine* 36:526–45.

———. 1992. "Os Mebengokre Kayapó: História e mudança social. De comunidades autônomas para a coexistência interétnica." In Manuela Carneiro da Cunha, org. *História dos Índios no Brasil.* São Paulo: Companhia das Letras: Secretaria Municipal de Cultura: FAPESP, 311–38. Translated by Beatriz Perrone-Moisés.

———. 1988. "History, Myth, and Social Consciousness among the Kayapó of Central Brazil." In Jonathan D. Hill, ed. *Rethinking History and Myth: Indigenous South American Perspectives on the Past.* Urbana: University of Illinois Press, 195–213.

———. 1985. "Animal Symbolism, Totemism, and the Structure of Myth." In Gary Urton, ed. *Animal Myths and Metaphors in South America.* Salt Lake City: University of Utah Press, 49–106.

———. 1980. "The Social Skin." In Jeremy Cherfas and Roger Lewin, eds. *Not Work Alone.* London: Temple Smith, 112–40.

———. 1979. "Kinship, Household, and Community Structure among the Kayapó." In David Maybury-Lewis, ed. *Dialectical Societies: The Gê and Bororo of Central Brazil.* Cambridge, Mass.: Harvard University Press, 179–214.

———. 1965. Review of "Les Kayapo du Nord, État de Para-Brésil: Contribution à l'étude des Indiens Gê" by Simone Dreyfus. *American Anthropologist* 67 (1): 149–50.

Umbuzeiro, Ubirajara Marques. n.d. *Altamira e sua História.* Altamira, Pará: Sociedade dos Poetas Cordelistas da Bacia Amazônica (SOPOCOBA)/Grupo de Teatro Amador dos Jovens Altamirenses (GRUTAJA).

Vandermeer, John, and Ivette Perfecto. 1995. *Breakfast of Biodiversity: The Truth about Rain Forest Destruction.* Oakland, Calif.: Institute for Food and Development Policy.

Veja. 1985. "Progresso na Aldeia." 6 November 1985, 77–78.

Ventura, Nerci Caetano. 1991. "Relatório da Situação Atual dos Xikrin do Bakajá—À Companhia Vale do Rio Doce." Ms. 4 pp. 26 April 1991. Copy in author's files.

Ventura, Nerci Caetano, and Benigno Pessoa Marques. 1993. Untitled Report. Report on investigation into the denunciations of logging activities on Indian reserves within the regional administration of Altamira between 25 August and 20 September 1993, 19 pp. Fundação Nacional do Índio, Altamira. Copy in author's files.

Veríssimo, Adalberto, Paulo Barreto, Ricardo Tarifa, and Christopher Uhl. 1995. "Extraction of a High-Value Natural Resource in Amazonia: The Case of Mahogany." *Forest Ecology and Management* 72:39–60.

Verswijver, Gustaaf. 1992. *The Club-Fighters of the Amazon: Warfare among the Kaiapo Indians of Central Brazil.* Gent: Rijksuniversiteit te Gent.

———. 1982. "The Intertribal Relations between the Juruna and the Kayapo Indians (1850–1920)." *Jahrbuch des Museums für Völkerkunde* 34:305–15.

Vidal, Lux B. 1992a. "Dramas do garimpo de Bacajá." *Boletim da Associação Brasileira de Antropologia* 12:13. Article without author attribution.

———. 1992b. "Relatório à Companhia Vale do Rio Doce." March. Ms. 17 pp. Copy in author's files.

———. 1985. "Relatório à Companhia Vale do Rio Doce. Setembro. A Situação Atual dos Índios Xikrin do Bacajá-Pará, Assistência ao Projeto de Apoio Ferro-Carajás." Ms. 27 pp. Copy in author's files.

———. 1981. "Contribution to the Concept of Person and Self in Lowland South American Societies: Body Painting among the Kayapó-Xikrin." *Série Ensaios* 4:291–303, Coleção Museu Paulista.

———. 1977. *Morte e Vida de uma Sociedade Indígena Brasileira.* São Paulo: Editora HUCITEC.

———. 1976. "As categorias de idade como sistema de classificação e controle demográfico de grupos entre os Xikrin do Cateté e de como são manipuladas em diferentes contextos." *Revista do Museu Paulista* 23:129–42.

Viveiros de Castro, Eduardo B. 1992. *From the Enemy's Point of View: Humanity and Divinity in an Amazonian Society.* Chicago: University of Chicago Press. Translated from the Portuguese by Catherine V. Howard.

Wachtel, Nathan. 1977. *The Vision of the Vanquished: The Spanish Conquest of Peru through Indian Eyes, 1530–70.* New York: Barnes and Noble Books. Translated by Ben and Sién Reynolds.

Wearne, Phillip. 1996. *Return of the Indian: Conquest and Revival in the Americas.* Philadelphia: Temple University Press.

Weinstein, Barbara. 1983. *The Amazon Rubber Boom, 1850–1920.* Stanford: Stanford University Press.

Werner, Dennis. 1984. *Amazon Journey: An Anthropologist's Year among Brazil's Mekranoti Indians.* New York: Simon & Schuster.

———. 1983. "Why Do the Mekranoti Trek?" In Raymond Hames and William Vickers, eds. *Adaptive Responses of Native Amazonians.* New York: Academic Press, 225–38.

———. 1980. "The Making of a Mekranoti Chief: The Psychological and Social Determinants of Leadership in a Native South American Society." Ph.D. diss., City University of New York.

Whittemore, Hank. 1992. "A Man Who Would Save the World," *Parade Magazine*, April 12, 4–7.

Wolf, Eric R. 1982. *Europe and the People without History.* Berkeley: University of California Press.

———. 1957. "Closed Corporate Communities in Mesoamerica and Central Java." *Southwestern Journal of Anthropology* 13:1–18.

INDEX